WORSHIP SERVICES
FOR YOUTH

WORSHIP SERVICES FOR YOUTH

By

ALICE ANDERSON BAYS

ABINGDON-COKESBURY PRESS
New York • Nashville

WORSHIP SERVICES FOR YOUTH

Copyright MCMXLVI by Whitmore & Stone

Library of Congress Catalog Card Number: 46-2855

E

SET UP, PRINTED, AND BOUND BY THE
PARTHENON PRESS, AT NASHVILLE,
TENNESSEE, UNITED STATES OF AMERICA

To
SENATOR AND MRS. W. E. BROCK
whose outstanding work in the Church is a constant source of inspiration to young people, this
book is affectionately dedicated

FOREWORD

THIS IS THE FOURTH in a series of planned worship services, written that young people may be led into a conscious relationship with God, discover his will and purpose for them, and gain strength for effective, abundant living. Like the former volumes, WORSHIP PROGRAMS AND STORIES, WORSHIP PROGRAMS IN THE FINE ARTS, and WORSHIP PROGRAMS FOR INTERMEDIATES, it is written to provide additional source material to enrich worship.

This book has grown out of actual experience in leading young people in worship in local churches, colleges, camps, and summer conferences. The services are not presented as models to be followed without adaptation, but are intended to supplement the worship suggestions of the various denominational boards and to aid local groups in developing an adequate program of worship based upon their needs.

These services were prepared for use in that part of the church school program known as the worship service, for the evening session of the youth group, and for vespers, morning watch, or other occasions in camps or summer assemblies. They may be shortened or simplified by omitting certain poems, musical selections, or other parts. I have endeavored to express the aspirations of young people in the prayers and meditations, but these may be omitted at any time, and the leader may offer his own prayer.

I wish to acknowledge indebtedness and to express deep gratitude to all who co-operated in the preparation of this volume—to the young people of Church Street Methodist Church, Knoxville, Tennessee, for their constructive suggestions during the use of this material; to the leaders of youth in other local churches who have also used the services; to Jack Anderson and to Elizabeth Wray Taylor for their helpful

FOREWORD

criticism; to Robert Bays for literary criticism; and to Elizabeth Platt for suggestions concerning anthems, solos, and special music.

Grateful acknowledgment is made to authors and publishers who have generously granted permission for the use of copyrighted material. Every effort has been made to trace ownership of all copyrighted material and to give proper credit. I am not conscious of any infringement directly or indirectly, but should there be question regarding the use of any material, I shall take pleasure in making proper acknowledgment in future editions.

Alice Anderson Bays

CONTENTS

CONTENTS

SERIES FOUR

FRIENDSHIP WITH ALL RACES

SERIES FIVE

AROUND THE YEAR WITH GOD

APPENDIX

SERIES ONE

FRIENDS OF GOD

Suggestions to the Counselor

IT IS not enough to teach young people about God; they must be brought into an awareness of his presence. Worship is not something which a leader may perform for others. It cannot be forced; each person must make his own response. The leader may arrange the setting, prepare the service, and bring the message, but unless we feel our need of God, turn our thoughts toward him, surrender our wills, and co-operate with his purpose, the worship will be meaningless to us.

Worship is a conscious effort to know God and to find his will concerning us. It is vital when it is related to our daily experiences and sheds light on our problems. It brings new insights, makes us sensitive to the needs of others, and provides inspiration and strength for creative living.

In this series the message centers around the lives of persons who have labored to make a dream come true and have dedicated themselves to some worthy cause. The group may be led to collect stories of the lives of leaders in various fields and build their own worship services. An interesting project for a worship commission would be to start a library of worship material and add to it books of poems, prayers, interpretations of pictures and hymns, biographical and inspirational stories. Denominational literature, current periodicals, and public libraries will yield a wealth of material if the group will take sufficient time to condense and arrange it in usable form. Stories which are copied from borrowed books or clipped from magazines may be filed in a commercial expanding file. Favorite poems may be classified and arranged alphabetically in a card index file.

The following books would be helpful as background reading for this series: Eve Curie, *Madame Curie;* Helen Keller, *The Story of My Life;* John Foxe, *The Book of Martyrs;* A. F. Beard, *The Story of John Frederick Oberlin;* Charles J. Connick, *Adventures in Light and Color.*

A subcommittee may be appointed by the worship commission to arrange a suitable worship center for each service. A cross placed on an altar or table with candles on either side is appropriate for most occasions. Variations may be worked out by using a picture related to the theme of the service instead of the cross. With the service "Singer in Light and Color" a picture of a stained glass window or slides of windows may be used. Or if possible the group may meet in the sanctuary where beautiful windows may be seen. With the service "A Lamp unto Our Feet" an open Bible may be the focal point in the center of worship. With "Friend of the Soil" a picture of a landscape or beautiful countryside would be appropriate. The counselor will strive to use the initiative of the group in working out the details for a proper setting for worship.

SERVICE 1

IMPRISONED SPLENDOR

PRELUDE: Hymn tune, "Creation."

CALL TO WORSHIP:

> From thee all skill and science flow,
>   All pity, care, and love,
> All calm and courage, faith and hope:
>   O pour them from above.
>
> And part them, Lord, to each and all,
>   As each and all shall need,
> To rise like incense, each to thee,
>   In noble thought and deed.
>
> —CHARLES KINGSLEY

HYMN: "Send Down Thy Truth, O God," or
"O Worship the King."

SCRIPTURE:

Pilate saith unto him, What is truth?

Jesus saith . . . , I am the way, the truth, and the life.

If ye continue in my word, then are ye my disciples indeed; and ye shall know the truth, and the truth shall make you free.

If the Son therefore shall make you free, ye shall be free indeed.

Study to shew thyself approved unto God, a workman that needeth not to be ashamed, rightly dividing the word of truth.

His truth shall be thy shield and buckler.[1]

POEM:

> Great truths are dearly bought. The common truth,
>   Such as men give and take from day to day,
> Comes in the common walk of easy life,
>   Blown by the careless wind across the way.

Bought in the market, at the current price,
　Bred of the smile, the jest, perchance the bowl,
It tells no tales of daring or of worth,
　Nor pierces even the surface of a soul.

Great truths are greatly won. Not found by chance,
　Nor wafted on the breath of summer dream,
But grasped in the great struggle of the soul,
　Hard buffeting with adverse wind and stream.

Not in the general mart, 'mid corn and wine,
　Not in the merchandise of gold and gems,
Not in the world's gay halls of midnight mirth,
　Not 'mid the blaze of regal diadems,
But in the day of conflict, fear, and grief,
　When the strong hand of God, put forth in might,
Plow up the subsoil of the stagnant heart,
　And brings the imprisoned truth-seed to the light.

Wrung from the troubled spirit in hard hours
　Of weakness, solitude, perchance of pain,
Truth springs, like harvest, from well-plowed field,
　And the soul feels it has not wept in vain.

—HORATIUS BONAR

LEADER:

On his eightieth birthday Victor Hugo said, "Winter is on my head but eternal springtime is in my heart. I have said only a thousandth part of what is within me. I hear within me many immortal symphonies which I have never expressed."

To the elements already known to science Mme Curie added her discovery of radium. It is a challenge to consider that there are many more truths yet to be discovered by man. Shall we follow the gleam of truth, or shall we be like the persons of whom Emerson spoke when he said, "Men stand on the brink of mysteries and harmonies into which yet they never enter, and with their hands on the doorlatch, they die outside"?

Jesus said, "To this end was I born, and for this cause came I into the world, that I should bear witness unto the truth."

HYMN: "O Jesus, Prince of Life and Truth," or
"Take Thou Our Minds, Dear Lord."

STORY:

IMPRISONED SPLENDOR

MARIE SKLODOVSKA, the daughter of a professor of mathematics and physics in Warsaw, was one of five children. Although her youth was filled with many obstacles, life was good to her by not being too kind. Her mother, who had been director of a private school in Warsaw, died of tuberculosis when Marie was eleven years of age. The anti-Russian sympathies of the family, her father's demotion in teaching rank, and the death of her mother were responsible for the family's continual poverty.

After graduation from high school Marie secured a position as governess and sent her sister to the Sorbonne in Paris to study medicine. Her evenings were spent pouring over scientific books in preparation for her own college career which did not begin until she was twenty-four and her sister had received her degree.

In Paris, Marie devoted her entire time to science, prepared her frugal meals over an alcohol lamp, and lived on three francs a day. Even though the long hours of study with little food and no recreation had affected her health, she ranked first in her classes. After two years of study she received her degree in mathematics and in another year her degree in physics and chemistry.

It was at the home of one of her professors that Marie met Pierre Curie, a brilliant scientist about thirty-five years of age. Her devotion to science and her unusual insight and understanding attracted Pierre, but she did not encourage him because she had decided to rule love out of her life. It was with difficulty that he persuaded her that they could contribute more to scientific research if they were married.

After their honeymoon which was spent bicycling through the country, the Curies took a small apartment in Paris. It was more a laboratory than a place for comfortable living; the only furniture in the living room was a long white table with one chair at either end. Perhaps no other chairs were necessary; for visitors, finding them hard at work, would not remain long.

Pierre's one aim in life was scientific research, working with his wife, whose purpose was the same. To support the family it was necessary for him to teach physics in a municipal school. Marie, in addition to her eight hours of research each day, had the duties of a mother and housekeeper as well. Three children were born, one of whom died in infancy. She did not have to choose between her family and her career; she managed both successfully.

On one occasion Professor Becquerel, knowing Marie's interest in physics, showed her a strange glow which came from uranium. At once she began to experiment and found that more powerful rays of a similar nature came from pitchblende, the substance from which uranium was extracted. This challenged her inquiring mind, and she determined to isolate the element which was more powerful than uranium.

Marie and Pierre began their research, not knowing where it would lead. Their savings were invested in tons of pitchblende, and when the ore was exhausted, they were no nearer a solution than when they began. Undaunted, they borrowed money, and for four years they mixed and boiled tons of ore and separated the elements from the impurities. They labored patiently to isolate the hidden substance which was responsible for the strange, powerful rays. The secret of the powerful energy locked in the mass of black ore continued to elude them.

The laboratory assigned to the Curies by the University was an abandoned shed with a leaky roof, formerly used as a dissecting room. In addition to the hardships which they bore, other scientists looked upon them with indifference and suspicion. Their adventure into the unknown cost them dearly, but they were willing to take risks, to sacrifice comforts and personal pleasures. They devoted their entire energies to the search for truth.

When Pierre, thinking the task was beyond them, remarked, "It can't be done. Nature has buried the truth in the bottom of the sea," Marie replied, "Man can dive. Think of the joy when one comes up with the pearl—the pearl of truth." She checked her data and instruments again and again for a possible mistake. Tons and tons of ore were separated, and still no residue—or so it seemed. "Just suppose there is another element, unlike the others—not inert matter but active energy such as radioactive waves," she suggested.

The Curies labored patiently, boiling the crushed ore, filtering and separating the elements from the impurities, until at last they extracted a small amount of bismuth salts which contained an active element three hundred times more powerful than uranium. Still they kept on working. One day Marie held in a crucible a substance with rays so powerful that they penetrated iron plate as well as flesh and bone tissue. "Radium," said she, "we will call this radium!"

In their release of this new element the Curies made the greatest contribution to science in their generation. Many honors came to them. Commercial interests offered huge sums of money for their discovery. But they refused to take out a patent for their formula, saying, "If our discovery has commercial future, that is an accident by which we must not profit. And if radium is going to be of use in treating disease, it seems to us impossible to take advantage of that. What we discover belongs to any one who can use it."

They continued to work together in their scientific research, but their dependence upon each other came to be a source of anxiety to Marie. On one occasion she said, "Pierre, if one of us disappeared, the other should not survive. We can't exist without each other, can we?"

Pierre replied, "You are wrong. Whatever happens, even if one has to go on like a body without a soul, one must work just the same."

Shortly afterwards Pierre was struck down in traffic and killed instantly. In spite of her intense grief Marie felt that their work must go on. She was elected to serve in her husband's place as professor of physics on the faculty of the Sorbonne. Since she was the first woman to serve on the historic faculty, it was a dramatic moment when her inaugural address was given. According to tradition she was expected to eulogize her predecessor, but in this case her predecessor was her husband as well.

At the exact moment set for the lecture, Mme Curie entered the room amid much applause and walked to her place behind the table covered with apparatus. When the ovation subsided, in a straightforward manner and in the cold words of science, she began, "When one considers the progress that has been made in physics in the past ten years, one is surprised at the advance that has taken place in our ideas concerning electricity and matter. . . ."

Thus she introduced her lecture at the exact sentence where Pierre had left off and with no outward show of emotion continued to the end. She spoke of new theories on the structure of electricity and radioactive substances and urged the students to carry the torch of scientific research into the great unknown. As a tribute to her husband's devotion to truth, she took up the work where he had laid it down and carried forward their scientific labors which had always been more important to them than life itself.

France failed to recognize the Curies until both England and Sweden had honored them, the latter awarding them the Nobel prize, which they shared with Becquerel. At first, French scientists excluded Marie from the Academy of Science, but later the Academy of Medicine honored her. In 1911 Marie was again awarded the Nobel prize—the only time it had been twice awarded to the same person, and that person a woman. Afterward France donated a Radium Institute in Paris, and her native country gave one in Warsaw.

The interest in radium spread to other countries. Skilled scientists in the United States, working under her direction, using her formula, produced a gram of radium from ore found in Colorado. When it was presented to her, she turned it over to the Curie Institute at the University of Paris. Later she was called to America to receive another gram of radium. This she gave to the Warsaw Cancer Hospital.

Though urging precautions upon others, Mme Curie refused to heed them herself. On July 4, 1934, at the age of sixty-seven she died of a strange anemia which was probably caused by her constant contact with radium. She brought healing to countless thousands but was a victim of her own discovery. From the black ore she opened a way that released the imprisoned splendor for the welfare of mankind. Those who work for human progress will find encouragement in her absolute devotion to truth and in her determination to persevere until the goal was reached.[2]

POEM:

> Truth is within ourselves; it takes no rise
> From outward things, whate'er you may believe.
> There is an inmost centre in us all,
> Where truth abides in fulness; . . . and to KNOW
> Rather consists in opening out a way
> When the imprisoned splendor may escape,
> Than in effecting entry for a light
> Supposed to be without.

—ROBERT BROWNING

ANTHEM: "Come, Holy Ghost, Our Souls Inspire," by Webbe, or

HYMN: "God of the Searching Mind," or
"Awake, Awake to Love and Work."

PRAYER:

"O God, thou who dost heal the bodies and souls of men, pour out thy spirit upon all who seek to relieve pain. We thank thee for the great company of those who through the years have added to our knowledge of the body. Our souls are lifted by the courage of those who in dangerous experiments have risked their lives that others might live. We rejoice in the integrity and devotion which keep doctors and nurses at their tasks when their own weary bodies cry out for rest.

"In humble gratitude we accept the opportunities for health so long denied to men and still available to so few. Quicken in us a due sense of our responsibility to share these blessings. In shame we acknowledge that among the poor, the ignorant, those in far countries, and those of other races, millions of thy children suffer grievously. Forgive the sin of our indifference. Spread the knowledge of healing, O Lord, and open the way to it among all men.

"If we are ill, guide us to those who can assist us to health. Keep calm and serene our spirits, that the healing forces with which thou hast endowed our bodies may have their way without hindrance. If need be, give us patience to accept disappointment and the failure of human wisdom to restore us speedily to health. As strength returns, make us grateful to thee and to them that have served our need.

"Impart bountifully thy wisdom, we pray, to all who minister to bodily ills. Make them wise to serve and strong to endure in time of great necessity. May they, like thy Son, minister in thy name and in his spirit of compassion heal the multitudes." [3] Grant wisdom to thy workmen and reveal sufficient truth that suffering humanity may eventually be free from disease and bodily ills. In Jesus' name, we pray. AMEN.

CLOSING HYMN: "Holy Spirit, Truth Divine," or
              "O Master, Let Me Walk with Thee."

SERVICE 2

SINGER IN LIGHT AND COLOR

PRELUDE: "Sanctus" from *The Holy City,* by Gaul.

CALL TO WORSHIP:

Leader: A thing of beauty is a joy forever:
           Its loveliness increases; it will never
           Pass into nothingness; but still will keep
           A bower quiet for us, and a sleep
           Full of sweet dreams, and health, and quiet breathing.
                                —JOHN KEATS

Group: Beauty is not a need but an ecstasy.
      It is not a mouth thirsting nor an empty
          hand stretched forth,
      But rather a heart enflamed and a
          soul enchanted.
      It is not the image you would see nor
          the song you would hear,
      But rather an image you see though
          you close your eyes and a song you
          hear though you shut your ears.
      It is not the sap within the furrowed bark,
          nor a wing attached to a claw,
      But rather a garden for ever in bloom and
          a flock of angels for ever in flight.[1]
                             —KAHLIL GIBRAN

SCRIPTURE:

    O sing unto the Lord a new song: sing unto the Lord, all the earth.

    Sing unto the Lord, bless his name; shew forth his salvation from day to day.

Declare his glory among the heathen, his wonders among all
  people.

For the Lord is great, and greatly to be praised.

He hath made every thing beautiful in his time: also he hath set
  the world in their heart.

Honour and majesty are before him: strength and beauty are in
  his sanctuary.

Give unto the Lord, O ye kindreds of the people, give unto the
  Lord glory and strength.

Give unto the Lord the glory due unto his name: bring an offering, and come into his courts.

O worship the Lord in the beauty of holiness: fear before him,
  all the earth.

Let the heavens rejoice, and let the earth be glad; let the sea roar,
  and the fulness thereof.

Let the field be joyful, and all that is therein: then shall all the
  trees of the wood rejoice before the Lord: for he cometh, for he
  cometh to judge the earth: he shall judge the world with righteousness, and the people with his truth.[2]

PRAYER:

  Creator of all joy and all beauty,
  We bless thee this morning for thy bright
    world.
  We thank thee that
  We may look as thou lookest
  Upon all the beauty of the earth.
  We thank thee that we may listen
  To its songs of praise,
  Both vocal and silent.

  O Master, lover of beauty and joy,
  Make our hearts simple and trustful,
  That we may think with thee thine
    eternal thoughts,
  Thy wise childlike thoughts,
  Whereby the worlds are upheld.
  Make our wills lowly and pure,
  That we may share in thy will
  Whereby is created and upheld

All the joy and the beauty
Of this thy great universe.[3]

ANTHEM: "O Worship the Lord in the Beauty of Holiness,"
by Hollins, or

HYMN: "For the Beauty of the Earth," or
"All Creatures of Our God and King," or
"This Is My Father's World."

STORY:

SINGER IN LIGHT AND COLOR

"ONE MORNING I awoke to a dirty, foggy Pittsburgh, when the smoke hung like a shroud over everything. I was utterly discouraged with myself as a mere worker in a glass shop. There was something within me that was aching for expression. The little shop in which I worked did not give me much chance to bring out what I felt to be a worthy expression.

"I was ready to admit defeat when, looking into my mother's garden, I saw a great red poppy lifting its defiant head into the dirt, smoke and fog. It sang to me of courage and valor so clearly that, from that morning, I have wanted to sing in active color and light."

Thus in his own words a great artist of our generation began to express the relation he felt between color and light and the spiritual qualities of mankind. Charles J. Connick first became interested in glass when he was a cub cartoonist on the *Pittsburgh Press*. One night he visited the workroom of a glassman, and as the gas jet was lighted, there came from the loose pieces of glass lying in the room, a world of vibrating color.

The question immediately came to his mind, "Why cannot this quality of color be had in stained glass windows? Though ancient color formulas have been lost, could we not regain the mastery of the art?"

So determined was he to find the answer that young Connick resigned as a cartoonist and began to work for glassmen in Boston and in Pittsburgh. He learned their craft and skill, but restlessness haunted him, for he found that there was no opportunity for creative work. The chief concern of his trade was to give customers what they wanted —not to express new ideas through color.

Still in the mood of discouragement he took his mother to a hotel on Cape Cod for a long rest after his father's death. One of the hotel guests, a Mr. Swift, noticed the courteous attention the young man gave his mother and was impressed by their simple good times together as the son sketched in oils and water colors. When the vacation ended, Mr. Swift visited Connick and announced abruptly, "The All Saint's Church at Brookline in Boston is being built, and I want you to make a window for it."

Astounded, the youthful artist replied, "I am an unknown worker in a commercial shop. How do you know that I can make a window that is worthy to be placed in a Gothic church designed by a noted firm of Boston architects? They will probably want an established English artist to make the window."

"Can you make the sort of window that they ought to have?" Mr. Swift retorted.

"Yes, I can, and I am eager for the chance."

"Then, if the window is made, you will make it," the new friend replied with a note of firmness in his voice.

Connick made the design, selected the glass, and painted it in the studio of a friendly craftsman. When the window was completed, the artist asked Mr. Swift, "How did you have the courage to back me, an unknown artist in stained glass, when you yourself had no means of knowing whether or not I was equipped for such a commission?"

The businessman replied, "I knew, for I could tell the sort of man you were from the way you treated your mother on the vacation that summer. I liked the chivalrous attention you paid to her. I enjoyed seeing you sit and paint while she looked on, holding an umbrella over you. I made up my mind that you were to be trusted with anything."

"But the way I treated my mother had nothing to do with my skill or my talent," the artist said with a laugh.

"But it had something to do with character," replied the businessman. "Honesty and integrity are valuable assets and have much weight with sincere persons in the business world."

The experience of making his first window gave the young man confidence. He used the money which he received to travel in Europe to study world-famous stained glass windows. His longest stay was at Chartres Cathedral, about fifty miles from Paris. When he saw what the master craftsmen of the Middle Ages had done in stained glass, he felt that there was no need to search further. Here was a message of jeweled light vibrating through the glass—not a portrait painted on glass.

Connick returned to America, determined to experiment until he could produce the same results through the use of his own original designs. He opened a shop in Boston. When donors of windows insisted that he copy the works oi ancient craftsmen, he replied, "I have no desire to be a mere copyist, for with the textures and colors made by glass makers, I believe there is something to be worked out in this generation that has never been done before."

Dr. Connick could not have been born at any time since the twelfth century and have found more ugliness in Protestant churches to make the sensitive person cringe. In many instances the windows shut out the light and spread such gloom that light has to be supplied artificially. He says: "Since the craft of stained glass belongs to the field of light and color, why make windows that blot out the light? As sound speaks in Beethoven's symphonies, so light in windows should speak."

One of the artist's favorite stories is about the "Love" window that dominates the choir group of the Princeton Chapel. On a certain morning when it was on exhibition in his studio, the sun flooded the room with radiance. The glass seemed to have acquired fresh beauty and significance in the path of that splendor. A stranger was standing before it, motionless and silent as though fixed to the spot. As Dr. Connick approached him, he turned and said in a vibrant voice, "Do you know Brahms—his *First Symphony*?"

"Yes, I love it," replied Connick.

"Do you recall the place where the sky opens in the fourth movement?" With a sweep of his arm he continued, "This is that place. I never expected to see it on this earth, but here it is!"

"And you," said Connick eagerly, "are the man for whom that window was made. You know its language. You are a musician?"

"Yes, I am a member of the Boston Symphony Orchestra," he replied.

The actual symbolism of the window had escaped the musician. When Dr. Connick called his attention to it, he accepted the explanation but continued to talk of the radiant vibrations of the window as though he still thought of it as music. He insisted that the good will, the fullness of warmth and light, and the radiant and hopeful good cheer of Brahms's fourth movement was the window's real message. He showed no surprise when Connick stated that the records of

Brahms's *First Symphony* had strengthened his heart and quickened his imagination as he developed the design for the window.

The musician replied, "Certainly, music is yours to use in your craft of stained glass. You have your own way of being a musician."

Connick's mother came into the studio following the visit of the musician. In relating the story to her the son said, "Mother, you have always been to me an opener of windows. You have put into a quiet life the qualities of faith, love, and courage that Brahms sang into his *First Symphony*. I have tried to put that conception of glorious music into this window which to me is a symphony of light and color. And I shall always think of this window as your own song of a good life beautifully lived." [4]

The studio on Harcourt Street in Boston has grown from a small beginning to a four-story building in which many workers are employed. Connick's windows are found in the most magnificent churches and chapels in America. [5]

Concerning the symbolism of colors Connick says:

"From the rich spiritual regions of the Middle Ages we have inherited a symbolism of color that is still recognized in our workaday world. The red cross of devotion and sacrifice now carries its message around a stricken world to remind us that in the twelfth century pure red was the color of divine love, passionate devotion, self-sacrifice, courage, martyrdom, and all of the warm impulses that belong to the greathearted everywhere.

"The blue of the Middle Ages was a pure cobalt, shading from deep to light, approaching sapphire. Blue supports red, so we acquiesce with those wise colorists who said that blue is the contemplative color—the color of Divine Wisdom. Blue symbolizes truth, constancy, eternity, Heaven itself, and the steadfastness of enduring loyalty that in our speech today we call 'true blue.'

"Green is the color of hope, springtime, youth, and victory. Gold symbolizes spiritual treasures, worthy achievement, and the good life. Violet, a combination of blue and red, symbolizes love, justice, and truth and is the color of royalty; while purple stands for pain, penitence, mystery, and death. Violet in ancient windows formed a beautiful background for shimmering silvery white, the symbol of faith, the light of truth, or peace and serenity."

There is a quality in Connick's windows that draws one back again and again to study and to enjoy them. As the light comes through the glass, the colors, pure and vibrant, inspire and lift one out of himself.

Connick is a master craftsman who works with a sincerity of purpose and finds great joy in his work. We can only conjecture whether he started a new era in glass or only happened to be there when the era came along. He has the distinction of being recognized during his lifetime as the greatest artist in his field in the world. The honorary degrees "master of fine arts" and "doctor of fine arts" have been conferred upon him by Princeton and Boston universities. He was awarded the gold medal at the San Francisco Exposition in 1915, the Logan medal at Chicago in 1917, and the Arts and Crafts medal at Boston in 1920.

The artist revealed in his windows is also seen in the man. The personality of Dr. Connick is as vibrant and radiant as any color combination designed in his studio. Many interests claim his attention. He may be in a distant city giving a lecture on stained glass, or in a library searching for material. He may be at his desk sketching a design or dictating to his wife an article on stained glass. He may be with friends, his face alight, speaking of a great theme which he will portray in a window. These varied interests form a complete mosaic of abundant living.

His abounding energy, enthusiasm, and keen sense of humor make him a delightful companion. His interest in people enables him to enter into their experiences. His zest in life, ready smile, and happy outlook on life reflect the radiance of a joyous life. He delights in doing simple things, such as driving through the country, hiking in the mountains, chatting with friends beside an open fire. He is the kind of person one would be pleased to number among his close friends.

PRAYER:

O Thou who art the all-pervading glory of the world, we bless thee for the power of beauty to gladden our hearts. We praise thee that even the least of us may feel a thrill of thy creative joy when we give form and substance to our thoughts and, beholding our handiwork, find it good and fair.

We praise thee for our brothers, the masters of form and color and sound, who have power to unlock for us the vaster spaces of emotion and to lead us by their hand into the reaches of nobler passions. We rejoice in their gifts and pray thee to save them from the temptations which beset their powers. Save them from the discouragements of a selfish ambition and from the vanity that feeds on cheap applause, from the snare of the senses and from the dark phantoms that haunt the listening soul.

Let them not satisfy their hunger for beauty with tricks of skill, turning the art of God into a petty craft of men. Teach them that they, too, are but servants of humanity, and that the promise of their gifts can fulfil itself only in the service of love. Give them faith in the inspiring power of a great purpose and courage to follow to the end the visions of their youth. Kindle in their hearts a passionate pity for the joyless lives of the people, and make them rejoice if they are found worthy to hold the cup of beauty to lips that are athirst. Make them the reverent interpreters of God to man, who see thy face and hear thy voice in all things, that so they may unveil for us the beauties of nature which we have passed unseeing, and the sadness and sweetness of humanity to which our selfishness has made us blind.[6] AMEN.

CLOSING HYMN: "We Thank Thee, Lord, Thy Paths," or
"Walk in the Light!"

SERVICE 3

SEEING THE INVISIBLE

PRELUDE: Hymn tune, "St. Asaph."

CALL TO WORSHIP:

O God, our Father,
We would ascend into thy holy hill,
We would enter into thy holy place,
And stand in thy glorious presence,
That we may commune with thee;
Therefore cleanse our hands
And purify our hearts;
And reveal thy beauty and thy truth
To guide us unto thyself. AMEN.[1]

—CHAUNCEY R. PIETY

HYMN: "My God, I Thank Thee, Who Hast Made," or
"Praise the Lord! Ye Heavens, Adore Him."

LITANY:

Leader: Lift up your hearts.

Group: We lift them up unto the Lord.

Leader: O Lord, open thou our eyes,

Group: That we may see the beauty of goodness.

Leader: O Lord, open thou our ears,

Group: That we may hear the appeal of truth.

Leader: O Lord, open thou our lips,

Group: And our mouth shall show forth thy praise.

Leader: Praised be the Lord.

Group: The Lord's name be praised. AMEN.

SEEING THE INVISIBLE

> The Lord is my light and my salvation; whom
>   shall I fear? the Lord is the strength of
>   my life; of whom shall I be afraid?
> Hear, O Lord, when I cry with my voice:
>   have mercy also upon me, and answer me.
> When thou saidst, Seek ye my face; my heart
>   said unto thee, Thy face, Lord, will I seek.
> Hide not thy face far from me; put not thy
>   servant away in anger: thou hast been my
>   help; leave me not, neither forsake me,
>   O God of my salvation.
> When my father and my mother forsake me, then
>   the Lord will take me up.
> Teach me thy way, O Lord, and lead me in a
>   plain path, because of mine enemies.
> Deliver me not over unto the will of mine
>   enemies: for false witnesses are risen up
>   against me, and such as breathe out cruelty.
> I had fainted, unless I had believed to see
>   the goodness of the Lord in the land of
>   the living.
> Wait on the Lord: be of good courage, and he
>   shall strengthen thine heart: wait, I say,
>   on the Lord.[2]

Hymn: "O Love That Wilt Not Let Me Go," or
   "He Leadeth Me."

Story:

BLIND—YET SHE SEES

Anne Sullivan was called to Tuscumbia, Alabama, to begin the education of a seven-year-old child who, born normal, was left blind, deaf, and dumb by an illness that attacked her at nineteen months of age. It was a baffling task, for the teacher herself had been almost blind until an operation gave her sight enough to read coarse print. Miss Sullivan began the patient search to find a way to reach the mind of Helen Keller. For four weeks she spelled words into Helen's palm, and still the child had no idea of what it meant. Her only response was to fly into a rage and throw herself on the floor. Patiently and diligently the teacher worked until she won the child's affection and was able at last to communicate with her.

Helen says of these early years:

"Have you ever been at sea in a dense fog, when it seemed as if a tangible white darkness shut you in, and the great ship, tense and anxious, groped her way toward the shore with plummet and sounding line, and you waited with beating heart for something to happen? I was like that ship before my education began, only I was without compass or sounding line, and had no way of knowing how near the harbour was. 'Light, give me light' was the wordless cry of my soul, and the light of love shone on me in that very hour.

"We walked down the path to the well-house, attracted by the fragrance of the honeysuckle with which it was covered. Someone was drawing water and my teacher placed my hand under the spout. As the cool stream gushed over one hand she spelled into the other the word *water,* first slowly, then rapidly. I stood still, my whole attention fixed upon the motions of her fingers. Suddenly, I felt a misty consciousness as of something forgotten—a thrill of returning thought; and somehow the mystery of language was revealed to me. I knew then that "w-a-t-e-r" meant the wonderful cool something that was flowing over my hand. That living word awakened my soul, gave it light, hope, joy, set it free! There were barriers still, it is true, but barriers that could in time be swept away.

"I left the well-house eager to learn. Everything had a name, and . . . every object which I touched quivered with life. That was because I saw everything with the strange, new sight that had come to me." [3]

That was the beginning of a modern-day miracle. New life began for both teacher and pupil on that day.

The teacher's work required ingenuity, infinite patience, and perseverance. Her knowledge of books was scanty, and there was no one to advise her, but day after day she devised means of opening up to her pupil the wonder-world of childhood. With her brilliant mind and willing spirit Helen soon learned to read; afterwards she was sent with her teacher to the Perkins Institute in Boston, where she made rapid progress.

Hearing of a blind, deaf, and dumb Norwegian girl who had learned to speak, Helen determined to learn to talk. She studied at the Horace Mann School in New York City and after much effort was able to pronounce words. In a short while she was able to carry on a conversation with others by placing her fingers on their lips. After accomplishing the difficult task, her favorite sentence was, "I am not dumb now."

Helen studied at Radcliffe College, taking the same course as other students and, declining to accept any favors, mastered every subject. At that time the textbooks were not written in Braille, so Miss Sullivan spelled into her palm the lectures in the classes and also the material from the textbooks. Finishing the courses of study in the same length of time as other classmates, Helen graduated with honors. She not only mastered English but learned Spanish, French, Italian, Latin, and Greek. She is the author of several books, and much of her time is given to lecturing in the interest of the blind.

Even though deprived of sight and hearing, Miss Keller is not shut out from the world of beauty. She says, "God did not put much of his world in raised print;

> My ears are dead, the birds are mute,
> And still they sing;
> It is within my heart they sing
> As I pass by."

Though her impressions come through touch and the sense of smell, her days vary as much as anyone's. She says, "I am conscious of days when the air feels like a veil of gossamer softly dropped in a shower of silver mist. I am conscious of glad days when the sun brings a message of spring. I know great, shouting days that goad me into activity—days when the wind beats against me, challenging me to leap up and wrestle with them.

"To me motion is the beauty of the trees, the cornfields, and the sea. My fingers thrill as I feel the wind toss nature's 'soft hair of grass.' It is both an emblem of growth and of eternity, roving far over land and sea; it is to my touch what I imagine the horizon is to the eye. It brings me a sense of infinite space, of mystery, of sublimity. The wind symbolizes gladness, the urge and aspiration with which the spirit of God keeps my inner life aglow.

"It is in the country that I am at home. Everything my foot touches is alive with interest. Bright-hued flowers march beside me and hold up lovely faces; the violets open their eyes and look at me wonderingly. I love to put out my hand and catch the rustling tread of small creatures in the leaves. I love to follow dark roads that smell of moss and wet grasses, hill roads and deep valley roads so narrow that the trees and bushes touch me as I pass. I love to sit on a fallen tree so long that the shy wood-things forget that it may be impudent to step on my toes.

"With body still and observant I hear myriad sounds that I understand—leaf sounds, grass sounds, and twigs creaking faintly when birds alight on them. I like to stand waiting, expectant of the birth of the day. The skies grow bright, I see the sun raise his beautiful face above a silvery misty sea; and I find the thing I have long sought and hoped for—the light!" [4]

Miss Keller is much disturbed by the unhappiness in the world today. She says, "Faith to hold fast to the ideal of democracy is the thing most needed in the world." To the question often asked, "If you knew that you could have one wish granted, what would it be?" her reply is, "I should wish for peace and liberty in all the lands of the world."

When Miss Keller was asked to enumerate the things she would like to see if by a miracle her sight should be restored for at least three days, she replied, "First, the face of my teacher who opened up the outer world to me. Perhaps then I might see the evidence of the sympathetic tenderness and patience with which the difficult task was accomplished." She would like to see the faces of all the friends who have been kind to her; her home with its familiar objects, and the birds and flowers and all the beauty of the out-of-doors.

History and art mean much to Miss Keller. Naturally she would like to spend some time in a historical museum that she might see the pageant of the progress of the world, and in an art museum where she would see the history of the nations expressed in art. She is interested especially in seeing a bust of Homer, for he was blind also. She would like to spend one day in the business world that she might fill her mind full of the images of people and things.

The conventional atmosphere of the cities disturbs Miss Keller, largely because she feels the lack of personal liberty, which next to idleness is the hardest part of being blind. She grows indignant over the contrast between the way the rich and the poor live. She says, "The half-clad, underfed men and women who live in the tenements are denied the sun and air which are God's free gifts to all. I have felt their rough hands and realized what an endless struggle their existence must be."

Miss Keller spends much of her time helping those who are handicapped by blindness and deafness. She has lectured throughout the United States, Canada, England, and Scotland in behalf of the blind.

She has become a world leader in this field, and the money earned from her lectures is given to the American Foundation for the Blind. She is interested in the phonographic "talking book" system, for she feels that through it a vast field of literature will be opened to the blind. Unable to hear even the loudest sounds, she enjoys music through the vibrations coming from an instrument, or by placing her fingers on the throat of a singer. She has expressed preference for Beethoven's symphonies, for she feels that he triumphed over his own deafness.

There was a close relation between Miss Keller and her teacher, Anne Sullivan Macy. The teacher was both eyes and ears for the pupil. However, in 1936 the friendship of forty-nine years was broken by the death of the teacher. Rising above the weight of sorrow caused by the separation, Miss Keller continued to carry on her work. Naturally she has not ceased to long for the touch of her teacher's hand—the hand that changed the darkness of her mind to happiness and usefulness. She thinks of her teacher now as being able to see without effort and using all her powers freely and joyously.

Miss Keller's greatest difficulty was learning to speak, but the mastery of it gave her spirit wings and helped her to reach the mind of others. Her limitations do not make her unhappy, for she feels that God is working out some good purpose through them. With Job she says, "Though he slay me, yet will I trust in him." Her troubles have made her sympathetic, have helped her to understand, and have given her the desire to serve those who are handicapped. It may be that she does not consider it a cross to be blind and deaf. But if it be a cross, she bears it with a degree of patience that is amazing.

In spite of her limitations Miss Keller accomplishes more than most of us with all of our faculties. Her happy outlook on life cheers those who are despondent; her firm faith in God points the way to those who are facing difficulty. She brings hope to those who are discouraged and helps them to live courageously and joyously under adverse circumstances. She has developed an inner vision which enables her to see beauty where others pass it by unnoticed. She is able to see God where others see stone.

POEM:

> Happy are they that have eyes to see:
> They shall find God everywhere.
> They shall see him where others see stone.

Happy are they that have deep insight.
They shall rejoice in undiscovered ways of God.
Happy are they who know the power of love:
They live in his spirit, for God is love.
Happy are they that live for truth:
They find a way to relieve the hearts of men.
Happy are the souls fully given to thee.
They shall be filled with peace and perfect love!

—AUTHOR UNKNOWN

LITANY:

Leader: Our Father, for the beauty which thou hast created to enrich our lives,

Group: We are grateful.

Leader: For eyes to see and minds to understand,

Group: We thank thee.

Leader: For the light which dispels the darkness,

Group: We are grateful.

Leader: If some of us continue to walk in darkness,

Group: Open our eyes that we may see.

Leader: Give us a vision of ourselves as thou seest us,

Group: We pray thee, O Lord.

Leader: Grant us a vision of the persons we can become,

Group: We beseech thee, O Lord.

Leader: Give us strength to overcome our limitations,

Group: We pray thee, O Lord.

Leader: Help us to surmount the obstacles that are in our path,

Group: We beseech thee, O Lord.

Leader: Grant that we may take whatever the day sends and make it contribute to our growth and development,

Group: We beseech thee, O Lord.

Leader: As we think of those who have served humanity, may we determine to use our talents in such a manner as to make the world a better and happier place,

Group: In Jesus' name, we pray. AMEN.

HYMN: "Joyful, Joyful, We Adore Thee," or
"Open My Eyes That I May See."

—34—

SERVICE 4

THE CHOICE GOES BY FOREVER

PRELUDE: Hymn tune, "Vesper Hymn."

CALL TO WORSHIP:

> Blessed are the undefiled in the way, who walk
> in the law of the Lord.
> Blessed are they that keep his testimonies, and
> that seek him with the whole heart.
>
> . . . .
>
> Wherewithal shall a young man cleanse his way?
> by taking heed thereto according to thy word.
> With my whole heart have I sought thee: O let
> me not wander from thy commandments.
> Thy word have I hid in mine heart, that I
> might not sin against thee.
>
> . . . .
>
> Teach me, O Lord, the way of thy statutes;
> and I shall keep it unto the end.
> Give me understanding, and I shall keep thy
> law; yea, I shall observe it with my
> whole heart.[1]

HYMN: "Awake, Awake to Love and Work," or
"Go, Labor On."

PRAYER:

O Thou, who art the light of the minds that know thee, the life of
the souls that love thee, and the strength of the hearts that serve thee;
help us so to know thee that we may truly love thee, so to love thee
that we may fully serve thee, whom to serve is perfect freedom; through
Jesus Christ our Lord. AMEN.

LEADER:

Are great men produced in a crisis or conflict? Is that why there are more heroes in times of war? Does one have to be confronted with a crisis in order to prove the stuff of which he is made?

Thought usually comes before action. Heroes are not made overnight but are in the process of becoming heroes when they choose their way of life. The testing time comes when they are given an opportunity to perform an act which is above and beyond the call of duty. For that kind of test there is no time to cram—one is either prepared or unprepared. The result of their thinking in the past comes out in action. Thus heroes are made over a long period of time, but they are not recognized until the testing time comes.

STORY:

ABOVE AND BEYOND THE CALL OF DUTY

MANY stories of heroism have come out of World War II, and Sergeant Henry Eugene Erwin's story ranks with any of them. He was the first B-29 crewman to win the Congressional Medal of Honor. In Northington General Hospital he was lying in a position calculated to put the least strain on the seared muscles of his right arm where the phosphorus bomb had burned to the bone. He spoke quietly, saying, "They made some fuss about my being a hero. It didn't occur to me that way at the time. I knew the bomb was burning, and I had to get it out of there. It was one man against eleven. I think any man in that ship would have done the same."

On the morning of April 12, 1945, twelve men were aboard a Superfortress that was leading a formation of B-29's on a mission against a gasoline plant 125 miles north of Tokyo. The co-pilot instructed Erwin to fire some flares and a smoke bomb. Erwin got off the colored flares all right. Then he picked up the phosphorus marker, a bomb about the size of two water tumblers. The chute through which the flares and the bombs are dropped is a metal tube about three and one-half inches in diameter. Erwin, working bare-armed and bare-headed, pulled the pin of the bomb and dropped it through. The fuse was faulty. The bomb exploded midway and blew back up the chute.

Phosphorus is sticky, slow-burning, and persistent. When the bomb exploded, it blew phosphorus particles into Erwin's face. His face and head and right arm were covered with the burning chemical.

The plane filled with a thick smoke, and the pilot, for the moment

—36—

blinded and choked, temporarily lost control. The B-29 was at 1,000 feet but soon dropped to 300 feet. It was carrying 6,000 pounds of general purpose bombs from which the pins had already been pulled. The bombs could not be thrown overboard, because at that altitude the explosion would wreck the plane, and if they weren't jettisoned, they would explode when the ship hit the water. There wasn't much time to waste.

The section of the cabin in which the radio operator sits is about nine by thirteen feet. But the center is blocked by a huge, circular turret from which the ship's forward guns are fired. The rest of the floor space is so cluttered with tables, seats, and other items of equipment that it is difficult to move about. One would say that it was impossible for a man, blinded and with flesh and clothing burning, to get by all the objects and carry the spewing bomb from the chute to the co-pilot's window. Somehow Erwin squeezed by the turret, only to find his way blocked by the navigator's table. It takes both hands to open this table, for it has a spring lock and drops down from the side wall. Erwin tucked the burning bomb under his right arm, lifted the table, and left the imprint of one hand on the table in seared flesh.

Then he staggered forward, yelling "Open the window!" for he could not see that it already was open. He groped for the window, hurled out the bomb, and then slumped to the floor. This took about ten seconds. By now he was on fire. His face, arms, and hands were smoldering, and his rubber life preserver was in flames.

"I never passed out, or felt any pain. I just knew I had to get that thing out of there. First they turned the fire extinguisher on me to put out the fire. What did I think of when the bomb hit me in the face? I could tell this thing was going to come back in the plane—I don't know whether I really saw it or just sensed it. I tried to stop it by putting my foot over the bomb chute, but it was no use. It caught me in the face and spewed all over me and put out my eyes, or so I thought at the time.

"It's hard to say just what was going through my mind. About all I remember thinking was 'I've got to get it out. If I don't get it out, we're all going to die.' I can't say why I didn't feel the pain. I was in plenty agony later. When I was lying there on the floor, I tried opening my eyes. There was phosphorus on them, and it was still smoldering, but I discovered I could see out of the corner of my left eye.

"I could hear Colonel Strouse asking the flight engineer how fast we could go back to Iwo and not use up our gas. We got there in an hour and a half. Our formation, though, went on to the target and knocked it out.

"They gave me some morphine, but it didn't put me out. Maybe it was a good thing, for I was the first-aid man on the ship, and I told the right gunner how to give me plasma.

"On the flight to Iwo I was praying to the Lord to let me get home and see my wife and my mother. That's all I wanted. We got to Iwo in the middle of a heavy air raid. They didn't want us to land, but Colonel Strouse told them we had to land. Our bunch had to get in the foxholes, but they got me to the hospital."

It was four days before they thought it safe to fly Sergeant Erwin to Guam. They still didn't know whether he would live. Meanwhile, General LeMay had sent to Washington the recommendation that Sergeant Erwin receive the Medal of Honor. Red tape was slashed, and on April 16 the award was approved. The actual presentation did not take place immediately, for there were no Medals of Honor in Guam, and one had to be flown from Hawaii.

Erwin said: "I was stunned. With General Hale, General LeMay, and some one-star generals present, there was more brass around my bed than I had ever seen in one spot before; but, best of all, my officers and crew were standing up there with them. I can remember General Hale reading the citation. I opened one eye and could make out the medal."

The sergeant digressed to talk about the boy who gave him plasma: "He's a Jewish boy from Jamaica, N. Y. You know, in Alabama I hadn't known many Jewish people. Not many Catholics, either. In the Army you learn something about people. When you get a buddy on your plane and eat and sleep together, and borrow each other's clothes, and fight together, you learn there's not much difference in religions. This Sergeant Schnipper is a really swell guy; he'd give me the shirt off his back, and there's nothing I wouldn't do for him.

"I think the country's going to be better off for what our boys are learning about these things. Take Negroes. You know, down South most people don't think so much of the Negro; they think he doesn't work. Well, when I saw what the Negro engineers did in getting the blacktop down on our field in Guam, I changed my mind about them."

To understand how Erwin was able to perform his heroic action in such quick, dogged, automatic fashion, it is helpful to know something about him. His life has been a hard struggle—mostly work and very little play. He has taken what life has given him without flinching, just as he took that burning bomb, and he has managed to come out pretty well in everything.

"I was born on May 8, 1921, in Docena, Alabama, a little coal-mining town," Erwin said from his hospital bed. It was a study in itself to watch him. He had a powerful set of shoulders and a tremendous, almost bulging forehead. Red hair cropped out from between his bandages. His right lid was raw from the fire but his hazel eyes looked straight at you. He didn't smile once during the entire recital, for it was not a pretty story. Besides, his lips were still slightly seared.

His father, a coal miner, who worked hard but earned little, died when Erwin was ten. His mother, left with seven children, took in washing while the boy worked in the coal company commissary. Somehow he managed to get through two years of high school before he quit at sixteen to work on his uncle's farm. When he joined the CCC in 1938, his mother received twenty-two dollars a month out of his thirty dollars pay. By taking advantage of study courses he was able to earn sufficient credits for a high school diploma.

Erwin was always religious—from as far back as he could remember. He talked about the Lord as a close personal friend and did it with a simple sincerity that was utterly genuine. As a member of the Bethlehem Methodist Church at Bessemer, Alabama, he has served as president of the Youth Fellowship of the West Birmingham district. When he entered the service, this group presented him with a gold-plated pocket Testament, inscribed "For God and Country."

In October 1941 Erwin went to work for the Fairfield Steel Works—a hot, back-breaking job—hooking white-hot steel that was rolled into plates for ships and tanks. The pay was enough to enable him to buy a five-room frame house in Bessemer. As a war worker and the main support of a family he was draft-exempt, but he enlisted in 1942. His grades in radio school were such that he was given a chance to go to Yale as a communications cadet, where he could have earned an officer's commission. However, when volunteers were needed for a B-29 crew, Erwin let the lieutenant's bars go by to join the crew of the B-29's. He went into training at Pratt, Kansas, in September, 1944, and all the eleven officers and men who started together went overseas in February. Before going over, he married Elizabeth Starnes, whom he had met at his church. He moved his family into his house, and Elizabeth divided her time between his family and her own family.

Because of the miracles of modern medicine Sergeant Erwin is going to be almost as good as he ever was. They flew him from Guam on

May 6 in a special transport plane with a doctor and nurse in attendance. Four days later he arrived in Tuscaloosa. At Northington by skillful skin grafting his burns have nearly all been hidden. He'll be able to use his badly burned arm, though his right hand will be stiff. The town of Bessemer, where he lives, has bought a furnished home for him.[2]

Sergeant Erwin had built his philosophy of life around the Christian ideals of love and self-sacrifice. He did not take time to stop and consider whether he would follow his convictions and sacrifice himself that the other crew members might live. His Christian ideals were so strong that he acted automatically, and by sacrificing himself he saved not only himself but the others as well. Are our Christian convictions strong enough to determine our automatic actions?

"For whosoever will save his life shall lose it; but whosoever shall lose his life for my sake and the gospel's, the same shall save it." [3]

POEM:

Once to every man and nation comes the moment to decide,
In the strife of Truth with Falsehood, for the good or evil side;
Some great cause, God's new Messiah, offering each the bloom or blight,
. . . .
And the choice goes by forever 'twixt that darkness and that light.
Then to side with Truth is noble when we share her wretched crust,
Ere her cause bring fame and profit, and 'tis prosperous to be just;
Then it is the brave man chooses, while the coward stands aside,
. . . .
And the multitude make virtue of the faith they had denied.

—JAMES RUSSELL LOWELL

PRAYER:

Our Father, help us to realize that the only way to self-realization is through the giving of self. Forgive us for the times when we have given in a half-hearted way, or when we have given for the approval of others. Help us to realize that we should not keep our possessions to ourselves. Forgive us for our selfishness and littleness. May thy spirit so dominate our lives that all of our thinking and acting may be Christian. Reveal to us thy will and purpose. May the Christian ideal of self-sacrifice be so strong in our lives that we will put our selfish interests in the background and lose ourselves in the service of others. Grant that we may begin each day joyously and zestfully because of the opportunities it offers to serve others. Grant that our convictions may become strong enough to guide even our automatic actions. In Jesus' name. AMEN.

HYMN: "Rise Up, O Men of God," or
  "March On, O Soul, with Strength."

BENEDICTION:

May thy spirit lead and guide us in every decision we make. AMEN.

SERVICE 5

SHARING THE CHAINS OF OUR BROTHERS

PRELUDE: "Largo," by Dvořák.

CALL TO WORSHIP:

> We are watchers of a beacon whose light must
>   never die;
> We are guardians of an altar that shows thee
>   ever nigh;
> We are children of thy freemen who sleep
>   beneath the sod;
> For the might of thine arm we bless thee:
>   our God, our fathers' God.
>
> —CHARLES SILVESTER HORNE

HYMN: "Come, Thou Almighty King," or
      "All Hail the Power of Jesus' Name."

SCRIPTURE:

> Out of the depths have I cried unto thee, O Lord.
> Lord, hear my voice: let thine ears be attentive
>   to the voice of my supplications.
> If thou, Lord, shouldest mark iniquities, O Lord,
>   who shall stand?
> But there is forgiveness with thee, that thou
>   mayest be feared.
> I wait for the Lord, my soul doth wait, and in
>   his word do I hope.
> My soul waiteth for the Lord more than they that
>   watch for the morning:
> I say, more than they that watch for the morning.

Let Israel hope in the Lord: for with the Lord
there is mercy, and with him is plenteous
redemption.
And he shall redeem Israel from all his iniquities.[1]

PRAYER:

Saviour divine,
Who perpetually for suffering humanity
Dost bear the burden,
The dread, relentless burden of redemption,
We pray thee that we thy servants today
May with these weak hands
Uplift a little corner of the weight which crushes
thee.

Grant unto us that we may share in thy holy
mystery of pain,
Thy sacrament of agony,
Which redeemeth the world.
Give us courage of heart,
That we may drink with thee a little of thy cup,
Thy bitter cup of humiliation, of loneliness, of
suffering.
Help us to see thee as thou art,
Incarnate in the starving, the disease-stricken, the
hopeless:
Give us grace in serving them to serve thee.

In our own loneliness and pain,—
If thou bestowest upon us these tokens of thy
fellowship,—
Help us to pay honestly, unstintingly and bravely
Our part of the great price,
Which of old and forever thou, O our God,
Payest in man for man.

Ennoble us this day with a share in thy work of
redemption. AMEN.[2]

HYMN: "Where Cross the Crowded Ways of Life," or
"God of the Strong, God of the Weak."

LEADER:

We are inclined to take for granted our religious heritage and fail to show appreciation for the leaders who have improved social conditions, made the world happier, and enriched our lives. Let us give honor to whom honor is due as we hear the story of the woman who started prison reform.

STORY:

ELIZABETH FRY, FRIEND OF PRISONERS

BECAUSE of her happy outlook upon life, Elizabeth Gurney rebelled against the soberness of the strict family life in which she was reared. Judged by the standards of the Quaker sect to which her parents belonged, her life filled with music, opera, and parties was considered quite gay. At the age of seventeen Elizabeth became seriously interested in studying the beliefs of the different religious sects. She finally assumed the Quaker garb, became a full-fledged member of the Society of Friends, and dedicated her life to social work.

Elizabeth had a great desire to do full-time religious work but instead married Joseph Fry, a London merchant. A family of eleven children took up much of her time, but she initiated and financed a number of projects for the relief of the poor. In her ministry to those neglected by the church she visited the sick, distributed clothing to the needy, and taught Bible classes in her home.

All of her spare time was taken up in social work, but when the call to the ministry came, Elizabeth responded at once. She was accepted by the Society of Friends as a minister, traveled over England and Scotland, established schools, and preached a practical message which appealed to the people. In her work she saw many deplorable situations, but nothing stirred her sympathy more than the conditions of the prisons.

In her efforts to bring about a change she began with Newgate prison in London, where she found men, women, and children, clothed in dirty rags and crowded into one large room. Herded together with little privacy, no employment, and no recreation, the prisoners spent their time quarreling, drinking, and gambling. It was the custom when a mother was sent to prison to send her children with her if there was no one to care for them. Mrs. Fry asked, "Is it fair to force these children to live with the worst criminals of the slums and listen to their degrading conversations? What have they done to merit such punishment?"

At that time it was the accepted opinion that a criminal was an enemy of society, and for him to reform was a remote possibility. Since he was thought to be incurable, he must be punished, and in some instances it seemed expedient to get rid of him. Mrs. Fry believed that a man broke the law, not because he preferred wrongdoing, but because of ignorance or the lack of opportunity to do right. She felt that instead of blaming him, we should reproach those who had failed him by leaving him in his ignorance. Although he had transgressed once, he did not need to remain a criminal. The prisons and reform schools should be moral hospitals where people could be healed and taught how to live.

In the face of bitter opposition which branded her reforms as radical, this courageous pioneer insisted on kindness to the insane, fair and humane treatment of criminals, and a continued program of education for discharged prisoners. She also believed that crime could be prevented by taking children out of improper environment, placing them in wholesome surroundings, and giving them a well-rounded education.

In transforming the prisons Mrs. Fry started many projects, chief of which was a school for prisoners under twenty-five years of age. Classes were formed, teachers employed, and a very creditable piece of work was carried on. A class in handwork for the women brought large returns. Among the women prisoners she distributed cloth and yarn and used the most skillful of them as instructors in sewing and knitting. The women shared the proceeds from the sale of the articles which they were taught to make.

The effect on the prisoners was greater than anticipated; the morale improved to the extent that the guard was reduced by half. Formerly, when prisoners were transferred to other prisons, they burned buildings, wrecked furniture, and destroyed anything within their reach. Following Mrs. Fry's reforms, the prisoners withdrew quietly, thanked the keepers, and shared their savings with those who stayed behind.

On her preaching tours Mrs. Fry visited jails in other cities and talked with those in authority about the improvements at Newgate. Visitors came from practically every city in the British Isles to study the methods employed. As the story of the reforms spread, Russia, Denmark, and other countries sent representatives to talk with the woman who had transformed the English prisons. Her fame spread until she was the best-known woman of her day. The British Parliament commended and encouraged her in the work.

Elizabeth Fry lived to see most of her prison reform ideas carried out, not only in Great Britain, but in other countries. The improvements in our present penal system may be attributed to the work of this unusual Quaker woman. Extremely sensitive to the needs of the unfortunate, she had a breadth of vision, a charity and tolerance toward those who differed with her, that few have attained. Her success may be attributed largely to her ability to work with people of various social levels. On the same day she might associate with noblemen and outcasts, with high-ranking officials and jailers. She felt equally at home with all of them. Elizabeth Fry changed the public opinion of her day regarding the treatment of prisoners, and her example encourages those who are carrying forward the work which she began.

SCRIPTURE:

Love your enemies, do good to them which hate you, bless them that curse you, and pray for them which despitefully use you. And unto him that smiteth thee on the one cheek offer also the other; and him that taketh away thy cloke forbid not to take thy coat also. Give to every man that asketh of thee; and of him that taketh away thy goods ask them not again. And as ye would that men should do to you, do ye also to them likewise. For if ye love them which love you, what thank have ye? for sinners also love those that love them. And if ye do good to them which do good to you, what thank have ye? for sinners also do even the same. And if ye lend to them of whom ye hope to receive, what thank have ye? for sinners also lend to sinners, to receive as much again. But love ye your enemies, and do good, and lend, hoping for nothing again; and your reward shall be great, and ye shall be the children of the Highest: for he is kind unto the unthankful and to the evil. Be ye therefore merciful, as your Father also is merciful. Judge not, and ye shall not be judged: condemn not, and ye shall not be condemned: forgive, and ye shall be forgiven: give, and it shall be given unto you; good measure, pressed down, and shaken together, and running over, shall men give into your bosom. For with the same measure that ye mete withal it shall be measured to you again.[3]

SOLO: "I Shall Not Pass Again This Way," by Effinger, or

HYMN: "O Master, Let Me Walk with Thee," or
    "Truehearted, Wholehearted, Faithful and Loyal."

SHARING THE CHAINS OF OUR BROTHERS

PRAYER:

O Lord, we are grateful for the great and good persons who have used their talents to make the world a better and happier place; we thank thee for their insight and their vision. Grant that the record of their lives will make us sensitive to the plight of the poor. May their example remind us of the importance of putting self into the background and becoming wholeheartedly interested in a worthy cause. Forgive us for our lack of sympathy, compassion, and tenderness toward the unfortunate, and grant that we may show our gratitude for the good things which we enjoy by sharing them with those who are in need. AMEN.

BENEDICTION:

The Lord bless us, and keep us: the Lord make his face to shine upon us, and be gracious unto us: the Lord lift up his countenance upon us and give us peace. AMEN.

SERVICE 6

THE SCAFFOLD SWAYS THE FUTURE

PRELUDE: Hymn tune, *"Ein' Feste Burg."*

CALL TO WORSHIP:

> They that wait upon the Lord shall renew
> their strength;
> They shall mount up with wings as eagles;
> They shall run, and not be weary;
> And they shall walk, and not faint.
> Wait on the Lord:
> Be of good courage,
> And he shall strengthen thine heart.[1]

HYMN: "A Mighty Fortress Is Our God," or
"Faith of Our Fathers."

RESPONSIVE READING:

Leader: Blessed are they which are persecuted for righteousness' sake:
for their's is the kingdom of heaven.

Group: Hymn, "Be Strong" (first stanza)

Leader: Blessed are ye, when men shall revile you, and persecute you,
and shall say all manner of evil against you falsely, for my sake.

Group: (second stanza of hymn)

Leader: Rejoice, and be exceeding glad: for great is your reward in
heaven: for so persecuted they the prophets which were before
you.[2]

Group: (third stanza of hymn)

PRAYER POEM:

> I pray for the mind of the rebel
> That will question the new and old,

And look underneath the plain label
   For the truth of that I hold.

I pray for the heart of the rebel
   That will crave the forbidden fruit,
And go seeking to save the unlovely
   Till victory crowns the pursuit.

I pray for the soul of the rebel
   Persistently trying to prove,
The soul that will challenge and challenge—
   That will not stay put in a groove.

I pray for the life of the rebel
   That will dare all worlds and space,
And trail wary Truth to her Temple,
   And see God face to face.[3]

                     —CHAUNCEY R. PIETY

STORY:

POLYCARP, SERENE MARTYR

POLYCARP, born of Christian parents about A.D. 70, grew up in the Church and, though it meant persecution, preached the gospel wherever he went. Finally, becoming a bishop, he was held in great reverence. When more than eighty years of age, he was arrested and brought to trial at Smyrna. An important Roman holiday, probably February 23, A.D. 155, was at hand. The governor, eager to please the people, had a group of Christians arrested and brought into the arena to be slain by the wild beasts in celebration of the holiday.

Since early morning a great multitude of jostling, shouting people had filled the stadium. There was an air of eager expectancy; the excitement reached fever pitch. When it was known that in addition to the games twelve Christians would be offered up, the people cheered wildly, for this was their favorite sport. Quintus, one of the victims, recanted when he saw the fury of the beasts, but to the delight of the curious, morbid crowd his companion, Germanicus, walked boldly up to the lion and defied the creature.

When eleven of the victims had been disposed of, it seemed that the day would end with an anticlimax. Polycarp, the chief victim, had not yet appeared. His friends had secured permission for him to retire to a farmhouse outside the city to await his execution. The manager of the festivities had hesitated before sending for the victim. Hating to make a spectacle of one so old, so gentle and refined, the manager felt that it was a shame that Polycarp insisted on being such an active Christian.

At last the soldiers were sent to bring in the prisoner. When they reached the farmhouse, Polycarp met them as graciously as if they were friends, insisting that they partake of refreshments while he retired to pray. While enjoying his hospitality, they heard him praying for them and for all with whom he had associated—friends and enemies alike. As they listened, they thought of his approaching death. It would not be easy to put to death a kind old man who had harmed no one, but the laws of the empire must be maintained.

When the Bishop had ended his prayer, he rode passively away with the soldiers. As they entered the city, Roman officials met them, asking for the privilege of talking with the prisoner. Taking him into their chariot, they tried to persuade him to give up the strange religion and thus save himself from certain death. They said: "If you will give up your belief in Christ, we shall not have to take you into the arena to face the wild beasts. Quintus, one of your group, seeing the horror of the spectacle, recanted today. If you will also give up your faith, we will set you free."

The officials threatened and coaxed, but Polycarp calmly refused to deny his religion. Seeing that their entreaties availed nothing, the officers became enraged, pushed the Bishop from the chariot, and ordered him to walk the remainder of the way to the stadium. When they reached the arena, a shout went up from the mob that awaited the arrival of the prisoner. They cried out: "Away with Polycarp! He is the one who opposed the worship of the emperor. He would not let our people worship our gods. Christians are multiplying every day because of his influence. Put him to death, and stamp out this strange religion. Burn him at the stake!"

When Polycarp entered the arena, his dignity astonished the people. A few of his friends standing by watching the procedure declared that an invisible supporter spoke to the aged man saying, "Be strong, Polycarp, and play the man." Before his accusers he was calm and fearless; his face shone like Stephen's.

The proconsul, making a last appeal, begged him to denounce the religion to which he clung so tenaciously, saying, "Don't you hear the people clamoring for your death, insisting that you be burned at the stake? Curse Christ, and I will set you free."

Polycarp answered, "Eighty and six years have I served Christ, and he did me no wrong. How then can I revile my King, that saved me?"

When the proconsul persisted, saying, "Swear by the fortune of Caesar," Polycarp replied, "If you vainly imagine that I shall swear by the fortune of Caesar, you are mistaken. Hear a plain answer: 'I am a Christian.' "

The friends of Polycarp were much impressed by his courageous manner; he was full of confidence and joy and not at all troubled by the things said to him. The proconsul was so amazed that he sent his herald to proclaim to the people, "Polycarp has confessed himself to be a Christian."

Upon this proclamation the whole multitude cried aloud: "This is the father of the Christians, the destroyer of our gods, who teaches many not to sacrifice or worship our gods. Away with him!" So saying they begged Philip to let loose a lion on Polycarp, but Philip replied that it was not lawful for him to do so, for he had concluded the wild beast combat. The people began then to cry, "Burn him at the stake! Burn him alive!"

Many hands helped to build the pyre on which the victim was placed, and when they piled the fagots about him, he asked that his hands not be tied behind him. "Let me remain as I am," he begged, "for he that has enabled me to brave the fire will so strengthen me that, without your tying my hands, I shall, unmoved, endure all the fierceness." They burned him according to their custom, and the serene old man met death calmly as the flames consumed his fragile body.

The Roman holiday closed, but the people were still not satisfied. They begged the proconsul, "Let us have the body of this man; we want to scatter his ashes. He died so bravely that his followers may come begging for his ashes that they may start a new religion for him." How little did they realize that the ashes were already scattered! History remembers the name of Polycarp, but the holiday makers have been forgotten in the ashes of time.

Scripture:

Now I want to assure you, brothers, that what has happened to me has actually resulted in furthering the preaching of the good news. Thus it is generally known throughout the Imperial Guard and elsewhere that it is for the sake of Christ that I am in prison, and so most of the Christian brothers have been exceedingly encouraged by my example to declare God's message without any fear of the consequences.

But what difference does it make? All that matters is that, in one way or another, ... Christ is being made known; ... For, as I see it, living means Christ and dying something even better. ... Whatever happens, show yourselves citizens worthy of the good news of Christ, so that whether I come and see you or am kept away and only hear news of you, I may know that you are standing firm with one spirit, one purpose, fighting side by side for faith in the good news. Never for a moment falter before your opponents, for your fearlessness will be a sure sign for them of their coming destruction, but to you it will be an omen, from God himself, of your deliverance. For you have been granted the privilege not only of trusting in Christ but of suffering for him. Take your part in the same struggle that you have seen me engage in and that you hear I am still keeping up.[4]

POEM:

> By the light of burning heretics Christ's bleeding feet I track,
> Toiling up new Calvaries ever with the cross that turns not back,
> And these mounts of anguish number how each generation learned
> One new word of that grand *Credo* which in prophet-hearts hath burned
> Since the first man stood God-conquered with his face to heaven upturned.
>
> .   .   .   .
>
> Careless seems the great Avenger; history's pages but record
> One death-grapple in the darkness 'twixt old systems and the Word;
> Truth forever on the scaffold, Wrong forever on the throne,—
> Yet that scaffold sways the future, and, behind the dim unknown,
> Standeth God within the shadow, keeping watch above his own.[5]

—JAMES RUSSELL LOWELL

LITANY OF SUPPLICATION:

Leader: For the courageous leaders who gave up everything for their religion,

Group: We are grateful, O God.

Leader: For the inspiration coming from the lives of these great men,

Group: We give thee thanks.

Leader: May their example challenge us to resist all forms of evil,

Group: We beseech thee, O God.

Leader: Grant us strength to admit our errors, to endure criticism, ridicule, and persecution,

Group: We beseech thee, O Lord.

Leader: Enable us to be honest in all our dealings, sincere in our promises, and steadfast in our convictions,

Group: We beseech thee, O Lord.

Leader: Help us to see clearly the difference between right and wrong, and lead us into the paths of righteousness,

Group: For Jesus' sake. Amen.

Solo: "These Are They," from *The Holy City*, by Gaul, or

Hymn: "My Soul, Be on Thy Guard," or
"A Charge to Keep I Have."

Benediction:

And now may the blessing of God the Father be with you all. Amen.

SERVICE 7

WAITING JUSTICE SLEEPS

PRELUDE: "Confidence," by Mendelssohn.

CALL TO WORSHIP:

> Give thanks, O heart, for the high souls
> That point us to the deathless goals—
> For all the courage of their cry
> That echoes down from sky to sky;
> Thanksgiving for the armed seers
> And heroes called to immortal years—
> Souls that have built our faith in man
> And lit the ages as they ran.
>
> —AUTHOR UNKNOWN

HYMN: "March On, O Soul, with Strength," or
"A Mighty Fortress Is Our God."

LEADER:

Throughout the ages great leaders have dreamed and labored for a better world. These daring, consecrated persons have been outnumbered by those who were content with the world as it is. They have been condemned, persecuted, and in some instances put to death by those who did not want any change. But their lives were not lived in vain, for we are enjoying the fruits of their labors. There is need today for those who will dream and strive to the point of martyrdom if necessary to bring about freedom and justice. There is today need for men of courage boldly to declare the truth, to break with all practices which enslave and crush people, to have no fear of what men will say or do, and to keep their ears and eyes open to the cries of the sorrow and suffering of mankind.

Near the close of one of the most triumphant chapters in the New Testament we read: Still others had to endure taunts and blows, and even fetters and prison. And the roll call follows of those heroic figures who endured and triumphed: by faith Abel—by faith Enoch —by faith Abraham—by faith Moses. One by one these great souls witnessed to the sustaining power of God in their lives.

SCRIPTURE:

All these people lived all their lives in faith, and died without receiving what had been promised; they only saw it far ahead and welcomed the sight of it, recognizing that they themselves were only foreigners and strangers here on earth.

And why should I go on? For my time would fail me if I told of Gideon, Barak, Samson, Jephthah, David, Samuel, and the prophets, who by their faith conquered kingdoms, attained uprightness, received new promises, shut the mouths of lions, put out furious fires, escaped death by the sword, found strength in their time of weakness, proved mighty in war, put foreign armies to flight. Women had their dead restored to them by resurrection. Others endured torture, and refused to accept release, that they might rise again to the better life. Still others had to endure taunts and blows, and even fetters and prison. They were stoned to death, they were tortured to death, they were sawed in two, they were killed with the sword. Clothed in the skins of sheep and goats, they were driven from place to place, destitute, persecuted, misused—men of whom the world was not worthy wandering in deserts, mountains, caves, and holes in the ground.

Yet though they all gained God's approval by their faith, they none of them received what he had promised, for God had resolved upon something still better for us, that they might not reach the fulfilment of their hopes except with us.

But you must remember those early days when after you had received the light you had to go through a great struggle with persecution, sometimes being actually exposed as a public spectacle to insults and violence, and sometimes showing yourselves ready to share the lot of those in that condition. . . . You must not lose your courage, for it will be richly rewarded, but you will need endurance if you are to carry out God's will and receive the blessing he has promised.[1]

PRAYER:

Our Father, thou who dost hear the cries of the oppressed people throughout the world, and who dost call us to work with thee in liberating the enslaved people, grant unto us the courage to be willing to be numbered with those who endure persecution and imprisonment if necessary that the masses of downtrodden men may have a chance to work, play, and worship as free men. Grant us vision and insight as we strive to co-operate with thee in bringing about a better world. In Jesus' name, we pray. AMEN.

POEM:

> Men! whose boast it is that ye
> Come of fathers brave and free,
> If there breathe on earth a slave,
> Are ye truly free and brave?
> If ye do not feel the chain,
> When it works a brother's pain,
> Are ye not base slaves indeed,
> Slaves unworthy to be freed?
>
> Is true Freedom but to break
> Fetters for our own dear sake,
> And, with leathern hearts, forget
> That we owe mankind a debt?
> No! true freedom is to share
> All the chains our brothers wear,
> And, with heart and hand, to be
> Earnest to make others free! [2]
>
> —JAMES RUSSELL LOWELL

HYMN: "For All the Saints," or
"Faith of Our Fathers."

STORY:

JOHN HUSS, FEARLESS REFORMER

JOHN HUSS was born of humble parents about 1369 in the little village of Husinetz, Bohemia. He was a charity pupil at the school in Prague, where he was known to have the keenest mind in the group. One evening while sitting before the fire reading about the lives of the saints, he surprised his mother by thrusting his hand into the flame, saying that he did it only that he might see what tortures of martyrdom he might be able to endure. Although coming from an obscure family, he became a noted scholar. He received the degree of master of arts at the University of Prague, served on the faculty, was ordained a priest, and became rector of the University. Great crowds flocked to hear him because of his ability as a speaker.

When the writings of Wycliffe, the English reformer, found their way into Prague, Huss studied them carefully. He agreed with Wycliffe that the word of God rather than the word of the pope should be the guide of moral conduct and that the people should be permitted to read the Bible in their native tongues. At times he read extracts from these writings to the students in the University and to his congregation. But when the archbishop ordered Wycliffe's books burned, the effect was quite different from what he expected, for it stimulated the friends of those doctrines to greater zeal.

From the pulpit Huss denounced the archbishop for burning the books in a center of enlightenment where a great university had stood for freedom of thought. He attacked the weaknesses of the Church, the luxury of the prelates and bishops, and the moral slackness from the pope down to the lowest priest. He announced the statement which from that time on became his chief contention—that the Bible alone is the true code of the Christian life and that Church councils and the commands of the pope were to be obeyed only when they agreed with it. When such commands ran counter to the Bible, they were to be disregarded.

Although such preaching made Huss unpopular with the pope, he continued his attack, and the opposition to the pope grew. Among the multitudes that flocked to hear him preach were the lords and barons, as well as the king and queen. Finally Prague was placed under interdict, which meant that marriages were banned, the dead could not be buried by a priest, and the churches were closed. The situation became so tense that the king of Bohemia asked Huss to leave the city.

Huss complied with the request and retired to the countryside where his boyhood had been spent. Here he continued to preach and to make his appeal through writing to the people, urging them to turn to the Bible and to look to Jesus for authority rather than to the pope. At last he was excommunicated by the pope, forbidden to baptize children or to bury the dead. His friends begged him to stop preaching and writing, but he felt that he would be a traitor if he followed their suggestion.

To bring the matter to a head a council was called in the city of Constance to which Huss was summoned. His friends tried to persuade him to remain in Bohemia, where he would be protected by the bravest knights of the realm, instead of delivering himself into the hands of the enemy. But Huss was firm in his decision to defend his beliefs before the Council of Constance. A guarantee of safe-conduct was secured from the emperor, two knights accompanied him as bodyguards, and he set out with the expectation of returning safely.

On a certain evening after his arrival in Constance, Huss was dining with his friend, Lord Chlum. The bishop and mayor of the city came asking Huss to appear before the pope for an informal discussion. Agreeing to their plans, Huss was questioned for awhile and then thrown into prison. Lord Chlum, discovering the treachery, demanded by what right the cardinals had violated the emperor's promise of protection. The only explanation given was that Huss had disobeyed the orders of the king, the emperor, and the pope, that he was a dangerous heretic, and therefore any promise made to him was not binding.

Lord Chlum wrote to the emperor, the king, and the queen but received no reply, for they too had fallen under the influence of the cardinals. Huss was removed from prison only to be thrown into a damp dungeon in a monastery where he contracted a fever. When it was known that he was near death, a physician was ordered to keep him alive until after his trial in order that justice might be done. He was removed from the dungeon and gained sufficient strength to appear before the council.

The charges against him were that he was a heretic; that he had preached and taught the condemned books of Wycliffe; had turned the Czech people against their masters, and had stirred up civil rebellion. His defense was that he had taught only spiritual matters and that he had tried to turn the people from the error of their way to individual righteousness. They questioned, "Since you have been excommunicated, by what authority do you teach?" He replied, "By the authority of my conscience." They retorted, "One hundred Church Fathers have testified against you. Do you dare to say that you are wiser than the Church council?" Huss replied, "I appeal to God and my conscience, and if you were many times more numerous than you are, I would still appeal to my conscience."

The bitterest disappointment came to Huss when he learned that three of his friends had been bribed and used as witnesses against him. He was taken back to jail and on the next day was brought again before the emperor, who begged him to confess the error of his teachings. Many people came urging him to recant, forms of confession were drawn up which were intended to make it easy for him, but he was unmoved by all of their arguments. He continued to fight for religious freedom which had become a compelling principle with him. He realized that a severe penalty would be meted out to him, but he felt that his life was a small price to pay for religious freedom. At last the sentence was pronounced: "The body of the heretic shall be burned at the stake."

As the wood was piled about him Huss was asked to recant. With the majesty of a king he replied: "God is my witness that I have never taught or preached those things that have been falsely ascribed to me, and the chief aim of all my preaching, writing, and acts was that I might save men from sin, and today I am willing to die for the truth of the gospel." As the torch was applied and the flames leaped up, he cried out, "O Christ, thou Son of the living God, have mercy upon us!"

POEM:

God give us men! A time like this demands
    Strong minds, great hearts, true faith, and ready hands;
Men whom the lust of office does not kill;
    Men whom the spoils of office cannot buy;
Men who possess opinions and a will;
    Men who have honor,—men who will not lie;
Men who can stand before a demagogue,
    And damn his treacherous flatteries without winking!
Tall men, sun-crowned, who live above the fog
    In public duty, and in private thinking;
For while the rabble, with their thumb-worn creeds,
Their large professions and their little deeds,—
Mingle in selfish strife, lo! Freedom weeps,
Wrong rules the land, and waiting Justice sleeps!

                        —J. G. HOLLAND

PRAYER:

Our Father, thou art our light in darkness, our help in temptation, and our strength in times of weakness. Grant us wisdom and understanding to meet the duties of this day; grant us courage to resist evil in every form and to maintain our standards in the face of criticism or ridicule. Help us to do the hard right when wrong is comparatively easy. Grant us the determination to resist the influence of any of our associates who are content to live on a low plane. Give us strength to live courageously, to be honest in all we say and do, that we may be worthy to be called thy children. Create within us a new heart, and renew a right spirit within us; through Jesus Christ our Lord. AMEN.

CLOSING HYMN: "Rise Up, O Men of God," or
"Once to Every Man and Nation."

SERVICE 8

A LAMP UNTO OUR FEET

PRELUDE: Hymn tune, "Munich."

CALL TO WORSHIP:

> O Word of God Incarnate,
>   O Wisdom from on high,
> O Truth unchanged, unchanging,
>   O Light of our dark sky:
> We praise thee for the radiance
>   That from the hallowed page,
> A lantern to our footsteps,
>   Shines on from age to age.
> —WILLIAM W. HOW

HYMN: "Break Thou the Bread of Life," or
      "My Soul, Be on Thy Guard."

RESPONSIVE READING:

Leader: For the prophecy came not in old time by the will of man: but holy men of God spake as they were moved by the Holy Ghost.

Group: A glory gilds the sacred page,
         Majestic like the sun;
         It gives a light to every age;
         It gives, but borrows none.

Leader: All scripture is given by inspiration of God, and is profitable for doctrine, for reproof, for correction, for instruction in righteousness.

Group: The Hand that gave it still supplies
         The gracious light and heat;

His truths upon the nations rise:
They rise, but never set.

Leader: These were more noble, . . . in that they received the word
with all readiness of mind, and searched the scriptures daily.

Group: Let everlasting thanks be thine
For such a bright display,
As makes a world of darkness shine
With beams of heavenly day.

Leader: It is written, Man shall not live by bread alone, but by every
word that proceedeth out of the mouth of God.

Group: My soul rejoices to pursue
The steps of him I love,
Till glory breaks upon my view
In brighter worlds above.[1]

PRAYER:

Our Father, we are grateful for all who have labored and endured
persecution that we may have thy Word in a language that we can
understand. We are grateful for the truths revealed in the Scriptures
and made available to us. Increase our insight and understanding as
we strive to live by these principles. Grant that thy Word may be a
lamp unto our feet and a light unto our pathway. In Jesus' name.
AMEN.

HYMN: "Book of Books," or
"A Glory Gilds the Sacred Page," or
"O Word of God Incarnate."

LEADER:

We are inclined to take for granted many contributions to our heritage. Some details about the making of the Bible cannot be known,
but there are many recorded facts concerning its history which are
available to us. As we learn more of the tedious task of transcribing
by hand, translating, and preserving the Bible, we grow in our appreciation of it as the Word of God and a guide for daily living.

We shall hear the story of one whose life was devoted to the
task of giving the English-speaking peoples the Bible in their native
tongue.

WILLIAM TYNDALE, TRANSLATOR OF THE BIBLE

MANY of the details are lacking of the life of William Tyndale, the one to whom we owe a large debt of gratitude for giving us the first Bible printed in English. With his unselfishness he would have been content to be forgotten if only the Word of God could be made known in the English language. Of his early life little is known except that he grew up in the county of Gloucester, where religious abuses flourished.

In Great Britain at that time religion was largely the observance of forms and ceremonies which had lost much of their meaning. Most of the Bible was practically unknown either to the clergy or to the people. No man was permitted to translate any part of the Scriptures into the English tongue or to read such translations without the authority of the bishop.

Tyndale, a shrewd and observant lad, found much to condemn in the Church of his day. He was a divinity student at Oxford and later at Cambridge, where Erasmus a few years previous had completed his translation of the New Testament into Greek. It may have been while studying the works of Erasmus that the idea came to Tyndale of translating the Bible into English.

At any rate he pondered over such statements as the following from Erasmus: "I totally dissent from those who are unwilling that the Sacred Scripture be translated into the native language and be read by private individuals, . . . as if the strength of the Christian religion lay in men's ignorance of it. I would wish even all women to read the Gospel and the Epistles of St. Paul. And I wish they were translated into all languages of all people, that they might be read and known, not merely by the Scotch and the Irish, but even by the Turks and the Saracens. I wish that the husbandman may sing parts of them at his plough, that the weaver may warble them at his shuttle, that the traveller may with their narratives beguile the weariness of the way."

After graduating from Cambridge, Tyndale served first as a chaplain and tutor in the home of Sir John Walsh of Gloucester County. Continuing his study of Greek, he calmly weighed the problems involved in the translation of the Bible into English. There was another difficulty—his views on religion were advanced far beyond the current views of his day, and his open criticism against the ignorance of the English clergy brought him into conflict with Church authority. At last it became inevitable that he must leave that section, so he gave up his work and went to London.

Calling on the Bishop of London, Tyndale hoped to secure his permission to translate the New Testament. The bishop coldly refused to give any sanction to the work or to appoint him to a chaplaincy, but this did not prevent the young scholar from carrying out his purpose. During the following year he lived with a friend in London while he worked diligently at the translation of the New Testament. It was hoped that the bishop would change his attitude, but instead the opposition grew. At last it became clear to Tyndale that he could not carry on his work in London; in fact, there was no place in all England for him to continue his work.

Six years prior to this time Luther had begun the Reformation in Germany, and it occurred to Tyndale that in that country he might find a more congenial environment in which to work. Taking his manuscript and Greek New Testament, he went to Wittenberg, the center of Luther's activities. Friends in London assured him that sufficient funds would be provided for the printing of his New Testament when it was completed.

Wycliffe's translation of the Bible from Latin into obsolete English was available but of little use, for the people needed to have the Bible in everyday speech. Tyndale used the Hebrew, Erasmus' Greek New Testament, and Luther's German translation, and with the help of an assistant who checked and copied the manuscript, the work was completed within the following year.

Since Wittenberg was the seat of the Reformation, Tyndale went to Cologne to have his work published that it might have a better reception in England. An enemy appeared, and Tyndale fled to the Protestant city of Worms with his manuscript, where in 1526 he brought out the first New Testament printed in English. In order to get the six thousand copies into circulation, he went to the fairs at Frankfort where he contacted the merchants from England. These men bought his forbidden writings and sold them to the English. The desire to own the Bible in a language they could understand was so strong that the people clamored for more copies.

The Church and royal authority ordered all copies burned, but a printer in Antwerp was persuaded to bring out another edition. Courageous booksellers smuggled many copies into England. It is difficult today to imagine the courage required to print an unauthorized version of the Bible. In those days to print anything without the authority of the Church or state was considered as great a crime as coining money without state authority.

Tyndale went on with his translation of the Old Testament, even though he was persecuted by those who were hostile to the spread of Protestantism. He completed the first five books and the Book of Jonah, and as far as we know, these are the only books of the Old Testament that he published. He was a marked man, especially in England. Henry VIII favored him until in 1530 he opposed the king's divorce from Catherine.

Wolsey took rigorous measures to seek out and burn all copies of the English New Testament and to have Tyndale brought back to England, but the wary scholar took refuge in the English House at Antwerp, a hostel to harbor Englishmen. Wolsey appealed to the emperor but was refused on the ground that he had no right to invade the sanctuary of the English House. Eventually Tyndale was lured out of the hostel by a man who had a grudge against him. He was arrested immediately and thrown into prison.

Of Tyndale's works only one letter remains today in his own handwriting. It is an appeal in Latin, written during his last imprisonment, to the governor of the castle. It reminds us of Paul, the Apostle to the Gentiles, in similar circumstances asking for his cloak and his books, "but especially the parchments" to comfort him during the tedious hours of his imprisonment. In like manner Tyndale, sitting in the cold, dark, damp cell of the prison, pleaded for warmer clothing, a lamp by which to study, and his Hebrew Bible, grammar, and dictionary.

His trial began in the early part of 1536 and dragged throughout the summer. Emperor Charles and Regent Mary were asked to decide whether in this case the statutes against heretics were to be enforced to the fullest extent. Thomas Cromwell and other friends appealed in behalf of the prisoner, but Charles and Mary were unwilling to offend the clergy. After more than a year of degrading imprisonment, Tyndale was convicted of heresy and condemned to death. On October 6, 1536, as he was led to his execution in the town of Vilvorde, Brussels, he cried with a loud voice, "Lord, open the King of England's eyes."

Those in authority could take his life, but his work was beyond their power to destroy. Nearly a century later when the translators were bringing out the King James Version of the Bible, Tyndale's phrasing and sentence construction were only slightly changed. The dignity, stateliness, beauty, and simplicity of the King James Version is largely his work. Relatively few changes needed to be made because his work had been done so carefully. His enemies criticized and tried to detract from his work, but the more we know of him, the more his genius is brought to light.

In every corner of the globe where English is spoken, the words of Tyndale's translation with slight changes are repeated with reverence. His simplicity, earnestness, independence, love of truth, and force of mind mark him as a great soul who was raised up and qualified for a noble work. No taint of weakness, no suspicion of selfishness, no parade of pride can be found within him. Humble, zealous, devoted in his work, beloved by his friends, and respected by his enemies, he was faithful unto death.

Though Tyndale was exiled from his country, sightseers now have pointed out to them his statue erected in a London square to the memory of the man who died that the English people might read the Bible in their native tongue.[2]

SOLO: "Be Thou Faithful unto Death," from *St. Paul,*
     by Mendelssohn, or

HYMN: "Soldiers of Christ, Arise," or
      "A Mighty Fortress Is Our God," or
      "Are Ye Able?"

POEM:

Where are you going, Greatheart,
With your eager face and your fiery grace?
Where are you going, Greatheart?

"To fight a fight with all my might,
For Truth and Justice, God and Right,
To grace all Life with His fair Light."
Then God go with you, Greatheart!

Where are you going, Greatheart?
"To beard the Devil in his den;
To smite him with the strength of ten;
To set at large the souls of men."
Then God go with you, Greatheart!

Where are you going, Greatheart?
"To cleanse the earth of noisome things;
To draw from life its poison stings;
To give free play to Freedom's wings."
  Then God go with you, Greatheart!

Where are you going, Greatheart?
"To lift Today above the Past;
To make Tomorrow sure and fast;
To nail God's colors to the mast."
  Then God go with you, Greatheart!

Where are you going, Greatheart?
"To break down old dividing lines;
To carry out my Lord's designs;
To build again His broken shrines."
  Then God go with you, Greatheart!

Where are you going, Greatheart?
"To set all burdened peoples free;
To win for all God's liberty;
To 'stablish His sweet sovereignty."
  God goeth with you, Greatheart![3]

  —JOHN OXENHAM

LITANY:

Leader: O God, thou who hast caused the Scriptures to be written for our instruction, help us to give heed to thy commandments,

Group: We beseech thee.

Leader: May we search diligently the record of experiences which others have had with thee and find guidance in everyday living,

Group: In Jesus' name, we pray.

Leader: For the men who have spent time in thy presence, meditating on the truth which thou hast revealed,

Group: We are truly grateful.

Leader: For the devout translators whose minds were saturated with thoughts of thee, for their courage and their willingness to sacrifice,

Group: We thank thee.

Leader: For the spiritual insight of these leaders and for their determination to follow the right as they saw it,

Group: We return our thanks, O Lord.

Leader: May we value this heritage and grow in understanding of the Bible. May its truths enter into our experiences, guide and control our actions,

Group: In Jesus' name, we pray. AMEN.

BENEDICTION:

May the peace of God remain with you. AMEN.

SERVICE 9

FRIEND OF THE SOIL

PRELUDE: Hymn tune, *"Laudes Domini."*

CALL TO WORSHIP:

O come, let us sing unto the Lord: let us make
a joyful noise to the rock of our salvation.
Let us come before his presence with thanksgiving,
and make a joyful noise unto him with psalms.
For the Lord is a great God, and a great King
above all gods.
In his hands are the deep places of the earth:
the strength of the hills is his also.
The sea is his, and he made it: and his hands
formed the dry land.
O come, let us worship and bow down: let us
kneel before the Lord our maker.[1]

HYMN: "This Is My Father's World," or
"We Plow the Fields and Scatter."

PRAYER:

Our Father, we thank thee that thou hast brought us through the
cycle of another year and that seedtime and harvest have not failed.
Out of thy bounty thou hast provided our daily bread, and because
of thy goodness we have shelter, clothing, and other comforts. Help
us to receive these gifts with gratitude and to be willing to share
them with others who are in need. May we not seek our good alone
but identify ourselves with all mankind, that we may be ready to
sacrifice ourselves for all members of the common family. AMEN.

LEADER:

The welfare of the ancient Hebrews was intimately connected with
the soil. If they obeyed God's laws in the care of the land, they were

blessed; but if they disobeyed, severe penalties were required. In order that the land might continue its fertility, every seventh year the fields were left uncultivated. In the Scripture we discover that the rules for the care of the land were God's laws:

"Therefore thou shalt keep the commandments of the Lord thy God, to walk in his ways, and to fear him. For the Lord thy God bringeth thee into a good land, a land of brooks of water, of fountains and depths that spring out of valleys and hills; . . . a land wherein thou shalt eat bread without scarceness, thou shalt not lack any thing in it; a land whose stones are iron, and out of whose hills thou mayest dig brass. When thou hast eaten and art full, then thou shalt bless the Lord thy God for the good land which he hath given thee. Beware that thou forget not the Lord thy God, in not keeping his commandments, and his judgments, and his statutes, which I command thee this day.

"Doth the plowman plow all day to sow? doth he open and break the clods of his ground? When he hath made plain the face thereof, doth he not cast abroad the fitches, and scatter the cummin, and cast in the principal wheat and the appointed barley and the rie in their place? For his God doth instruct him to discretion, and doth teach him.

"If ye be willing and obedient, ye shall eat the good of the land." [2]

MEDITATION:

We are the farmers.

We stand on the land—and from it we view, and judge, the world.

The soil about our feet becomes a part of us.

We were born on it, and almost, it seems to us, from it.

For what it is enters into us.

Its steadiness, its dependability, enter into our souls and cause us to expect the same from the world.

Its obedience to the laws of growth, moisture, sun, maturity, harvest—this also becomes a part of us.

Its readiness to receive and to give, to deal fairly with those who till it—this is another gift of the good earth to us.

And these which we have learned from the soil, we expect from the world.

When the world we live in proves undependable; when it follows the laws of chance instead of growth; when it tricks us instead of giving us an honest return for our labor—then we are confused, suspicious, desperate.

We trust our native soil and we tend to distrust all else.

We—and you—will wreck our world in strife, or we will together rebuild it in fairer and more Christian forms.

We are the farmers.[3]

Solo: "The Blind Plowman," by O'Hara, or

Hymn: "O Master, Workman of the Race," or
"For the Beauty of the Earth."

Story:

OBERLIN, FRIEND OF THE SOIL

John Frederick Oberlin was born in 1740 in Strasbourg when it was a city of France. His father was a professor in a preparatory school; his mother was a woman of rare literary and musical gifts. There was a small income and a large family, and the strict economy practiced in the home took deep root in the boy's life and affected his character.

Oberlin's work in the university was under eminent professors. At the age of eighteen he took his degree of bachelor of arts and five years later the degree of doctor of philosophy. When accepted as a minister in the Lutheran Church and urged to take a pastoral charge, he replied, "No, I am not qualified. I need more experience in order to preach to others. I do not want to labor in any pastoral charge where I can be at ease; I want a work no one else wishes to do and which will not be done unless I do it."

To prepare himself as a pastor, he served first as a private tutor in a surgeon's family in Strasbourg, where his leisure was spent studying botany and medicine. His journal shows that he disciplined himself rigidly, living on as little as possible, putting aside a portion of his income for the relief of the poor, and making plans to dedicate his life to the service of others. His sympathy with humanity, his practical way of living, his humor and cheerfulness, and his love of nature made him an interesting person in spite of the strict rules which he imposed upon himself.

When the call came to become pastor at Waldbach, Oberlin's desire for a difficult task was fulfilled. He found the people living as slaves, extremely poor, and taxed beyond their ability to pay. It did not take long for him to grasp the situation. He felt that little could be accomplished by merely preaching to the people. The evils which were deeply rooted in the community must be changed, and a new environment created. There was a close connection between the poverty and the low moral standards of the community.

Holding that the people must be taught, yet that they must not be taxed to pay for their education, Oberlin began with a scheme of education which staggered the faith of his friends. Since adequate buildings were necessary, he erected the first one by using his own salary, a donation from a friend, and a loan which he secured. It was even more difficult to secure teachers qualified to work in that situation.

Oberlin's ideas of education were far ahead of his day. Including the adults in his plan, he tried to make the entire community a unit of intellectual and moral co-operation. His schools were the first that were equipped to give industrial training. In addition to teaching several trades, he required each pupil to memorize essays on the care and planting of trees and to plant at least two trees, the first fruits of which were to be brought to him. His Strasbourg friends donated funds which enabled him to print and circulate practical books among his parishioners.

His next project was to build roads to connect the villages with the cities, for good roads were needed to get their produce to the market. Believing that he was out of his sphere of activity, the people refused to work with him, but their obstinacy did not in the least change his plan. Early one morning the people saw their pastor with pick and shovel, accompanied by three or four members, pass their village. Later when they saw him digging and shoveling, they could not resist. The next day twenty were working with him, and the following day there were fifty. Eventually all of the people not only believed in good roads but worked on the project, and the road was completed. Streams which had flooded the highway were guided into channels dug to receive them, and bridges were built across the largest streams.

Realizing that improvements in methods of farming were necessary in order to raise the level of living, Oberlin organized an agricultural club. He taught the farmers about the nature of the soil, the kinds of crops to grow, and introduced new products. He demonstrated how to apply fertilizer, how to prevent waste and erosion of the land. He urged the people to discard their crude implements and made it possible for them to buy modern equipment.

When he began his work, there was not a mechanic in the entire district. In his vocational schools he trained craftsmen and persuaded manufacturers to establish branch factories in that section. The young women were not overlooked, for those employed at a ribbon factory learned new habits of industry and thrift. Eventually the people who were impoverished were lifted to a higher level of living.

A remarkable change was noticed in a short while. The people spoke a different language. Instead of the Lorraine dialect, they spoke a pure and correct French. The churches were filled with thoughtful worshipers; the schools were well attended; good roads took the place of bypaths. With the use of improved implements the crops were profitable, and there was sufficient income for all of the needs of the people.

Oberlin developed with his parishioners, and honors came to him from beyond the mountain region in which he labored. The National Agricultural Society of France awarded him a gold medal for his improvements in agriculture. Attractive offers came from many quarters, but to all of them he replied: "I will never leave this place, for I have laid my plans for the future, and I shall need at least twenty years to carry them out. God has confided this flock to me, and why should I abandon it?"

Dr. Oberlin was a century ahead of his day in believing that a person cannot be considered apart from his home, his work, and his wages. Applying the teachings of Jesus, he helped the people work out their economic, social, and religious problems. The countryside with its rich and fertile fields shared also in the redemption of the people. Thus from the soil itself the people worked out their own salvation, and the change worked from within—down deep where are the roots of life.[4]

POEM:

> Men of the soil! We have labored unending:
> We have fed the world upon the grain we have grown.
> Now with the star of the new day ascending,
> Giants of the earth, at last we rise to claim our own.
> Justice throughout the land, happiness as God has planned.
> Who is there denies our right to reap where we have sown?
>
> Men of the soil! Now the torch we have lighted;
> Kindle fires in every land where rings the harvest song!
> Shoulder to shoulder in courage united

From every race we come to join the tillers' mighty throng.
Earth ne'er shall eat again bread gained through blood of
men.
We have sworn to right forevermore the ancient wrong.

Men of the soil! We are coming in judgment,
To tell the world till justice rules there is no liberty.
We in our strength are arising as prophets,
Marching on to show the world the dawn that is to be.
There's a lightning in the sky, there's a thunder shouting
high;
We will never stop until the sons of men are free.[5]

—HAROLD M. HILDRETH

PRAYER:

O eternal God, we thank thee that thou has given us many things
to enrich our lives. For the soil, which represents the true wealth of
the world, we are grateful; for all the bounty which thou hast provided, we return our thanks. Help us to do all in our power to protect
the soil from the ravages of erosion and flood. Realizing that the
farmer holds in his hands our well-being, help us to realize the dignity
and worth of his labor and to guard his interests in every way. Grant
us wisdom and understanding as we strive to live according to thy
laws, and fulfill thy purpose in the world. Forbid that we should
block any of thy plans through our selfishness or lack of vision. In
Jesus' name, we pray. AMEN.

HYMN: "Be Strong, We Are Not Here to Play," or
        "O Jesus, I Have Promised," or
        "Work, for the Night Is Coming."

BENEDICTION:

Now may the light which shone in Christ, shine in our hearts and
minds both now and forever more. AMEN.

SERIES TWO

COMPANIONS WITH GOD

Suggestions to the Counselor

THE PURPOSE of this series is to help young people appropriate the spiritual resources which are available for creative living. One need not go through life living on the ragged edge of insecurity when he can be free from fear and worry, enjoy peace and quietness of mind. Through communion with God strength will be given to live courageously and victoriously in any situation. Every experience of life can be made to contribute to one's growth and development. Through such fellowship life is ennobled, everyday tasks become significant; but without worship life tends to lose its meaning.

Proper lighting and well-planned worship centers add much to the effectiveness of meditative types of services. When the services are held in the evening, the room should be dimly lighted and a strong light thrown upon the worship center. If a spotlight is not available, candles may be arranged to give sufficient light. Speakers should stand on either side or in the back of the room, but never in front of a worship center.

It is well to enlist the interest of as many persons as possible in preparing the room and in arranging the center of worship. If suitable pictures are not on hand, it is possible to borrow them from art museums, art stores, public libraries, schools and colleges, or they may be ordered from denominational headquarters. When a picture is used for the first time, it gives added meaning to lead the group in a worship service based on the message of the painting. It is advisable to hang only one picture at a time in a room used for worship. For best effect pictures should be mounted or framed, placed over a dark velour background, and hung back of an altar or table. Candles or a low bowl of flowers on the table may give variety.

The following pictures are suggested to be used with this series, but others may be substituted: With "Practicing the Presence of God" use A. E. Borthwick, "The Presence." With "Be Still and Know" use Da Vinci, "The Head of Christ." With "Beside Still Waters" use William L. Taylor, "Beside Still Waters." With "He Shall Be like a Tree" use any good picture of trees. With "Let This Mind Be in You" use Copping, "Christ."

If possible, the service "He Shall Be like a Tree" should be held out of doors with trees in the background. The call to worship may be given by a trumpeter hidden at a distance, while a violin furnishes the accompaniment for the singing. The group will remain seated throughout the service, but the speakers will rise unannounced for their parts.

These books give background for this series: Brother Lawrence, *The Practice of the Presence of God;* R. M. Jones, *New Eyes for Invisibles;* A. E. Bailey, *The Gospel in Art;* Dorothy Pease, *Altars Under the Sky;* A. J. Sadler, *Out of Doors with God;* M. S. Rice, *My Father's World.*

SERVICE 10

PRACTICING THE PRESENCE OF GOD

PRELUDE: Hymn tune, "Consolation," by Mendelssohn.

CALL TO WORSHIP:

"Deep calleth unto deep," the Psalmist said,
    And I could picture endless sea and sky
Merged into one vast crystal depth of blue,
    With waves that feel the tug of tides on high.

But better have I learned what words can mean
    Than from the images of tide and weather;
For there are moments when my soul lifts up
    And God bends down, and we are one together.[1]
                        —ESTHER BALDWIN YORK

HYMN: "Still, Still with Thee," or
    "Saviour, Breathe an Evening Blessing."

POEM:

In the castle of my soul
Is a little postern gate,
Whereat, when I enter,
I am in the presence of God.
In a moment, in the turning of a thought,
I am where God is.
This is a fact.
When I enter into God,
All life has a meaning,
Without asking I know;
My desires are even now fulfilled,
My fever is gone
In the great quiet of God.

My troubles are but pebbles on the road,
My joys are like the everlasting hills.

So it is when my soul steps through the postern gate
Into the presence of God.
Big things become small, and the small things become great.
The near becomes far, and the future is near.
The lowly and despised is shot through with glory.
God is the substance of all revolutions;
When I am in him, I am in the Kingdom of God
And in the Fatherland of my Soul.[2]

—WALTER RAUSCHENBUSCH

SCRIPTURE:

O Lord, thou hast searched me, and known me.

There is not a word in my tongue, but, lo, O Lord, thou knowest
it altogether.

Such knowledge is too wonderful for me; it is high, I cannot attain
unto it.

Whither shall I go from thy spirit? or whither shall I flee from thy
presence?

If I ascend up into heaven, thou art there:

If I make my bed in hell, behold, thou art there.

If I take the wings of the morning, and dwell in the uttermost
parts of the sea;

Even there shall thy hand lead me, and thy right hand shall
hold me.

If I say, Surely the darkness shall cover me; even the night shall
be light about me.

Yea, the darkness hideth not from thee; but the night shineth as
the day: the darkness and the light are both alike to thee.

How precious also are thy thoughts unto me, O God! how great is
the sum of them!

If I should count them, they are more in number than the sand:
when I awake, I am still with thee.

Search me, O God, and know my heart: try me and know my
thoughts:

And see if there be any wicked way in me, and lead me in the way
everlasting.

The Lord of hosts is with us; the God of Jacob is our refuge.[3]

Lord,
We would this day lay in thy hands all that we have and are,
That our bodies and souls may become fair temples of thy
   indwelling;
We desire with a great desire, O our God,
That our wills may be utterly possessed by thy will,
That our eyes may look out on this world as thine eyes look,
That our being may be filled by thy being,
That through our feeble hearts may beat a pulse of thine eternal
   love,
And in our narrow souls may dwell a spark of thine eternal joy.

For, Master, what have we in heaven or earth but thee—?
Yet, not as an external possession do we desire thee:
Come not in condescension from above:
Come not in glory and power from without:
Come not as a belief to be comprehended:
Come not as a wave of emotion, to be felt and forgotten,
But come as the indwelling spirit within our souls,
Transforming them into thine own divine nature,
Creating in them thine own joyful and loving will.

May we know with an immediate and ineffable knowledge
That in thee we live and move and have our being.
May we prove before men, in daily practice of devoted living,
In peace and joy, patience and fortitude, humility and love,
The fact that thou art our Father and their Father.[4]

HYMN: "Dear Lord and Father of Mankind," or
         "O Thou, in Whose Presence," or
         "Abide with Me."

STORY:

PRACTICING THE PRESENCE OF GOD

THREE centuries ago a Frenchman, Nicholas Herman, became converted at the age of eighteen. The sight of a bare tree stripped of its leaves in midwinter caused him to reflect upon the miraculous power by which the tree is renewed in the spring, and there came to him a new insight into the power and providence of God.

Herman, who had been a soldier and a lowly footman prior to his conversion, was admitted to the order of Carmelites in Paris and was known thereafter as "Brother Lawrence." In the monastery he was assigned to work in the kitchen, a task which he despised because of the disagreeable odors, the greasy pots and pans, and the endless monotony. In spite of these conditions he was determined to learn the secret of communion with God.

At first Herman was not very successful because of his conflicting desires, his poor health, and his irritation with his work. Feelings of guilt and lack of faith hindered him constantly; it was only on rare occasions that he was aware of the presence of God. He felt that he must come to terms with himself and get rid of tensions, irritations, selfishness, and pride. At the beginning of his adventure with God his prayers had to do with conquering his own restless spirit.

Herman prayed: "O Lord, help me to get rid of the feeling of aversion that I have for my work. Help me to change my attitude until I can feel the importance of it. Guide me as I try to put myself in the background and center my mind on the service that it is possible for me to render through my work. Strengthen me for this task, for if you do not help me, I shall surely fail."

Gradually a change came about in his life. Amid the noise and clatter of pots and pans he remained calm, for he had found an inner harmony. His health improved to the extent that he was able to get rid of all bodily ills; even his menial tasks took on dignity and greatness. In the most trying situations he remained serene and poised. He said: "My soul, which till that time was in trouble, now felt a profound inner peace, as if it had found its center and place of rest."

What was the secret of the success of this humble workman? Will that which set him apart from the simple life of his day aid us in solving problems of a more complex life? His education was limited, and his contacts with the outside world were few. His experiences did not run the whole gamut of life as we know it today. He remained a cook throughout most of his lifetime. Living a narrow, restricted life, there was every possibility that he would remain obscure and never be known outside the monastery.

Of his writings sixteen letters and a few scraps of conversation remain, but they are evidence that he lived continually in the presence of God. When we think of worship, our minds immediately turn to his experience. Communion with God glorified whatever he did, so that the kitchen and the altar were as one to him. Such power came to him that he lived radiantly and victoriously. Many brought their problems to him, for they recognized a spirit that led them into closer fellowship with God.

Brother Lawrence had regular periods of prayer, but his devotions were not confined to these times. He sought God continually, but not for his gifts; he prayed for strength and courage to accept even the denial of his petitions. Believing that the chief end of man is to glorify God, he sought God that he might enjoy his presence. For him prayer was not something apart from life, but he was conscious of the presence of God in every contact throughout the day. At all times his mind was open to impressions coming from the Father; his daily prayer was, "O God, make me wholly thine."

What Brother Lawrence did, any of us can do. His psychology was good not only for his day, but for ours. He took all of his problems into the presence of God and there found a solution for them. He made a real contribution in that he did not try to use prayer as a means of obtaining special favors but rather as a means of knowing God's will and of developing inner resources that would enable him to live victoriously in any situation.

LEADER:

Let us not assume that prayer is to be used to bend God's will to our will, but in our communion with God let us strive to think his thoughts after him and discover his will and purpose for our lives. If we learn to practice the presence of God, we can be rid of tensions, fear, and worry, and sufficient strength will be given to meet the demands of each day. Whether amid pots and pans in the kitchen or in the confusion of modern life, we can live in harmony with God and be victorious in any situation.

In this quiet place let us turn our thoughts toward God, saying, "Surely the Lord is in this place, and he will be in our lives if we open them to him." Let us recognize him as the giver of every good gift and thank him for the blessings which we enjoy. Confessing our sins, let us ask for strength and guidance as we strive to overcome our weaknesses and avoid the mistakes that we have made in the past. Let us ask that we be led into a closer fellowship with him as we offer him our entire lives to be used in helping to bring the kingdom of God on earth.

POEM:

> The sky was touched with silver, rose, and gold;
> A smiling, kindly hush lay over all;
> A priest of God read collects writ of old;
> A people, worshiping, felt stillness fall
> From Holy Writ, from earth and sky and air,
> On noisy places of the life within,
> Found soul renewal as they tarried there
> And opened doors to let God's presence in.
> One spoke whose soul, aglow with living light,
> Made manifest to all the way he trod,
> Told in the heaven-lit quiet of the night
> The old-new message of man's need of God.
> Lord, enter in; be Thou not far away.
> "With thee began, with thee shall end the day." [5]
>
> —GEORGIA HARKNESS

SILENT PRAYER.

SOLO: "Lord, Make Me Strong," by Eville, or

HYMN: "If Thou But Suffer God to Guide Thee," or
"Draw Thou My Soul, O Christ," or
"Take My Life and Let It Be."

BENEDICTION:

May the peace of God which passeth all understanding keep your hearts and minds in the knowledge and love of God. AMEN.

SERVICE 11

BE STILL AND KNOW

PRELUDE: "Sarabande," from *First French Suite,* by Bach.

CALL TO WORSHIP:

> Serenity is that small drop which falls
>   From off the cup of duty's silver edge;
> We may not seek it in great banquet halls,
>   Or on adventure's narrow mountain ledge;
> It dwells not in an unbeliever's heart
>   Or in the selfish seeking after gold;
> It is Christ alone who can impart
>   That inward peace which is not bought or sold.
> But anywhere, in hearts of high or low
>   Where truth abides, serenity will glow.[1]
>   —HAZEL I. DANNEKER

HYMN: "Dear Lord and Father of Mankind," or
"We May Not Climb the Heavenly Steeps."

LITANY:

> We thank Thee, Lord,
> For all thy Golden Silences—
> Silence of moorlands rolling to the skies,
> Heath-purpled, bracken-clad, aflame with gorse;
> Silence of deep woods' mystic cloistered calm;
> Silence of wide seas basking in the sun;
> Silence of white peaks soaring to the blue;
> Silence of dawnings, when, their matins sung,
> The little birds do fall asleep again;
> For the deep silence of high golden noons;
> Silence of gloamings and the setting sun;
> Silence of moonlit nights and patterned glades;
> Silence of stars, magnificently still,

Yet ever chanting their Creator's skill;
Deep unto deep, within us sound sweet chords
Of praise beyond the reach of human words;
In our souls' silence, feeling only Thee—
We thank Thee, thank Thee,
Thank Thee, Lord.[2]

—JOHN OXENHAM

TALK:

USING SOLITUDE TO COMMUNE WITH GOD

THE TEMPO of living has increased until most of the time we feel driven. There is danger of living so intensely that we lose a sense of the presence of God. Who has not had the desire to get away from the loud noises and discordant sounds of the city and yield his spirit to the healing balm of nature? We need time enough to possess our soul in the rush of life.

I need not shout my faith. Thrice eloquent
Are quiet trees and the green listening sod;
Hushed are the stars, whose power is never spent;
The hills are mute; yet how they speak of God![3]

—CHARLES HANSON TOWNE

"Solitude has brought me to a certain way of regarding nature. . . . Through long years, assailed by grievous doubt, acquainted with sorrow, I have come at last to feel with all my heart the immediate presence of God; . . . and I am certain that he finds through the medium of solitude access to these wayward hearts of ours that he loves so long and so well.

"When the Master said, 'Come unto me, all ye who are weary and heavy-laden, for I will give you rest,' surely he must have known that as we retire to solitude, to us comes stealing unaware spiritual insight as well as the more obvious refreshment. It takes solitude, under the stars, for us to be reminded of our eternal origin and our far destiny."[4]

Although Wordsworth wrote more than a century ago,

"The world is too much with us; late and soon,
Getting and spending, we lay waste our powers,"

the same may be said about our own day. Our lives are crowded with

—84—

so many things that there is danger of losing sight of the most important things of life. We need periods of quiet meditation in order to see our lives objectively and to get a true perspective of life.

On many occasions Jesus withdrew to commune with his Father. Before beginning his ministry he spent forty days alone in the wilderness; before calling his disciples he spent the entire night in prayer. Frequently we read, "And in the morning, rising up a great while before day, he went out, and departed into a solitary place, and there prayed." Jesus called his disciples apart, not only to rest in order to build up the physical reserve that had been broken down, but also to strengthen their purposes, re-establish their ideals, and help them to have the right attitude toward their task.

When the disciples returned from their first preaching tour, Jesus invited them to come apart into a quiet place to rest awhile. From the standpoint of physical and mental health it was important to have times of withdrawal for the renewal of spirit which is so essential. Their ability to help others depended upon the poise and serenity which comes from quiet meditation and communion with God. Jesus knew that strained eyes may fail to see him, tense and anxious hearts may miss him, and only spirits that have been made serene by communion with God are able to help others.

The finer things of life grow slowly; profound thoughts develop during hours of meditation. Great works of art are not created in a rush, nor are great lives developed in a whirl of amusement. Newton discovered the law of gravitation, not by accident, but in a quiet garden, meditating on the wonders of the universe. Einstein's greatness may be attributed to the fact that he spends a great deal of time alone.

Beethoven spent much time alone. Early in his career he realized that he was losing his hearing, but he did not allow this affliction to interfere with his career. Eight of his best-known compositions were produced after he was deaf. In the silence, free from distraction and interruption, he was able to concentrate sufficiently to produce great compositions. At a public performance in Vienna in which the *Ninth Symphony* was given, the ovation was so great that the police had to restore order. Yet Beethoven was not aware of the impression that his music had made until someone had him turn around that he might see the audience. When the people realized that he had heard neither the music nor the ovation, they broke into a still greater demonstration.

When the Psalmist said, "Be still and know that I am God," he probably meant for us to be still in our own minds, quiet in our thoughts, desires, and petitions. We need to approach God with unhurried calm, free our minds of our ideas, and open them attentively to him. As we leave off talking and seek God in an attitude of listening, a sense of his presence is borne in upon our consciousness. "Closer is He than breathing, and nearer than hands and feet." At such time we are no longer seeking him, but are being found by him. We listen, and he speaks to us. New insights and new revelations come; feelings of fear, futility, and dissatisfaction vanish.

In making plans for our meditation, there needs to be a definite time and place set aside in which we can be free from distraction. We should avoid using a very late hour when we are too weary to concentrate. Reading may occupy a part of the time, but not the entire period. Our moods and needs will vary, and the reading should be selected to suit our needs.

There are Bible passages that are suitable for any need we may have. For example, if we lack courage we might read: "Have I not commanded thee? Be strong and of good courage; be not afraid, neither be thou dismayed. As I was with Moses, so I will be with thee; I will not fail thee, nor forsake thee." If fearful, we might read, in Goodspeed's translation of the passage: "Have no anxiety about anything, but make all your wants known to God in prayer and entreaty, and with thanksgiving. Then . . . the peace of God, so far above any human thought, will guard your minds and thoughts."

There may be times when we will want to think about a definite purpose for our life, a course of action to be followed, or a solution of a problem or difficulty. At such times we may center our thoughts on conversations of Jesus, or incidents in his life which will throw light on our problem. By so doing, the spirit of his teachings becomes the guide for our actions.

There are diverse ways of communing with God; each person will need to work out his own method of approach to God. We need not be discouraged if at first we are unable to achieve an awareness of God's presence. If our first attempts leave us with a feeling of futility, let us keep in mind that it takes time to form new thought patterns and to learn new ways of living.

The following suggestions may be helpful as you strive to commune with God:

1) Let mind and body be relaxed and free from strain.

2) Cast out irrelevant thoughts, concentrating on the problem or theme selected.

3) Open your mind to receive new insights freely, listening to what God reveals to you.

4) Turn your thoughts toward God, approaching him in humility, feeling your need of his help.

5) Praise God for his goodness, and be thankful.

6) Remove all barriers between yourself and God, confess sins and mistakes, and examine motives and actions.

7) Commit yourself to the new and better insights gained through communion with God.

8) Accept God's will and purpose in all areas of your life.

POEM:

> Be still and know
> That God is in his world,
> Though clouds shut out the light,
> Though ghoulish specters stalk,
> And all is night.
>
> Be still and know
> That God is in his world,
> Though Mammon clamors loud,
> And Mars lifts flashing steel,
> Untamed and proud.
>
> Be still and know
> That God is in his world,
> Though men with reckless waste,
> May seek they know not what
> In feverish haste.
>
> Be still and know
> That God is in his world.
> God speaks, but none may hear
> That voice except he have
> The listening ear.[5]

—GEORGIA HARKNESS

SCRIPTURE:

The Lord is in his holy temple; let all the earth keep silence before him.

My soul, wait thou in silence for God only; for my expectation is from him.

As the hart panteth after the water brooks, so panteth my soul after thee, O God.

My soul thirsteth for God, for the living God: when shall I come and appear before God?

Have mercy upon me, O God, according to thy lovingkindness: according unto the multitude of thy tender mercies blot out my transgressions.

Wash me thoroughly from mine iniquity, and cleanse me fom my sin.

For I acknowledge my transgressions: and my sin is ever before me.

Purge me with hyssop, and I shall be clean: wash me, and I shall be whiter than snow.

Hide thy face from my sins, and blot out all mine iniquities.

Create in me a clean heart, O God; and renew a right spirit within me.

Restore unto me the joy of thy salvation; and uphold me with thy free spirit.[8]

LITANY:

Leader: O Master of our lives, thou who didst find help through communion with the Father,

Group: Help us to be willing to tarry awhile with thee.

Leader: Thou who didst find strength in seclusion,

Group: Grant unto us a renewal of our spirits.

Leader: Thou who speakest not in the earthquake, wind, or fire, but in the still small voice,

Group: Save us from a feeling of futility.

Leader: Thou whose voice didst still the angry waves,

Group: Bid our anxious fears subside.

Leader: Thou who didst heal the broken spirits of men,

Group: Calm our troubled minds and hearts.

Leader: Thou who dost speak above the storm and stress of life,

Group: May we hear thy voice above the clamor and strife.

Leader: Thou who canst give a peace which the world cannot give,

BE STILL AND KNOW

Group: Grant us the serenity which comes only from communion with thee. AMEN.

POEM:

> Let us then labor for an inward stillness,
> An inward stillness and an inward healing,
> That perfect silence where the lips and heart
> Are still, and we no longer entertain
> Our own imperfect thought and vain opinions,
> But God alone speaks in us, and we wait
> In singleness of heart, that we may know
> His will, and in the silence of our spirits,
> That we may do his will, and do that only!
>
> —HENRY WADSWORTH LONGFELLOW

SOLO: "The Lord Is My Shepherd," by Liddle, or

HYMN: "Come unto Me," or
"Thou My Everlasting Portion," or
"O for a Closer Walk with God," or
"Be Still, My Soul."

BENEDICTION:

Thou who hast renewed our strength, send us out to bear a more worthy part in the struggle for righteousness and peace. AMEN.

SERVICE 12

BESIDE STILL WATERS

PRELUDE: Hymn tune, "Consolation," by Mendelssohn.

CALL TO WORSHIP:

> Make a joyful noise unto the Lord, all ye lands:
> Serve the Lord with gladness: come before his
> presence with singing.
> Know ye that the Lord, he is God:
> It is he that hath made us, and not we ourselves;
> We are his people,
> And the sheep of his pasture.[1]

HYMN: "Still, Still with Thee," or
"Draw Thou My Soul, O Christ."

SCRIPTURE:

Said Jesus unto them again, Verily, verily, I say unto you, I am the door of the sheep. All that ever came before me are thieves and robbers: but the sheep did not hear them. I am the door: by me if any man enter in, he shall be saved, and shall go in and out, and find pasture.

The thief cometh not, but for to steal, and to kill, and to destroy: I am come that they might have life, and that they might have it more abundantly. I am the good shepherd: the good shepherd giveth his life for the sheep.

I am the good shepherd, and know my sheep, and am known of mine. As the Father knoweth me, even so know I the Father: and I lay down my life for the sheep. And other sheep I have, which are not of this fold: them also I must bring, and they shall hear my voice; and there shall be one fold, and one shepherd.

My sheep hear my voice, and I know them, and they follow me: and I give unto them eternal life; and they shall never perish, neither shall any man pluck them out of my hand.

BESIDE STILL WATERS

My Father, which gave them me, is greater than all; and no man is able to pluck them out of my Father's hand. I and my Father are one.[2]

PRAYER:

Almighty God, unto whom all hearts are open, all desires known, and from whom no secrets are hid, cleanse the thoughts of our hearts by the inspiration of thy Holy Spirit, that we may perfectly love thee, and worthily magnify thy holy name; through Christ our Lord. AMEN.[3]

LEADER:

As we study the picture "Beside Still Waters," by Taylor, let us try to discover the message which the artist would convey.

PICTURE INTERPRETATION:

BESIDE STILL WATERS

A PICTURE embodies the imagery created within the artist's mind, and that imagery is the deposit left by experience. An artist can paint only what he has seen. Even his inventions, the works of his imagination, are new combinations of old experienced elements.

William Ladd Taylor lived in Wellesley, Massachusetts. As far as I know, he never saw Palestine. Of necessity, then, when he attempted to illustrate the Twenty-third Psalm, he had to visualize it as a New Englander. The lovely "still waters" of this picture have not the slightest resemblance to the streams of Canaan; and the grass that grows over the shallow banks and into the water is more lush than any Judean shepherd's feet ever trod. This meadow of peace may well be that of the painter's own Charles River in early June, or some other valley with the purple Berkshires next the sky. Only, instead of the elms that often rise like fountains out of such New England loveliness, Taylor has substituted a few palms to give an Oriental suggestion. All else is the homeland he loved.

And why not? The experience here pictured is a universal experience. If we translate the words of David's lyric into terms of our twentieth-century personal life, why should not the artist translate the imagery also? We might assert that he must translate it in order to save it, for we are a long way off from Judea's rugged hills. If we moderns could duplicate the actual thoughts and feelings of the

Hebrew David, visualize the situation that gave rise to the psalm, and be confronted with David's God, we would be startled, not to say shocked. His world was not ours, but his spiritual needs were like ours because he was human. David knew "still waters" like the pools of Artas; countless people down the centuries, and we too, have sometimes drunk at crystal fountains. It is this reality that counts, not its trappings, its imagery; and this reality transcends time and place and the individual.

Taylor invites you to contemplate this reality. He creates a spacious setting far from the world's tumult; he spreads above you the canopy of the heavens in which float untroubled clouds; he sketches the flock which trustfully follows the shepherd; and then in the face of the shepherd himself he admits you to that human experience, that attitude of soul, which constitutes the reality of "still waters," of which all this imagery is a nature symbol.

And just what is that reality? It is faith that the universe is friendly. There are many levels on which this faith may be exercised. There is the primitive biological level where the amoeba puts forth a feeler now here, now there, in the belief that the nutriment it needs exists somewhere. There is the instinctive level, as when the bird flings itself from its eyrie and trusts the air to put buoyancy beneath its flight; as when the golden plover feels the call to forsake its winter home in the Argentine and, trusting the radio beam in its own breast, finds itself and its mate on the shore of the Arctic Ocean. There is the human level where the babe finds its "still waters" in its mother's arms; the youth in the urge for adventurous living; the man and the woman in their daring partnership for life. The worker sees it as the postulate behind all work; the statesman as the dynamic of all his striving; and the artist and the poet as the inspiration of all idealism.

The older we grow and the more clearly we see the problems and the defeats of life, the more necessary we find this faith that, in spite of the worst we have experienced or known, the universe is friendly; its inexorable laws are the only foundation we can trust; underneath us are the Everlasting Arms, in the pulses of which we can feel the beat of the Eternal Heart.

To have this faith is to be led by "still waters." That is what "still waters" means to these unknowing sheep—a universe they can trust. That is what it means to this shepherd—a guidance for himself like that which he furnishes his flock. And to us moderns in a world of distraction and conflict and tragedy it must mean the same thing—

confidence in the ultimate goodness that reveals itself both as law and as love.[4]

SCRIPTURE:

> The Lord is my shepherd; I shall not want.
> He maketh me to lie down in green pastures:
> He leadeth me beside the still waters.
> He restoreth my soul: he leadeth me in the paths of righteousness for his name's sake.
> Yea, though I walk through the valley of the shadow of death, I will fear no evil: for thou art with me; thy rod and thy staff they comfort me.
> Thou preparest a table before me in the presence of mine enemies: thou anointest my head with oil; my cup runneth over.
> Surely goodness and mercy shall follow me all the days of my life: and I will dwell in the house of the Lord forever.[5]

SOLO: "Beside Still Waters," by Hamblen, or

HYMN: " 'Mid All the Traffic of the Ways," or
       "I Need Thee Every Hour," or
       "Dear Lord and Father of Mankind."

POEM:

> We bless thee for thy peace, O God,
>   Deep as th' unfathomed sea,
> Which falls like sunshine on the road
>   Of those who trust in thee.
>
> We ask not, Father, for repose
>   Which comes from outward rest,
> If we may have through all life's woes,
>   Thy peace within our breast.
>
> That peace which suffers and is strong,
>   Trusts where it cannot see,
> Deems not the trial way too long,
>   But leaves the end with thee.

That peace which flows serene and deep,
    A river in the soul,
Whose banks a living verdure keep,
    God's sunshine o'er the whole.
                              —AUTHOR UNKNOWN

PRAYER:

O God, the stay of all who put their trust in thee, the author of all good, from whom cometh every good and perfect gift, lead us by thy spirit. May thy love be in our hearts, and may the light which cometh from thee lead us into the paths of righteousness. Keep us in thy love, strengthen us with thy presence, blend our wills with thine, and may all we think, or speak, or do be acceptable in thy sight. Thou makest all things to work together for good to them that love thee. Knowing this, we can endure all things, face sorrow, illness, or other calamities unafraid, for thou art our strength and refuge. Draw us into a closer fellowship with thee, O God. AMEN.

HYMN: "Saviour, like a Shepherd Lead Us," or
       "Have Thine Own Way," or
       "O for a Closer Walk with God."

BENEDICTION:

May the peace which passeth understanding abide with us. AMEN.

SERVICE 13

HE SHALL BE LIKE A TREE

PRELUDE: Adagio movement from Beethoven's "Sonata," Opus 2, No. 1.

CALL TO WORSHIP:

> Holy, holy, holy Lord God of Hosts!
> Heaven and earth are full of thee!
> Heaven and earth are praising thee,
>   O Lord Most High!

HYMN: "For the Beauty of the Earth," or
      "All Creatures of Our God and King," or
      "Fairest Lord Jesus."

SCRIPTURE:

Blessed is the man that walketh not in the counsel of the ungodly, nor standeth in the way of sinners, nor sitteth in the seat of the scornful.

But his delight is in the law of the Lord; and in his law doth he meditate day and night.

And he shall be like a tree planted by the rivers of water, that bringeth forth his fruit in his season; his leaf also shall not wither; and whatsoever he doeth shall prosper.

The ungodly are not so: but are like the chaff which the wind driveth away.

Therefore the ungodly shall not stand in the judgment, nor sinners in the congregation of the righteous.

For the Lord knoweth the way of the righteous: but the way of the ungodly shall perish.[1]

LITANY OF THANKS:

> For meadows spread with gold and gemmed with stars;
> For every tint of every tiniest flower;

For every daisy smiling to the sun;
For every bird that builds in joyous hope;
For every lamb that frisks beside its dam;
For every leaf that rustles in the wind;
For spiring poplar, and for spreading oak;
For queenly birch, and lofty swaying elm;
For the great cedar's benedictory grace;
For earth's ten thousand fragrant incenses,—
Sweet altar-gifts from leaf and fruit and flower;
For every wondrous thing that greens and grows;
For wide-spread cornlands,—billowing golden seas;
For rippling stream, and white-laced waterfall;
For purpling mountains; lakes like silver shields;
For white-piled clouds that float against the blue;
For tender green of far-off upland slopes;
For fringing forests and far-gleaming spires;
For that deep sea—a shallow to Thy love;
For round green hills, earth's full benignant breasts;
For sun-chased shadows flitting o'er the plain;
For gleam and gloom; for all life's counter-change;
For hope that quickens under darkening skies;
For all we see; for all that underlies,—
We thank Thee, Lord! AMEN.[2]

—JOHN OXENHAM

SCRIPTURE:

O Lord, how manifold are thy works!
In wisdom hast thou made them all:
The earth is full of thy riches.
So is this great and wide sea,
Wherein are things creeping innumerable,
Both small and great beasts.
Thou sendest forth thy spirit, they are created:
And thou renewest the face of the earth.
The glory of the Lord shall endure for ever:
The Lord shall rejoice in his works.
He looketh on the earth, and it trembleth:
He toucheth the hills, and they smoke.
I will sing unto the Lord as long as I live:
I will sing praise to my God while I have my being.[3]

HE SHALL BE LIKE A TREE

LEADER:

The Psalmist said, "He shall be like a tree." In what ways are we like a tree? Does the Maker and Designer of trees expect us to keep our lives in tune with the laws of the forest? Does he expect us to live close to nature, to become calm in spirit, clean and upright as a tree? What is the purpose of our lives?

TALKS:

THE PARTS OF A TREE CO-OPERATE

WHEN we look at a tree and enjoy its beauty, we see only a part of it. There is almost as much of it underground as above ground. In many cases the root mass is similar in size and shape to the trunk and foliage. The leaves are marvelous in their great variety with endless patterns, all perfect in detail, but the roots with their intricate detail are equally wonderful.

If a tree lives and grows, every part of it must carry out the function which it is to perform. The roots anchor the tree to the ground, hold it in place, and reach deep into the soil to absorb the water and minerals necessary for growth. The food is carried by the water through the sapwood to every part of the tree, and growth takes place when it is changed into the substance of the tree.

It seems incredible that a tree should be able to take out of the ground such a vast amount of water and lift it to the highest branches. It is said that a medium-sized tree will lift eight hundred pounds of water out of the ground on a summer day. Of all the moisture taken in only two per cent is used to nourish the tree; the remainder is released into the air through openings in the leaves. During dry spells the valves in the cells of the leaves close and thus conserve the water supply.

Besides acting as a water fountain by throwing off the water it cannot use, the leaf performs other functions. Charles F. Kettering, the scientist, has been trying for some time to discover why the leaf is green. When he finds the answer, he may also discover how the leaf with its magical chemistry of chlorophyll changes the carbon dioxide of the air into the living protoplasm of the tree and at the same time gives off oxygen. There is much yet to be learned about the process, but growth takes place when chlorophyll, air, sunlight, and water furnish the nourishment the tree needs.

Looking at a cross section of a tree, we see the bark which protects the tree. Underneath this outer layer is a layer of cells which carry the food, a slippery jellylike substance, to every part of the tree. Next is a thin layer of cells, called the cambium layer, which is the growing part of the tree. Within these cells are the water conduits, called sapwood, through which the water flows upward from the root system.

Each year there is formed a new layer of cambium cells, and it is by these rings of growth that the age of the tree can be determined. The older sapwood stores water for the dry spells, and when no longer needed for a reservoir, it becomes a hard substance which supports and gives strength to the tree. In the center of the heartwood is the pith, the oldest part of the tree.

A tree has a remarkable ability to adapt itself to its surroundings. In arid sections it does not grow tall because of the limited supply of water; in a crevice of a rock it is stunted because of the lack of food; on a ridge or mountain peak, swept by wind and storms, it is bent in the direction the wind blows. A tree thus bent becomes gnarled and twisted, but it is stronger because of the stress it has withstood.

A PARABLE OF GROWTH

THE STORY is told that on a Midwestern farm on the top of a hill there stood a huge tree which stayed green when other trees withered. A new highway was being built which had to pass over the exact spot where the tree stood. Workers leveling the hill cut the tree down, and the secret of its enormous height was discovered. The roots of the tree had reached down to a spring which no drought could effect. While other trees withered, this particular tree continued to grow. It had a never-failing reservoir from which to draw. This tree reminds us of persons who are able to stand up against any adversity. They can face whatever the day sends because they have tapped a reservoir which is a never-failing source of strength.

POEM:

Defeat may serve as well as victory
To shake the soul and let the glory out.
When the great oak is straining in the wind,
The boughs drink in new beauty, and the trunk
Sends down a deeper root on the windward side.
Only the soul that knows the mighty grief

HE SHALL BE LIKE A TREE

Can know the mighty rapture. Sorrows come
To stretch out spaces in the heart for joy.[4]
—Edwin Markham

When Longfellow was well advanced in years, a friend inquired, "How do you manage to write so beautifully and to keep in such vigorous health at your age?" Pointing to a near-by apple tree that was in bloom, the poet replied, "You see that tree? It is very old, yet it has never been prettier than it is now. It bears the loveliest blooms that it has ever borne. The secret is that each year it grows a little new wood, and it is out of the new wood that the blooms come. Like the apple tree, I try to grow a little new wood each year."

In the western part of the United States the giant redwoods, or Sequoias, grow to enormous height. They are perhaps the oldest living things in the world. Their extreme age may be attributed to the fact that their roots reach out, intertwine, and thus help to hold each other up. Or perhaps their ability to recuperate may explain their age. When a top is broken off, the tree has the power to grow another top. When the bark is cut or injured, a new covering is grown to heal the scar. Their ability to throw off attacking borers before they injure the tree may also help to account for their old age. Then, too, since the redwoods grow straight, the power of gravity works with them instead of against them, and by growing over a long period of time, they reach their great height and size.

Like the roots of the Sequoias, are we striving to reach out and support our weaker brothers? Have we learned to work together, hold each other up, so that the strength of one becomes the strength of all? Do we recuperate as readily? When our plans are shattered, our hopes blasted, can we start over again and reach greater heights? Have we determined to rise above the calamities that beset us? Can we throw off the little borers of selfishness, or do we allow them to sap our strength? Do we stand upright, work with God, refuse to compromise?

We can grow quietly and serenely according to the plan of God. We can strive for perfection, beauty, and usefulness. A tree does not live for itself; it lives to bear fruit, to render some definite service. So also should we live.

Blessed is the man that trusteth in the Lord,
And whose hope the Lord is.

For he shall be as a tree planted by the waters,
And that spreadeth out her roots by the river,
And shall not see when heat cometh,
But her leaf shall be green;
And shall not be careful in the year of drought,
Neither shall cease from yielding fruit.[5]

PRAYER:

Our Father, Maker and Designer of the growing trees, help us to grow. Thou who shapest the twisted little scrub pine bent by the mountain gales, the dainty white birch mirrored in the placid lake, and the mighty Sequoias, monarchs of the forest, fashion our lives. Make us strong that we may not be bowed down by the winds of difficulty and discouragement. Instill us with a desire to serve our fellow men and not to be satisfied with vainglory. Make us upright— great souls of towering grandeur. May we measure our height by the Christ, ever reaching up to the sky.

We thank thee for the hard things of life, for struggle, for discouragement, and even for loneliness and seeming defeat. For it is only in weakness that we can feel thy strength; it is only in struggle that we need thy help; it is only in discouragement that we receive courage and confidence in thee; it is only in loneliness that we know fully thy companionship; it is only in seeming defeat that we experience the greatest triumph. As the moss and the flowers cover the scars caused by disaster, as the bending bush struggling for a hold on life sends its roots deep into the earth, as the trees receive their towering strength by meeting the gale, so wilt thou blot out from our sight the mistakes we have made and help us to root our faith deep in thee that we may face life bravely.

And rooted in thee, we face the morrow with confidence and follow the road unafraid, for we do not walk alone. AMEN.[6]

SOLO: "Trees," by Rasbach,[7] or
        "The Green Cathedral," by Hahn, or

HYMN: "God, Who Touchest Earth with Beauty."

BENEDICTION:

Thou who hast made everything beautiful in its time, help us to strive for beauty in all our relations one with another. AMEN.

SERVICE 14

LET THIS MIND BE IN YOU

PRELUDE: Hymn tune, *"Ar Hyd Y Nos."*

CALL TO WORSHIP:

> Come, Holy Ghost, in love,
> Shed on us from above
>   Thine own bright ray!
> Divinely good thou art;
> Thy sacred gifts impart
> To gladden each sad heart:
>   O come today!
>
> —RAY PALMER

HYMN: "O Young and Fearless Prophet," or "Breathe on Me, Breath of God," or "Thou My Everlasting Portion."

RESPONSIVE READING:

Leader: Now, brothers, let your minds dwell on what is true, what is worthy, what is right, what is pure, what is amiable, what is kindly—on everything that is excellent or praiseworthy.

Group: Jesus said, "It was for this that I was born and for this that I came to the world, to give testimony for truth. Everyone who is on the side of truth listens to my voice. . . . You will know the truth and the truth will set you free."

Leader: Let your minds dwell on what is pure.

Group: To the pure everything is pure, but to the evil-minded and unbelieving nothing is pure, but their very minds and consciences are unclean. They profess to know God, but they disown him by what they do.

Leader: Let your minds dwell on what is honest.

Group: Do not pay anyone back with evil for evil. See that you are above reproach in the eyes of everyone.

Leader: Let your minds dwell on what is excellent or praiseworthy.

Group: Do not act for selfish ends or from vanity, but modestly treat one another as your superiors. Do not take account of your own interests, but of the interests of others as well. Have the same attitude that Christ Jesus had.

Leader: Let your minds be steadfast.

Group: Thou wilt keep him in perfect peace, whose mind is stayed on thee.[1]

PRAYER:

O our God, we humbly beseech thee to purify our hearts from all vain and worldly and sinful thoughts, and thus prepare our souls to worship thee this day acceptably, with reverence and godly fear. O Lord, set our affection on things above, all the day long, and give us grace to receive thy word which we shall hear this day, into honest and good hearts, and bring forth fruit with patience. Hear us, O God, for the sake of Jesus Christ, our Saviour. AMEN.[2]

ANTHEM: "Christ of the Upward Way," by Mueller, or

HYMN: "Take Thou Our Minds, Dear Lord," or
"Have Thine Own Way."

TALK:

JESUS, THE SON OF MAN

WE wonder about the human appearance of Jesus during the time of his earthly ministry—the tone of his voice, the expression of his eyes, his entire personality. There is evidence that his voice had an unusual appeal, for we are told that "never man spake like this man." People were affected when Jesus looked upon them; all that was good in Zacchaeus rose up and asserted itself under the steady gaze of the Master's eyes. In Jesus' manner and in every detail of his appearance there was a simple dignity that accorded with the pattern of his life.

It is difficult to paint a satisfactory picture of Christ. It is not so much the artist's inability to depict ideal traits, but it is difficult to portray the many-sidedness of the ideal. As A. E. Bailey says: "Christ was the sanest and most wholesome man that ever lived; he was at the same time so completely filled with the spirit of God that the keenest analysis fails to tell where the human leaves off and the divine begins. He touched life throughout its vast orbit; he entered into all the relationships that men sustain with one another, and that man and God may enter."

He knew what work with his hands involved; he knew the duties of a son, a brother, a wage earner; he was friend, teacher, physician, preacher, reformer, story-teller, Jewish Messiah, Son of Man, Son of God! "What single portrait can compass this range? The problem reduces itself to the adequate embodiment of a single trait or two, the presentation of only an aspect of his personality."[3]

Recent artists, in order to make Jesus real to us, have emphasized his humanity. They have taken away the halo from his head and have given him the sun-tanned brow of one who lived much in the open. Instead of the sad, effeminate expression on his face, they have given him the steady gaze of the carpenter; and for the rich robes they have substituted the plain clothing of the workingman. They have shown him, not with slender fingers, but with the strong, firm hands of one who toils for his daily bread. They depict the Son of Man with desires and problems similar to ours, and we are naturally drawn to a Christ who understands.

When an artist paints Christ in a humble workingman's home, he is depicting the idea that plain working people are as much in Christ's thought as are the rich. Christ toiled for his daily bread, spoke the language and understood the problems of the workingmen. The poor heard him gladly, for he entered into their joys and sorrows. Just as Christ graced the homes of the humble during his earthly ministry, so he blesses any home by his presence today.

SOLO: "How Beauteous Were the Marks Divine," or
"Lord, for Tomorrow and Its Needs."

POEM:

> O come, thou wisdom from on high,
> And order all things far and nigh;
> To us the path of knowledge show,
> And cause us in her ways to go.
>
> O come, desire of nations, bind
> All people in one heart and mind;
> Bid envy, strife, and quarrels cease;
> Fill the whole world with heaven's peace.[4]

TALK:

THE MIND OF JESUS

ST. PAUL says, "Let this mind be in you, which was also in Christ Jesus." What was this mind?

"It must not be forgotten that Jesus had some significant mental images which he was able to match with reality in a way so unique as to fill our hearts with sublime envy. . . .

"He thought what it would be like to be a true son of God. No nobler mental image than that could ever enter the mind. Most of us are content with something very much less. Could we be sons of Socrates or of Shakespeare or Beethoven or Lincoln we would count ourselves blessed among mortals. Could we create or think or act in our times as they did in theirs how rich life would be! But evidently from earliest childhood Jesus had but one mental image for himself— that he should think and act and love like a son of God. How well he succeeded in giving that picture actuality we need not pause to relate. Without the slightest evidence of pose or straining after effect, without a sign of . . . one who is playing a rôle, he talked and lived in such fashion that this critical twentieth century does not bother to ask whether Jesus was like God, but in a bold leap of desire and faith expresses a hope and a conviction that God is like Jesus." [5]

POEM:

Stay, Master, stay upon this heavenly hill;
A little longer, let us linger still;
With all the mighty ones of old beside,
Near to God's holy presence still abide;
Before the throne of light we trembling stand,
And catch a glimpse into the spirit-land.

Stay, Master, stay! we breathe a purer air;
This life is not the life that waits us there:
Thoughts, feelings, flashes, glimpses come and go;
We cannot speak them—nay, we do not know;
Wrapt in this cloud of light we seem to be
The thing we fain would grow—eternally.

"No!" saith the Lord, "the hour is past," we go;
Our home, our life, our duties lie below.

LET THIS MIND BE IN YOU

While here we kneel upon the mount of prayer,
The plow lies waiting in the furrow there!
Here we sought God that we might know his will;
There we must do it, serve him, seek him still.

If man aspires to reach the throne of God,
O'er the dull plains of earth must lie the road:
He who best does his lowly duty here,
Shall mount the highest in a nobler sphere:
At God's own feet our spirits seek their rest,
And he is nearest him who serves him best.

—SAMUEL GREG

DIRECTED MEDITATION (after each prayerful meditation by the leader,
the group responds by singing a stanza of Earl Marlatt's hymn):

Leader: Let us remember Jesus, who during his childhood was subject unto his parents. O Lord, may we recognize persons of
authority and live in such manner as to honor our parents.
Jesus increased in wisdom and stature and in favor with God
and man; O Lord, guide us that we may come to our best
growth and development.

Group: Spirit of Life, in this new dawn,
            Give us the faith that follows on,
            Letting thine all-pervading power
            Fulfill the dream of this high hour.

Leader: Jesus lived in the flesh, yet was a true son of God. O Master,
grant that we may have the same mental image for ourselves; help us to think, act, and love like a son of God.

Group: Spirit Creative, give us light,
            Lifting the raveled mists of night;
            Touch thou our dust with spirit-hand
            And make us souls that understand.

Leader: Jesus gave his life on the cross that we through his death
might have eternal life.

Group: Spirit Redeeming, give us grace
            When crucified to seek thy face;
            To read forgiveness in thine eyes
            Today with thee in Paradise.

Leader: Jesus on several occasions withdrew from the crowd to be alone with his Father. O God, grant that we may have a sense of thy presence at all times but especially when facing a crisis, or a difficult decision.

Group: Spirit Consoling, let us find
      Thy hand when sorrows leave us blind;
      In the gray valley let us hear
      Thy silent voice: "Lo, I am near."

Leader: Jesus declared his mission to be to preach deliverance to the poor, to set the captives free; O Master, grant that we may have a keener insight into our divine mission. The Son of Man lived without sin; help us, O Lord, to have the same standard of perfection for ourselves.

Group: Spirit of Love, at evening time,
      When weary feet refuse to climb,
      Give us thy vision, eyes that see,
      Beyond the dark, the dawn and thee.[6]

LEADER:

Putting his life at the disposal of his Father, Jesus was so in tune with God's purpose that he accomplished things which seem miraculous to us, but to him they were natural, because he drew upon the resources made available by the indwelling Spirit of God. To him the body and the spirit were one; he lived in the spirit to such an extent that his mind, desires, purposes, and actions were all in accordance with the will of his Father. If the things which he did seem impossible to us, it is because we look at them from the standpoint of the physical or material. But if we live by God's will, allow him to work out his purpose through us, new forces will be at our disposal and we may expect the unusual to happen.

Let us ask for guidance as we try to discover the will of God for ourselves. Are we ready to be used as instruments in his hands, to be led by his spirit, not only to give what we have but to give ourselves also in his service? "For as many as are led by the Spirit of God, they are the sons of God."

SOLO: "Spirit of God, Descend," by Neidlinger, or

HYMN: "Spirit of God, Descend upon My Heart," or
    "Lord, Speak to Me, That I May Speak."

LET THIS MIND BE IN YOU

Leader: Come, all ye who bear the name of Christ,
           and order your lives by it,
        For you are his epistles known and read
           of all men;
        Let this mind be in you which was also in
           Christ Jesus,
        That it may direct your thinking, speaking,
           living,
        That all who take knowledge of you
        May learn the salvation of God.[7]

—CHAUNCEY R. PIETY

Group: O wondrous Lord, my soul would be
        Still more and more conformed to thee,
        And learn of thee, the lowly One,
        And like thee, all my journey run.

—A. CLEVELAND COXE

BENEDICTION:

And the peace which passeth all understanding shall keep your hearts and minds; through Christ Jesus. AMEN.

SERIES THREE

CREDO

Suggestions to the Counselor

THE PURPOSE of this series is to guide young people in a search for a better understanding of their relation to God, to strengthen their faith, and to help them discover ways to work with God. The leader should help them to anticipate the series as a whole and to know the purpose of each service.

The success of these services depends upon each person's studying his part until the message becomes his own. The parts should be assigned well ahead of time. All who participate should be in their places before the prelude begins. Quiet music at the beginning will help to set the mood for worship. Announcements and irrelevant material should be posted on a bulletin board and not included in the worship service.

To build a worship center appropriate for this series, cover an altar or table with a cloth and place upon it a cross and lighted candles. With the service "I Believe in Jesus," use a picture which portrays Jesus as a strong character—e.g., Beecroft, "And Christ Turned and Looked upon Peter."

The following books will be helpful with this series: W. A. Smart, *The Contemporary Christ;* J. G. Gilkey, *The Certainty of God;* and H. D. Gray, *A Theology for Christian Youth.*

It will add to the effectiveness if the group is led in a discussion of the topic following each service. The leader will prepare his own questions ahead of time. The following are merely suggestive:

With "I Believe in Man," illustrate the difference between Jesus' idea of the worth of personality and the prevailing idea today. Did race, color, or station matter to him? What would be changed if Christians today accepted Jesus' idea of the worth of persons and treated them accordingly?

With "I Believe in the Church," consider what the world would be like without the Christian Church. Mention some of the values that have come to you from the Church. Is the influence of your local church as vital as it could be? What changes would you like to bring about in your church?

With "I Believe in the Kingdom of God," review the parables on the Kingdom of God. What changes must take place before the Kingdom of God comes on earth? What can you do to hasten its coming?

With "I Believe in Jesus," read John 18:37 and explain what was meant by this statement. What was the purpose of Jesus' life? What do you mean when you say that you believe in Jesus? Is one's life always modified when he accepts Jesus' way of life?

With "I Believe in God," mention some experiences that have helped you to a better understanding of God. Recall some of your earliest ideas of God. Have they changed? Why? Does the way you think about God make any difference in your conduct? When are you most aware of the presence of God?

SERVICE 15

I BELIEVE IN MAN

PRELUDE: Hymn tune, *"Ton-Y-Botel."*

CALL TO WORSHIP:

> We are all blind until we see
> That in the human plan
> Nothing is worth the making if
> It does not make the man.
>
> Why build these cities glorious
> If man unbuilded goes?
> In vain we build the work, unless
> The builder also grows.[1]
>
> —EDWIN MARKHAM

HYMN: "O Son of Man, Thou Madest Known," or
"O Young and Fearless Prophet."

SCRIPTURE:

> When I consider thy heavens, the work of
> thy fingers, the moon and the stars, which
> thou hast ordained;
> What is man, that thou are mindful of him?
> and the son of man, that thou visitest him?
> For thou hast made him a little lower than
> the angels, and hast crowned him with
> glory and honour.
> Thou madest him to have dominion over
> the works of thy hands; thou hast put all
> things under his feet:
> All sheep and oxen, yea, and the beasts of
> the field;

> The fowl of the air, and the fish of the sea,
>   and whatsoever passeth through the paths
>   of the seas.
> O Lord our God, how excellent is thy name
>   in all the earth! [2]

PRAYER:

Our heavenly Father, who by thy love hast made us, and through thy love hast kept us, and in thy love wouldst make us perfect; we humbly confess that we have not loved thee with all our heart and soul and mind and strength, and that we have not loved one another as Christ hath loved us. Thy life is within our souls, but our selfishness hath hindered thee. We have resisted thy Spirit. We have neglected thine inspirations. Forgive what we have been; help us to amend what we are; and in thy spirit direct what we shall be; that thou mayest come into the full glory of thy creation, in us and in all men; through Jesus Christ our Lord. AMEN.[3]

HYMN: "All Hail the Power of Jesus' Name," or
      "O Master Workman of the Race."

AN AFFIRMATION OF BELIEF:

> I believe in man,
> Made a little lower than God,
> Crowned with glory and honor,
> And given dominion of the earth.
>
> I believe in man,
> Created spiritually like God,
> With a mind that hungers for truth,
> With a heart that loves good more than evil,
> With a dynamic will that dares to do,
> And with a boundless capacity for growth and
>   progress.
>
> I believe in man,
> Who dreamed and prayed and planned,
> And from the jungle built the world we know;
> And being conscious of present evils,
> He still dreams and struggles and prays

I BELIEVE IN MAN

To build integrity, justice, good will, brotherhood, and everlasting peace.

I believe in man, the offspring of God,
Potentially and eventually triumphant.[4]

—CHAUNCEY R. PIETY

TALKS:

THE DIGNITY OF MAN

I BELIEVE in man. So does everyone else, of course, in one way or another. But the way in which one believes in man is quite important.
What one believes about man makes an enormous difference in the
way one treats other people. It is very important that one should
believe those things about man that are in harmony with reality.
Only thus can he be free to behave toward his fellow men in an appropriate way.

I believe in the dignity of man. Faith in the universal dignity of
man does not rest on observation. It is not gained by the scientific
study of man or by the acquaintance with people in general. The most
powerful faith in the dignity of man is a religious conviction. It is the
conviction that man is created in God's image, and that God's image
is implanted in every individual.

I believe that God created man in his own image, and that man is
responsible to God for the way in which he lives. Man, therefore,
has an inalienable right to freedom—freedom of conscience, and freedom of life. The image of God in man, therefore, sets limits on the
demands that can rightfully be made on him by other men, or by
institutions or by groups such as the political state. This is the basic
principle of democracy; it is the principle that underlies the civil rights
of men; it is also the source of whatever brotherhood does or can exist
among people and the peoples of the world. All men are created to love
and to serve God. Therefore, they cannot be degraded into mere instruments of loyalty and service to other men, or to the state.

It is true that the image of God is often dimmed in the character
of individual men. But however warped and vague it may appear
to be, yet it is there, established, not by us but by the divine Creator.
It can never be completely effaced or destroyed. Therefore, I believe
in the dignity of man.

—113—

MAN'S NEED TO GROW

I BELIEVE in the ability and the need of man to grow. Man is a creature who bears in his very nature a likeness to God the Creator. He is not only creature but creator as well. As a creator man has freedom to make critical judgments among possible goals, to make choices on the basis of his judgment, and to act in accordance with his choices. Man can say No, and think a situation over. His freedom is limited by his interests, his character, and his experience, but within these limits he is free to make a large proportion of his knowledge and ideals effective in what he does.

Thus man has the ability to direct his life toward worthy goals in which he sees meaning, and which he has come to value and appreciate. It is our very nature to revalue our values, to change our minds, to develop our habits, to build our own characters. It is only in the process of living that the image of God so deep within us comes to actuality. Perhaps the most glorious fact about living is that we can have no experience, even though it be tragedy, that cannot be made to contribute to our growth of character. Even death itself, the last experience in this world, can make its own inexpressible contribution to the richness, beauty, and strength of character when it is faced, understood, accepted, and prepared for. I believe in the ability and need of man to grow.

WORTH OF MAN

I BELIEVE in the worth of man. Man is by nature a lover and worshiper. He is never happy until he gives himself away. Before he can find his own true being, he must find something so important in his eyes that he is willing to give his very life for it. While man chooses many persons and causes for such devotion, he never finds his true meaning until he loves and worships God.

But man can love and worship God in this deep and profound way only in response to the love and grace of God. In every age, and among all peoples, men have discovered that God loves men more than man knows how to love himself. And in this discovery, and in it alone, man has learned the true worth of man. If God values man, man is of infinite value. And if in the love of God man is of infinite value, he is also immortal. Because I believe in that love of God for man, I believe in the worth of man—in the worth of every living soul.[5]

I BELIEVE IN MAN

HYMN: "O Jesus, Master, When Today," or
"More Love to Thee, O Christ."

MAN CAN BE REDEEMED

I BELIEVE that man is a sinner who can be redeemed. God has implanted his image in man. That image carries with it the responsibility for developing by man the dignity and character which should characterize him as a child of God. But through sin man fails in the responsibility which God places upon him.

Sometimes man fails to realize his creaturehood. He thinks of himself more highly than he should. He puts himself in God's place. Such arrogance is the worst sin of all. Man has creative powers, but when he fails to exercise his freedom, when he fails to discriminate among possible goals, to be as critical as he can in his thinking, to exercise courage and loyalty in his work for the good, he denies his station as God's child, and so falls into sin. Again man misdirects his freedom. He shifts his attention from the good to the bad, and dwells upon it, toying with temptation. When he uses his freedom improperly, he falls into sin. He is a sinner, too, if he neglects to grow, if he is careless about himself, about what he is to become; if he fails to realize the need to change his mind, to deepen his appreciations, to rebuild his character. Being a lover puts upon man the tremendous responsibility to love the good. But man may love the things that are evil, build up appreciations for the uncouth and unclean, and so fall into sin. He may worship idols, and let them obscure the true God that should be first in his loyalty and love. Or he may think so little of himself as to deny God's love, and deny his own essential importance. Men lose faith in themselves; they fail to believe that God loves them. And this, too, is sin. I believe in man as a sinner—but as a sinner who can be redeemed.

MADE IN THE IMAGE OF GOD

GOD's grace, like light, is spread throughout the universe. But for us it radiates in healing from one central figure, like sunlight. Jesus Christ is our sun. He is the light of the world. In him God's grace shines for the healing and health of men. When we move into the light by believing in him and purposing to live by his standards he breaks the power of sin over us, and we move joyously toward a new life. If any man be in Christ he is a new creature.

I believe that man can be saved from sin through the grace of God revealed in Jesus Christ for the healing and health of men. Salvation is not so much a transaction as a relation and a direction. As a relation, salvation is putting God at the center of things and finding our place in relation to his being and love and will. As a direction, salvation for the individual . . . "is to be on the way now to ever higher and expanding life, to more abundant life."

Christians believe that in Jesus Christ God's character and will are made known, man's vocation is made effective, and God's grace is made available for man's salvation. Christ came to seek the lost (those who are on the way to a life which is "starved, narrow, and diseased at the core"; those who are miserable but unable by themselves to find the way out of their misery) and to save them (by setting them on the way toward goodness and blessedness in a spirit of buoyant hope and sustaining vital strength). This means that Jesus took upon himself the burden of man's sin and suffering, endured its consequences on the Cross, and in the Resurrection demonstrated the eternal vitality of love. The message of the Cross is that God pays a great price to redeem men out of their sins, and set them on the road to life.

Thus man becomes a new creature—a new creature, but not a perfect man any more than a man recovering from typhus is thereby given a perfect physical body. Health is equilibrium, balance, wholeness. A healthy organism is one in which all the parts function in proper relation to one another, and which does the work as a whole that it is fitted for. So it is with a redeemed man. His various powers function properly together and his life as a whole moves with the trend of the world, as he joyously loves the kind of values and does the kind of work for which God created him.

I believe in man: a creature made in the image of God who is also a creator with freedom to make critical judgments among possible alternatives, to choose among these alternatives, and thus through self-direction help to create his own future and change the world; a developing spirit that has forever the ability and the need to grow; a lover and worshiper whose happiness is possible only in love and service to God, and whose infinite value and eternal life are assured in God's grace and love; a sinner who can be saved by faith in the redeeming love of God in Christ.[6]

PRAYER:

O God, deliver us from a low appraisal of ourselves. Grant that we may think of ourselves as sons and daughters of thine and learn to live in love and brotherhood. Forgive us for narrowness of vision and contentment with low desires and low aims. Grant unto us a clear understanding of our divine possibilities for growth and development. Help us to study to show ourselves approved unto God, a workman that needeth not to be ashamed, rightly dividing the word of truth. Make clear thy plan and purpose for us and strengthen us as we strive to live by thy plan. Be thou our guide as we dedicate the powers of mind, heart, and hand to thee. In the name of the Master of us all, we pray. AMEN.

HYMN: "Spirit of Life, in This New Dawn," or
      "Are Ye Able?"

BENEDICTION:

The grace of the Lord Jesus Christ, and the love of God, and the communion of the Holy Spirit, be with you all. AMEN.

SERVICE 16

I BELIEVE IN THE CHURCH

PRELUDE: Hymn tune, "Italian Hymn" (Trinity).

CALL TO WORSHIP:

> Come, O thou God of grace,
> Dwell in this holy place,
>   E'en now descend!
> This temple, reared to thee,
> O may it ever be
> Filled with thy majesty,
>   Till time shall end!
>
> Be in each song of praise
> Which here thy people raise
>   With hearts aflame!
> Let every anthem rise
> Like incense to the skies,
> A joyful sacrifice,
>   To thy blest name!
>   —WILLIAM E. EVANS

HYMN: "Glorious Things of Thee Are Spoken," or
"Jesus, with Thy Church Abide."

SCRIPTURE:

When Jesus came into the coasts of Caesarea Philippi, he asked his disciples, saying, Whom do men say that I the Son of man am?

And they said, Some say that thou art John the Baptist: some, Elias; and others, Jeremias, or one of the prophets. He saith unto them, But whom say ye that I am? And Simon Peter answered and said, Thou are the Christ, the Son of the living God.

And Jesus answered and said unto him, Blessed art thou, Simon

—118—

Barjona: for flesh and blood hath not revealed it into thee, but my Father which is in heaven. And I say unto thee, That thou art Peter, and upon this rock I will build my church; and the gates of hell shall not prevail against it. And I will give unto thee the keys of the kingdom of heaven: and whatsoever thou shalt bind on earth shall be bound in heaven: and whatsoever thou shalt loose on earth shall be loosed in heaven.

Then Peter said unto them, Repent, and be baptized every one of you in the name of Jesus Christ for the remission of sins, and ye shall receive the gift of the Holy Ghost. Then they that gladly received his word were baptized: and the same day there were added unto them about three thousand souls. And they continued stedfastly in the apostles' doctrine and fellowship, and in breaking of bread, and in prayers. And fear came upon every soul: and many wonders and signs were done by the apostles. And all that believed were together, and had all things common; and sold their possessions and goods, and parted them to all men, as every man had need. And they, continuing daily with one accord in the temple, and breaking bread from house to house, did eat their meat with gladness and singleness of heart, praising God, and having favour with all the people. And the Lord added to the church daily such as should be saved.[1]

PRAYER:

O Lord, we thank thee for thy Church Universal and for the inspiration and fellowship which we enjoy in our local church. Help us to be more worthy of the rich heritage left us, and may we give of ourselves and our possessions that the influence of the Church be carried to others.

We thank thee that thou dwellest not afar off, but that thou art in our midst to strengthen and encourage us. Thou who hast overcome the world, grant that sin shall not have dominion over us. Increase our faith, confirm our hope, and give us the assurance of thy power working through us. In Jesus' name. AMEN.

TALKS:

I BELIEVE IN A CHURCH THAT SERVES

CHRIST spoke of the Church as his body, for it is the instrument through which his Spirit moves among men and by which men are brought into a knowledge of God. It is both human and divine, for its membership is made up of imperfect human beings, and yet at the same time it is the channel through which the Spirit of God works. There will always be problems in the Church, for the people are not perfect, yet the vision of the ideal Church is kept before Christians all the while as the goal for which to strive.

The Church has no rivals in the work of reclaiming lost humanity. With its schools, hospitals, orphanages, and leper asylums it carries on a world-wide program of service. It seeks to meet the needs of people regardless of race, station, or color. The Church has given the people a new conscience on social issues. It has spoken against corrupt practices and evil of every kind; it has inspired and promoted practically all of the movements to uproot evil; it has taught the worth of human personality and the rights of the individual; it has stirred the people to bring about better living conditions. Along with its missionary and reform movements, it has promoted education and democracy. The Church is still the greatest force for good in the world, for it has within it the power to correct the evil which remains.

The Church has many functions to perform: it seeks to help people to know and to do God's will, to foster a Christian fellowship among all races, and to usher in a great spiritual awakening. It is universal in its appeal, for its message is adapted to the peculiar needs of all people. It helps them to solve their problems of poverty, fear, and insecurity. In spite of all its shortcomings, it is the best agency for fellowship that men have found, for it includes members of every race and every country. The Church is founded on a necessity, for it meets needs which otherwise would not be met. It trains people in their worship of God and leads to a desire to serve mankind and to bring in the Kingdom of God on earth.

When the revolution came in Germany, Albert Einstein, the scientist, looked to the universities to defend freedom, for they had always boasted of their devotion to the cause of truth; but the universities were silenced. Then he looked to the editors of the great newspapers whose editorials had proclaimed their love of freedom, but they were also silenced. Realizing that only the Church stood across the path of the campaign to suppress truth, Einstein said: "I never had any special interest in the Church before, but now I feel a great affection and admiration because the Church alone has had the courage and persistence to stand for intellectual truth and moral freedom. I am forced thus to confess that what I once despised I now praise unreservedly."

While kingdoms have risen and fallen, political groups have come and gone, the Church has stood an ever-growing influence for good. What would the world be today without the influence of the Christian Church?

POEM:

> Love is the doctrine of this church,
> The quest of truth is its sacrament,
> And service is its prayer.
>   To dwell together in peace,
>   To seek knowledge in freedom,
>   To serve mankind in fellowship,
> To the end that all souls shall grow
>   into harmony with the Divine;
> Thus do we covenant with each other
>   and with God.
>
> —AUTHOR UNKNOWN

APPRECIATION OF THE CHURCH

BEFORE I was born, the Church gave to my parents ideals of life and love that made my home a place of strength and beauty. In helpless infancy the Church joined my parents in consecrating me to Christ and in baptizing me in his name.

The Church enriched my childhood with the romance and religion and the lessons of life that have been woven into the texture of my soul. Sometimes I seem to have forgotten and then, when else I might surrender to foolish and futile ideals of life, the truths the Church taught become radiant, insistent, and inescapable.

In the stress of adolescence the Church heard the surge of my soul and guided my footsteps by lifting my eyes toward the stars. When first my heart knew the strange awakenings of love, the Church taught me to chasten and spiritualize my affections; she sanctified and blessed my home.

When my heart was seamed with sorrow, and the way ahead was not clear, the Church drew me to the Friend of all the weary and whispered to me the hope of another morning, eternal and tearless.

When my steps have slipped and I have known the bitterness of sin, the Church has believed in me and wooingly she has called me back to live within the heights of myself.

My Church calls me to her heart. She asks my service and my loyalty. She has a right to ask it! I will help her to do for others what she has done for me. In this place in which I live, I will help her keep aflame and aloft the torch of a living faith.

Deep in my heart I know that the Church is of God. That in spite of human frailties, she has brought blessings untold to all generations including our own. That she has made my community and my country a better place in which to live, to work, and to establish a home. That I would not want to live in a land where no church spires point its people heavenward. I also know that the Church continues to live triumphantly even when men and nations reject her by indifference or open hostility. In this knowledge I gladly give myself to my Church and offer her my loyal support by intelligent membership, regular attendance, generous giving, ardent prayer, and devoted service.[2]

POEM:

> O where are kings and empires now,
> Of old that went and came?
> But, Lord, thy Church is praying yet,
> A thousand years the same.
>
> We mark her goodly battlements
> And her foundations strong;
> We hear within the solemn voice
> Of her unending song.
>
> For not like kingdoms of the world
> Thy holy Church, O God!
> Though earthquake shocks are threatening her,
> And tempests are abroad;
>
> Unshaken as eternal hills,
> Immovable she stands,
> A mountain that shall fill the earth,
> A house not made with hands.
>
> —A. CLEVELAND COXE

PRAYER:

O God, we pray for thy Church, which is set today amid the perplexities of a changing order, and face to face with a great new task.

We remember with love the nurture she gave to our spiritual life in its infancy, the tasks she set for our growing strength, the influence of the devoted hearts she gathers, the steadfast power for good she has exerted. When we compare her with all other human institutions, we rejoice, for there is none like her. But when we judge her by the mind of her Master, we bow in pity and contrition. Oh baptize her afresh in the life-giving spirit of Jesus! . . . Put upon her lips the ancient gospel of her Lord. . . . Fill her with the prophets' scorn of tyranny, and with a Christlike tenderness for the heavy-laden and down-trodden. . . . Bid her cease from seeking her own life, lest she lose it. Make her valiant to give up her life to humanity, that like her crucified Lord she may mount by the path of the cross to a higher glory.[3] AMEN.

HYMN: "O Spirit of the Living God," or
      "The Church's One Foundation."

BENEDICTION:

And now the God of peace keep your hearts and minds in the knowledge and love of God. AMEN.

SERVICE 17

I BELIEVE IN THE KINGDOM OF GOD

PRELUDE: Hymn tune, "Duke Street."

CALL TO WORSHIP:

>Come, let us tune our loftiest song
>   And raise to Christ our joyful strain;
>Worship and thanks to him belong,
>   Who reigns, and shall forever reign.
>   —ROBERT A. WEST

RESPONSIVE READING:

Leader: Surely the Lord is in this place.
This is none other but the house of God
And this is the gate to heaven.
Enter into his gates with thanksgiving, and into his courts
with praise.

Group: (to be sung)

>I love thy kingdom, Lord,
>   The house of thine abode,
>The Church our blest Redeemer saved
>   With his own precious blood.

Leader: For a day in thy courts is better than a thousand. I had rather
be a doorkeeper in the house of my God, than to dwell in the
tents of wickedness.

Group:

>I love thy Church, O God!
>   Her walls before thee stand,
>Dear as the apple of thine eye,
>   And graven on thy hand.

Leader: How amiable are thy tabernacles, O Lord of hosts! My soul
longeth, yea, even fainteth for the courts of the Lord: my
heart and my flesh crieth out for the living God.

I BELIEVE IN THE KINGDOM OF GOD

Group: For her my tears shall fall,
            For her my prayers ascend,
          To her my cares and toils be given,
            Till toils and cares shall end.

Leader: Yea, the sparrow hath found an house, and the swallow a nest for herself, where she may lay her young, even thine altars, O Lord of hosts, my King, and my God.

Group: Beyond my highest joy
          I prize her heavenly ways,
         Her sweet communion, solemn vows,
           Her hymns of love and praise.

Leader: Blessed are they that dwell in thy house: they will be still praising thee.[1]

Group: Sure as thy truth shall last,
           To Zion shall be given
         The brightest glories earth can yield,
           And brighter bliss of heaven.

                            —TIMOTHY DWIGHT

PRAYER:

Almighty God, from whom all thoughts of truth and peace proceed; kindle, we pray thee, in the hearts of all men the true love of peace, and guide with thy pure and peaceable wisdom those who take counsel for the nations of the earth; that in tranquility thy kingdom may go forward till the earth is filled with the knowledge of thy love; through Jesus Christ our Lord. AMEN.[2]

HYMN: "O Zion, Haste, Thy Mission High Fulfilling."

TALK:

I BELIEVE IN THE KINGDOM OF GOD

I BELIEVE that the Kingdom of God is a reality which exists here and now.

Jesus asked us to pray for it as we pray for our daily bread. In his prayer he makes it synonymous with "Thy will be done," and in that phrase we see the basic condition of its citizenship. The Kingdom is composed of those who earnestly strive in all things to know the will of God and to do it. This must be a continuing and ever-expanding quest for the individual person—never ended, never perfectly or finally realized, but always inspiring, enlarging, growing, flowering out in new achievement and larger vision.

I believe that the Kingdom is a part of the future to be realized more perfectly and more concretely than in the present; that the search for the will of God will become central and of highest value in the desires of peoples and nations. I believe also that the Kingdom has evidenced its saving power in the past and that our heritage is rich and precious.

I believe that the Kingdom of God is established whenever and wherever a single soul earnestly resolves to discover the will of God and commits his whole mind and heart to that will as he perceives it. But I believe, also, that the Kingdom is a divine fellowship of those who are committed above all things to carrying out God's will among men. The saying of Luke, "the kingdom of God is within you," means "within your group, among you." Moffatt's translation reads, "the Reign of God is now in your midst."

The Old Testament itself is the finest evidence of the development a single people can make in its search to discover the will of God and to do it. One sees at once that the arduous search for that which was at first dimly perceived to be God called forth prophets, priests, statesmen, and finally a Teacher and Saviour whose work was to slough off the temporary, the expedient, and the accidental from the great tradition and to make of it, not a tribal Messiah, but a universal revelation of God's will for all men.

In our day, for the first time in history, essential techniques and processes have been perfected which make a modicum of health and security available for all men without conflict. Man's fighting has arisen not from a depraved nature that prefers violence and blood, but from hunger and a ceaseless desire for abundance in life. Thus, what we formerly called man's baser instincts and accepted as inevitable parts of his nature give way to processes and means of co-operative living.

We must not assume, on the other hand, that mere social and economic progress will abolish the evil in men's hearts. That will come only through the work of the spirit of God and through those men and women who, because they work in harmony with his will, find their power and faith multiplied through fellowship in the Kingdom of God. When all physical causes of insecurity are abolished, men's need of God will not be less but greater. No amount of international co-operation will answer the insistent cry: Whence came I, and whither am I bound? [3]

Amid the confusion and breakdown of the old order to what does the Christian look for a basis of a new order? He looks for nothing less than God's order, the Kingdom of God. The Kingdom of God was Jesus' answer to the world's ills. The Kingdom confronted the whole of the life of sinful man with God's redemptive offer and demand. It was offered both to the individual and the collective will: the nation as well as the individual was to embody this new order.

The Kingdom of God is within history and yet it is beyond history. On the other hand the Kingdom is an eternal Kingdom, but it is God's purpose that it should come within time and within the world. While the Kingdom is not of this world, yet it acts both as ferment and as dynamite in every social structure. [4]

POEM:

> We can never build God's Kingdom
> Till we learn to love man more,
> Till we trample the injustice
> That now tramples down the poor;
>
> Till employers and employees
> Stifle selfish greed and strife,
> And co-operate as brothers
> As they seek abundant life;
>
> Till we banish brutal passions
> That make armies, navies, wars;
> Till we conquer racial hatreds,
> And break down the color bars.
>
> We can never build God's Kingdom
> In a corner by itself;
> It must master earth and mankind,
> Social orders, power, and self. [5]
>
> —CHAUNCEY R. PIETY

SOLO: "I Believe, O Lord," by Saint-Saëns, or

HYMN: "Truehearted, Wholehearted, Faithful and Loyal," or "Lead On, O King Eternal."

God, who at sundry times and in divers manners spake in time past unto the fathers by the prophets, hath in these last days spoken unto us by his Son.

Unto the Son he saith, Thy throne, O God, is for ever and ever: a sceptre of righteousness is the sceptre of thy kingdom.

Thou hast loved righteousness, and hated iniquity; therefore God, even thy God, hath anointed thee with the oil of gladness above thy fellows.

Then said he, Unto what is the kingdom of God like? and whereunto shall I resemble it?

It is like a grain of mustard seed, which a man took, and cast into his garden; and it grew, and waxed a great tree; and the fowls of the air lodged in the branches of it.

And again he said, Whereunto shall I liken the kingdom of God?

It is like leaven, which a woman took and hid in three measures of meal, till the whole was leavened.

Again, the kingdom of heaven is like unto treasure hid in a field; the which when a man hath found, he hideth, and for joy thereof goeth and selleth all that he hath, and buyeth that field.

Again, the kingdom of heaven is like unto a merchant man, seeking goodly pearls:

Who, when he had found one pearl of great price, went and sold all that he had, and bought it.

Again, the kingdom of heaven is like unto a net, that was cast into the sea, and gathered of every kind:

Which, when it was full, they drew to shore, and sat down, and gathered the good into vessels, but cast the bad away.

And seek not ye what ye shall eat, or what ye shall drink, neither be ye of doubtful mind.

For all these things do the nations of the world seek after: and your Father knoweth that ye have need of these things.

But rather seek ye the kingdom of God; and all these things shall be added unto you.

For the kingdom of God is not meat and drink; but righteousness, and peace, and joy.

Let us therefore follow after the things which make for peace, and things wherewith one may edify another.[6]

I BELIEVE IN THE KINGDOM OF GOD

PRAYER:

Almighty God, we have erred and strayed from thy ways by following our own devices. We have left undone the things which we should have done, and we have done the things from which we should have refrained. Forgive us, for we come to thee confessing our sins.

Thou, in whose hands is the destiny of men and of nations, hear our prayer as we acknowledge our sins of omission and commission. May we not suffer in vain for our faults. Grant that our shortcomings may serve as guideposts to those who come after us to help them avoid our mistakes. We pray that the leaders of our nation whom we trust and follow may recognize their responsibility and not lead us into the wrong paths.

Grant us the wisdom to know whether the causes for which we stand are thy causes. We thank thee for those who are bearing hardships and difficulties for thy Kingdom. Give us the courage to join their ranks, patience and willingness to bear our burdens, and faith to believe in the coming of thy Kingdom on earth. In Jesus' name, we pray. AMEN.

HYMN: "Lift Up Our Hearts," or
        "God of Grace and God of Glory."

SERVICE 18

I BELIEVE IN JESUS

PRELUDE: Hymn tune, "Crusader's Hymn."

CALL TO WORSHIP:

Leader:

Jesus, we look to thee,
  Thy promised presence claim;
Thou in the midst of us shalt be,
  Assembled in thy name.

Present we know thou·art;
  But, O, thyself reveal!
Now, Lord, let every waiting heart
  The mighty comfort feel.
                                    —CHARLES WESLEY

Group:

Let all mortal flesh keep silence,
  And with fear and trembling stand;
Ponder nothing earthly minded,
  For with blessing in his hand,
Christ our God to earth descendeth,
  Our full homage to demand.

HYMN: "Spirit of Life, in This New Dawn," or
      "We Would See Jesus," or
      "Fairest Lord Jesus."

SCRIPTURE:

And he came to Nazareth, where he had been brought up: and, as his custom was, he went into the synagogue on the sabbath day, and stood up for to read. And there was delivered unto him the book of the prophet Esaias. And when he had opened the book, he found the place where it was written.

I BELIEVE IN JESUS

The Spirit of the Lord is upon me, because he hath anointed me to preach the gospel to the poor; he hath sent me to heal the broken-hearted, to preach deliverance to the captives, and recovering of sight to the blind, to set at liberty them that are bruised, to preach the acceptable year of the Lord.

And he closed the book, and he gave it again to the minister, and sat down. And the eyes of all them that were in the synagogue were fastened on him. And he began to say unto them, This day is this scripture fulfilled in your ears. And all bare him witness, and wondered at the gracious words which proceeded out of his mouth. And they said, Is not this Joseph's son? [1]

AN AFFIRMATION OF FAITH:

We believe in the one God, Maker and Ruler of all things, Father of all men, the source of all goodness and beauty, all truth and love.

We believe in Jesus Christ, God manifest in the flesh, our teacher, example, and redeemer, the Saviour of the world.

We believe in the Holy Spirit, God present with us for guidance, for comfort, and for strength.

We believe in the forgiveness of sins, in the life of love and prayer, and in grace equal to every need.

We believe in the Word of God contained in the Old and New Testaments as the sufficient rule both of faith and of practice.

We believe in the Church as the fellowship for worship and for service for all who are united to the living Lord.

We believe in the Kingdom of God as the divine rule in human society, and in the brotherhood of man under the fatherhood of God.

We believe in the final triumph of righteousness, and in life everlasting. AMEN. [2]

POEM:

> "As the shadow of a rock," the Scriptures say,
> "Of a great rock within a weary land,"
> Will be our Christ in days of tribulation.

> O Saviour, pardon mankind in this day!
> He walks a world his own designs have planned.
> He thirsts in desert wastes of every nation.

Stretch forth Thy sheltering shadow's cooling length,
And let men find Thy pity and Thy strength! [8]
                                        —ESTHER BALDWIN YORK

HYMN: "O Master Workman of the Race," or
      "By Roads That Wound Uphill and Down," or
      "Sun of My Soul, Thou Saviour Dear."

TALKS:

I BELIEVE IN JESUS

WHEN we talk about believing in Jesus, we usually think of something removed from us by nineteen centuries of time and thousands of miles of space. Belief in Jesus is identified with belief in his miraculous birth or his miraculous powers, his existence as a heavenly being before he came to earth, or the fact that he was made of divine "substance," not human.

There are right and wrong answers to all such problems, and some of them are important, but they are all far removed from the life which I must live today. I am looking for something in which I can believe because it tells me the truth about life, some key which will unlock at least part of life's mysteries and help me to understand its meaning and to find its values. I want something in which I can believe as confidently as the scientist believes in truth, as enthusiastically as the artist believes in beauty, as unreservedly as a mother believes in her love for her child. I want something so compelling that once I have seen it I cannot help believing in it.

In that sense, everyone has his creed. The multitudes who think that the possession of money will make life worth-while, those who live to gratify impulse and find pleasure, even the cynic who, like the Preacher of Ecclesiastes, thinks that it is all a striving after wind and that nothing is worth serious effort, all have found what they think to be the truth about life, and they follow the paths which they believe will yield the largest satisfactions. And when I look about me and try to understand the things which men really believe, I find that increasingly I believe in Jesus, because he seems to be the way.

WHY I BELIEVE IN JESUS

IN the first place, I believe in Jesus, because he makes it easier for me to believe in myself, for nowhere else do I find such high value attributed to human life as in his estimate of it. It is a bit of irony that a worm-of-the-dust theology should ever have crept into a religion which had its origin in Jesus, for to him all men were potentially divine, and the worth which he found in even the most unlovely human specimens was something of a scandal in his day.

We must never forget that Jesus dealt largely with the rubbish heap of humanity, the people on the wrong side of the railroad tracks. It is easy to generalize about the outcasts of other days, but it is not so easy to equate them with the outcasts of our own society. But to him they were divine, and in an amazing number of cases his faith was justified. People who had slunk in dark alleys suddenly discovered themselves. Those who had hid from contempt or the patronage of the complacent found a new dignity in themselves. Publicans welcomed him into homes where the socially respectable had never entered. The common people heard him gladly, and those who were weary and heavy laden found burdens slipping from their backs in his presence. The penitent tears of a common prostitute bathed his feet. The political grafter was reborn an honest man. Woman, whose social status was a kind of preferred slavery, came into her own, and the children who had been repressed took precedence over their self-important elders. It was for the most part a motley crew that Jesus dealt with, the wreckage of the social system, but as many as received him, to them gave he power to become sons of God. The coming of Jesus was the Magna Charta of the common man.

HIS LIFE

But it is not only the value which Jesus found in the most drab and discouraging human specimens which gives us a sense of worth; it is even more what he is able to make of his own life, for he has made more out of this experiment of living on this earth than anyone else who has tried it. This is not the place to describe the winsomeness of the personality of Jesus, even if it could be described. Too often we have allowed theological interpretations to blur our vision of the matchless beauty of that life, but the important thing is not the theological explanation of it, but merely that it was actually lived. Century after century looks on him in wonder, and finds no other to put beside him. A few years ago a writer, standing in imagination by the roadside as he dragged the cross up toward Calvary, listening to the ribald jests of the crowd and seeing the marks of exquisite suffering in his face, said that he could not feel sorry for him, because he could not escape the suspicion that this Jesus had found the thing the absence of which made the lives of the rest of us restless and unsatisfied.

Jesus made that out of this business of living here on this earth, and when I look on him I feel a new dignity in myself. I shall never be like him, but I, too, am part of the human race which he has transfigured.[4]

POEM:

Light of the world, thy beauty
   Steals into every heart,
And glorifies with duty
   Life's poorest, humblest part;
Thou robest in thy splendor
   The simplest ways of men,
And helpest them to render
   Light back to thee again.

Light of the world, illumine
   This darkened earth of thine,
Till everything that's human
   Be filled with the divine;
Till every tongue and nation,
   From sin's dominion free,
Rise in the new creation
   Which springs from love and thee.

           —JOHN S. B. MONSELL

SOLO: "The Lord Is My Light," by Allitsen, or

HYMN: "I Bind My Heart This Tide," or
"O Young and Fearless Prophet," or
"Dear Master, in Whose Life I See."

HIS SENSE OF VALUES

I BELIEVE in life interpreted in terms of the values which Jesus has shown us as I cannot believe in any other kind of life, and wherever I find reflections of his spirit in other lives, I recognize them as supremely good. Even if I should wish to, I could not help believing in Jesus.

I BELIEVE IN JESUS

Not only do I believe in Jesus because human life takes on new dignity because of him, but I also believe in him because I believe that he offers the one hope of salvation from the social chaos in which we find ourselves. Of course I am aware that Jesus never heard of many of our social problems, for they had not risen above the horizon in his day. And what is more important, Jesus does not undertake to create social patterns for us to follow. The repeated attempts to find in Jesus a blueprint by which we can erect our social structure have always ended in failure. Jesus does not tell us what kind of international organization would end war, nor what wages should be paid cotton pickers or coal miners, nor what interest on money (if any) should be allowed. He did not mention tariffs, nor labor unions, nor social security, nor the control of the liquor business. Christians are always wanting to make Jesus a revised Moses, and always failing.

Yet Jesus is more relevant to our modern scene than any other character who has lived. For our social patterns have bogged down all along the line, and when we stop to examine them in the light of Jesus, we find that they are failing just where they are in defiance of his insights. We are speaking now of social patterns and not of personal morals. And by social patterns we mean those ways in which society is undertaking to live together and get its work done. Our industrial system, for instance, is one such pattern. Though it may sound strange to our pagan ears, the function of business is not to make money, but to supply human needs. The reason for shoe factories is that people might have shoes, not that men might make fortunes. While the motivation is somewhat different in the professions, we have turned over the supplying of our material needs largely to self-interest and the desire for material gain as a motive.

Jesus does not mention industry, but the merest child can see that we have made practically no effort to bring our industrial life into harmony with his teachings. With him, the normal relation between men is that between brothers. Wealth is desperately dangerous because of what it does to character and to personal relations; and the purpose of effort is to serve society and not to make profit out of it. To be successful does not mean to have money. Such ideas are not intelligible in the average directors' meeting, but certainly we are not happy about the pass to which directors' meetings have brought us. So far as I am concerned, I do not believe there is any ultimate salvation for our industrial system unless we can incorporate at its heart Jesus' insights.

HE IS THE WAY

OUR war system is another of our social patterns. We were born into a world divided artificially into national units. These nations must get along with each other in some way, and we are familiar with the way that has been tried. National greed, jealousy, dishonesty, and jingoism lead periodically into wars, and each war is worse than the last. We are wondering whether they can survive and what can take the place of narrow race and national pride. What of the future? Do we still believe that there is a way out through revenge and brute force? When I look for something in which I can believe as the political world falls to pieces around me, I turn again to Jesus, not because it is a religious duty, but because I can see nothing else in which to believe. We will never have the world we want until we found it on his teaching of human brotherhood and the sacredness of those lives which our present system outrages and slaughters.

It is so with our other social patterns. It is doubtful whether there is a major relationship in our so-called Christian society which has made any serious attempt to take the insights of Jesus as determinative. Even the home and the church are only partial exceptions. And there is scarcely a social relationship, including both the home and the church, which is not staggering under its inability to solve its own problems. Today pessimism is easy. War is the most dramatic of our failures, but only temporarily does it divert attention from other points of tension in our confused world. And the extent of our confusion is largely the measure of our variance from Jesus.

Finally, I believe in Jesus because he makes it easier for me to believe in God. Certainly it is not easy to believe in God in a world like this one. The still small voice does not shout above bombardments. The God who feeds the birds and clothes the lilies but will not help the millions of the dispossessed to feed and clothe their helpless children seems too idealistic to be of service. Jesus' dream of a reign of God makes little headway against the reign of force and cruelty. Yet Jesus dreamed his dream. In a world more depressed than anything we have known, crushed economically and politically, with religion thinking that only a miracle can save it, he was sure of God's triumph in the future. Surrounded by the noisy, dirty, superficial mob of the Near East, his own faith never faltered. And he could dream of a perfect world because he could get away into a mountain apart and link his soul with the great God of love and goodness, the God who had seen kingdoms come and kingdoms go, but who patiently through the ages worked out his eternal purposes. Jesus endured as seeing him who is invisible.

And when I see the mastery over self and over the world and over all the works of evil which Jesus found in companionship with God, I believe in him because he has what I so desperately need.

If Jesus is not the truth about life, then I know of nothing else.[5]

HYMN: "How Beauteous Were the Marks Divine," or
      "O Son of Man, Our Hero," or
      "No Distant Lord Have I."

PRAYER:

O Master of our lives, thou who didst come into the world to reveal the Father, grant unto us a new revelation of thyself; thou who camest to do not thy will but the will of thy Father, open up our lives to the inspiration of thy life; thou who art the Son of God, help us to be worthy to be children of our Father. In times of temptation, help us to make wise choices; in times of weakness, give us strength to do right; in times of danger, help us to be courageous. Fill us with a devout love for thee, keep us steadfast in that love, increase our faith, strengthen our hope, and make us bold to attempt great things for thee. Teach us to serve thee faithfully and not to ask for any reward, except that of knowing that we do thy will. AMEN.

BENEDICTION:

Now unto him that is able to keep you from falling, and to present you faultless before the presence of his glory with exceeding joy, to the only wise God our Saviour, be glory and majesty, dominion and power, both now and evermore. AMEN.

SERVICE 19

I BELIEVE IN GOD

PRELUDE: Hymn tune, *"Nun Danket."*

CALL TO WORSHIP:

> Gather us in: we worship only thee;
> In varied names we stretch a common hand;
> In diverse forms a common soul we see;
> In many ships we seek one spirit-land;
> Gather us in!

HYMN: "Still, Still with Thee."

INVOCATION:

Almighty God, who hast brought us through the darkness of the night to the light of the morning, grant us a sense of thy presence. We worship thee in true humility and in reverence; we are grateful for all the good gifts which come from thee. Grant us a fuller knowledge of thee, wisdom to know thy will, courage to follow it, and strength to live according to thy purpose for us. Lead us into a closer fellowship with thee. AMEN.

AFFIRMATION OF FAITH: (in unison)

We believe that God is Spirit, and they that worship him must worship him in spirit and in truth.

We believe that God is Light, and that if we walk in the light, as he is in the light, we have fellowship one with another.

We believe that God is Love, and that everyone that loveth is born of God and knoweth God.

We believe that Jesus Christ is the Son of God, and that God hath given to us eternal life, and this life is in his Son.

We believe that he is the Resurrection and the Life, and that whosoever believeth on him, though he were dead, yet shall he live.

I BELIEVE IN GOD

We believe that we are children of God, and that he hath given us of his Spirit.

We believe that if we confess our sins, he is faithful and just to forgive us our sins, and to cleanse us from all uncleanness.

We believe that the world passeth away and the lust thereof, but he that doeth the will of God abideth forever. AMEN.[1]

SOLO: "Whither Shall I Go from Thy Spirit?" by MacDermed, or

HYMN: "Holy, Holy, Holy," or
"Lord of All Being, Throned Afar."

POEM:

Love of God, give to me
Thyself in living essence
That all my activity
May radiate thy presence.

Zeal of God, fill me now
With spirit warming, burning;
Make sure my daring may somehow
Match all my dreaming, yearning.

Wisdom of God, share with me
Thyself, my mind renewing;
And manifest thy cogency
In all my thinking, doing.

Life of God, live within
My life, thy grace bestowing;
Toward life's goal and origin
Keep me forever growing.[2]
—CHAUNCEY R. PIETY

TALKS:

WHAT GOD MEANS TO ME

GOD is for me a satisfying explanation of the strange universe within which I find myself. Why do I call the universe "strange"? Because it is so vast and at the same time so orderly. An airplane, flying day and night at a constant speed of 200 miles per hour, would need more than 52 years to make the journey from the earth to the sun. Yet that journey, long as it seems, is only one-fourteen billionth of the distance from the earth to the farthest star. Such is the size of our universe . . . and in that universe order is the prevalent thing. Every fresh advance of science discloses new elements of adjustment, arrangement, structure, apparent purpose.

How can I explain such a universe? The only explanation which satisfies me is the one offered by modern Protestantism. It says, "This vast and orderly universe is not, cannot be, the product of blind chance. Rather it is the deliberate creation of an Unseen Mind-and-Power-and-Goodness to which we give the name 'God.' It was God's mind which conceived the plan of this strange universe, God's power which brought the universe into being, God's goodness which made its basic processes work toward order rather than disorder, beauty rather than ugliness, the victory of truth rather than the victory of falsehood, the triumph of right rather than the triumph of wrong." Thus for me God is a satisfying answer to the basic riddles of life.

The second thing God means to me is much more difficult to define. God is an Invisible Companion, indescribably near and real—an Unseen Presence permeating the realm of Nature and continually enfolding my life and the life of every human being.

Gazing at persons I find myself saying, "These human beings are not chance fragments of living matter. They are God's children. Through a carefully planned life-process he brought them into the world, and now he surrounds them with his purpose, his love, his interest, his eagerness to help. Many of them are sinful, and others are ignorant. Only a few really deserve God's friendship and aid. But to all of them God offers these things, asking only that in return they live steadily at their best."

Holding this view of life, I find God an Invisible Companion as I make my way through the years. Without my faith in him, without the sense of comradeship with him which my faith gives me, existence would be for me indescribably lonely. Glimpses of the vast and relatively empty space that surrounds our drifting earth would be nothing less than terrifying. But the sense of God's reality and nearness changes all this. The threatening loneliness and fear vanish, and the old words "Underneath thee are the everlasting arms" seems utterly true.

To me God is also a source of inward help at moments of tension

and need. In moments of supreme crisis there emerges a saving quietness, strength, wisdom, and courage. So day by day, God brings every
human being who lives at his best the inward resources he needs.

God does not give any of us immunity from disaster, or deliverance
from the strains and frustrations which the complex scheme-of-things
continually thrusts upon us. But God does give us power to face hardship, power finally to master it. To me, as to numberless other individuals, God is thus "a very present help in trouble."

The final thing God means to me—he is my ground and hope and
confidence as I face an admittedly uncertain future. Like every observant human being I realize that hostile forces are not only present
but continually active here in our world. Their ultimate origin I cannot entirely explain; their grim power over us is a factor with which I
know I must continually reckon. Eventually some of those forces may
wreck beyond repair the social structures which the human race has
slowly and laboriously built. But believing in God I face that admittedly uncertain future with hope and confidence rather than with
fear and despair. I am convinced that God has so planned and shaped
the scheme-of-things that the forces making for life are stronger than
those making for death, that the forces making for order are more
powerful than those making for disorder, that the forces making for
right are more resourceful than those making for wrong, that human
society will grow better rather than worse as the slow centuries pass.
Without my faith in God the future would be for me even more dis-
turbing than the present; with my faith in God the numberless to-
morrows seem not only secure but also bright with promise.[3]

POEM:

> As the marsh-hen secretly builds on the watery sod,
> Behold I will build me a nest on the greatness of God:
> I will fly in the greatness of God as the marsh-hen flies
> In the freedom that fills all space 'twixt the marsh and the skies:
> By so many roots as the marsh-grass sends in the sod
> I will heartily lay me a-hold on the greatness of God:
> Oh, like to the greatness of God is the greatness within
> The range of the marshes, the liberal marshes of Glynn.[4]
>
> —SIDNEY LANIER

HYMN: "The Spacious Firmament on High," or
    "O God, Our Help in Ages Past."

I BELIEVE IN GOD

I BELIEVE in God. Most people believe in some kind of God. Even those who prefer not to use the word "God" believe in some Power which sustains the universe. Something seems to be at work here.

The Christian religion accepts the person of Jesus as the interpretation of what this Sustaining Power is like. God is not blind, unconscious force such as we see in the physical world, nor is he whimsical and arbitrary as the ancients thought him, nor is he self-centered and autocratic like the Oriental monarch. God is active at all times and in all places, but he has "broken into history" supremely in the historic Jesus.

But none of this gives me religion. To believe that there is a God in the universe and that he has revealed himself in past history does not satisfy the religious hunger of my soul. Religion for me must be *my* commerce with God. The God who is active in his universe must be active in me also. The God who was present in the life of Jesus long ago must also be present for me. Otherwise my religion degenerates into mere opinions about history. Religion means that I may find God, giving direction, discipline, strength and joy to my living today.

We Christians know but one God, the God who revealed himself supremely in Jesus. But this God is Spirit. And when I realize that this Spirit-God can press upon my little life, that "Spirit with spirit may meet," then I know God as Holy Spirit, Center and Source of the whole kingdom of spirits and the eternally present Father of his spiritual children.

In the New Testament this Spirit of God is identified with the risen, spiritual Christ, and so becomes personal and takes the nature of God himself. For Paul "the Lord is the Spirit," and in John's gospel "God is Spirit." God himself, the Holy Spirit, is seeking to reproduce in us that fulness of life which was in Christ Jesus. It is this belief in God as ever-active Holy Spirit which keeps religion alive.

I want a religion which can function in my life today, which can give me a religious interpretation of patriotism, and can bring God into my business life, and can make me know God's will for the colored races. I want God to suggest to me what wages I should pay, and how I should use my leisure time, and what my besetting sins are. And I want a God who can actively help me in overcoming them.

The author of John's gospel, writing some two generations after the death of Jesus, out in the Gentile world with problems in many ways very different from those of Jesus in Galilee, has Jesus anticipate this need to keep religion constantly contemporaneous. Jesus could not tell his little band of Galilean followers what Christianity should do in Ephesus, nor how it should face the fall of Rome centuries later, nor how it should be adjusted to science in the nineteenth century. He had to leave them without even attempting to tell them all that would be involved in Christian living. "I have yet many things to say unto you, but ye cannot bear them now."

Christians are not leaderless, groping their way through a constantly changing world. Their glory is that God, the Holy Spirit, still leads them on. "Howbeit when he, the Spirit of truth, is come, he shall guide you into all the truth." Christianity does not consist in merely reproducing ancient patterns of conduct and of thought. It finds new ways of acting and of thinking in each new situation. But its changing patterns are not haphazard. They are in conformity with its fundamental genius, because they are directed by the God who is Spirit guiding them into all the truth.

A Christlike God at work in the world today, that is the hope of our world. But it is not easy. When I look honestly into the impulses of my own heart, or when I look out on the chaos into which we have brought our world, it is not always easy to see the evidences that a Christlike Spirit is at work. Is it possible that the work of creation as described in Genesis is never ended, and that always the Spirit of God is brooding over the face of a chaos, trying to create God's order out of it? [5]

HOW MAY I FIND GOD?

THE POET finds God in the flower, the astronomer finds him in the stars, the botanist in the plants, and the biologist in various forms of life. Some persons find him when they see his Spirit reflected in the lives of other persons. Others find him when facing a moral crisis; in their effort to overcome evil there comes to them the feeling that he is backing them up and helping them to reach right conclusions. Others find him by co-operating with him in a moral venture, by joining with him in the creative process of helping to build a better world, by giving themselves wholeheartedly to serve in a worthy cause.

We believe that the universe is built along moral lines. God's laws are written into our physical nature as well as into the universe. We feel responsible to God for our actions, and when we violate his laws we suffer the consequences. There is a Power lifting our spirits in the direction of goodness as surely as the power of the sun draws the water from the sea to the skies. We experience God in a definite sense and he becomes real to us when we experience the higher levels of living—when love, brotherhood, and good will are put into effect in our lives. Then God is the source of each day's meaning, the central reality of life.

POEM:

A fire-mist and a planet,
  A crystal and a cell,
A jelly-fish and a saurian,
  And caves where the cave-men dwell;
Then a sense of law and beauty
  And a face turned from the clod,—
Some call it Evolution,
  And others call it God.

A haze on the far horizon,
  The infinite, tender sky,
The ripe, rich tint of the cornfields,
  And the wild geese sailing high;
And all over upland and lowland
  The charm of the golden-rod,—
Some of us call it Autumn,
  And others call it God.

Like tides on a crescent sea-beach,
  When the moon is new and thin,
Into our hearts high yearnings
  Come welling and surging in;
Come from the mystic ocean
  Whose rim no foot has trod,—
Some of us call it Longing,
  And others call it God.

A picket frozen on duty,
  A mother starved for her brood,
Socrates drinking the hemlock,
  And Jesus on the rood;

I BELIEVE IN GOD

And millions who, humble and nameless,
   The straight, hard pathway plod,—
Some call it Consecration,
   And others call it God.[6]

          —WILLIAM HERBERT CARRUTH

SCRIPTURE:

> O God, thou art my God; early will I seek thee: my soul thirsteth for thee, my flesh longeth for thee in a dry and thirsty land, where no water is;
>
> To see thy power and thy glory, so as I have seen thee in the sanctuary.
>
> Because thy lovingkindness is better than life, my lips shall praise thee.
>
> Thus will I bless thee while I live: I will lift up my hands in thy name.
>
> . . . .
>
> Because thou hast been my help, therefore in the shadow of thy wings will I rejoice.
>
> My soul followeth hard after thee: thy right hand upholdeth me.
>
> O give thanks unto the Lord, for he is good: for his mercy endureth for ever.[7]

HYMN: "Now on Land and Sea Descending," or
      "There's a Wideness in God's Mercy."

BENEDICTION:

Now unto him who is eternal, immortal, invisible, the only just and all-wise God, be glory and honor, dominion and power, now and forever. AMEN.

SERIES FOUR

FRIENDSHIP WITH ALL RACES

Suggestions to the Counselor

THE PURPOSE of this series is to help young people appreciate the world-wide mission of the Christian Church. It would be helpful for the local group to build worship services based upon the lives of the leaders of their own denomination who have pioneered in carrying the Christian message to other countries. A great heritage is ours because Christians of the past have endured persecution, trials, and imprisonment rather than relinquish the teachings of Christianity which they have cherished.

The following books would be helpful for background reading: Elmer Clark, *The Chiangs of China;* Philip Lotz, *The Founders of Christian Movements;* Frank C. Laubach, *The Silent Billion Speak;* W. W. Pinson, *Walter R. Lambuth;* John Foxe, *Book of Martyrs;* E. H. Griggs, *Moral Leaders;* H. P. Van Dusen, *The Church Was Already There;* Thomas, *Living Biography of Religious Leaders;* Basil Matthews, *Missionary Heroes.*

The following pictures are suitable to be used with this series, but others may be substituted: Copping, "The Sower" and "The Healer"; Zimmermann, "Christ and the Fishermen"; and Soord, "The Lost Sheep."

A discussion in connection with these services will help the group to realize the importance of sharing the Christian message with other races. The following questions are merely suggestive: In what countries is your denomination carrying on missionary work? Mention the various types that are being carried on in these places. Are the young people responsible for any part of the work? What evidence is there that the spirit of God is at work in these countries? Would you want to live in a non-Christian country? Do you feel responsible for sharing with other races the values which you have found in Christianity?

When using the service "Overcoming Handicaps," it would add to the interest to have some of Marian Anderson's records played on a portable victrola. The following are suggested: "Ave Maria (Victor 14210), and "Were You There When They Crucified My Lord?" (Victor 1966 B).

SERVICE 20

THE HAND OF GOD IN THE AFFAIRS OF MEN

PRELUDE: "Agnus Dei" (O Lamb of God), by Bizet.

CALL TO WORSHIP:

Seek ye the Lord while he may be found, call ye upon him while he is near:

Let the wicked forsake his way, and the unrighteous man his thoughts: and let him return unto the Lord, and he will have mercy upon him; and to our God, for he will abundantly pardon.[1]

HYMN: "Holy Spirit, Faithful Guide," or
"Send Down Thy Truth, O God."

SCRIPTURE:

Know ye not that ye are the temple of God, and that the Spirit of God dwelleth in you.

There is therefore now no condemnation to them which are in Christ Jesus, who walk not after the flesh, but after the Spirit. For the law of the Spirit of life in Christ Jesus hath made me free from the law of sin and death. For what the law could not do, in that it was weak through the flesh, God sending his own Son in the likeness of sinful flesh, and for sin, condemned sin in the flesh: that the righteousness of the law might be fulfilled in us, who walk not after the flesh, but after the Spirit. For they that are after the flesh do mind the things of the flesh; but they that are after the Spirit the things of the Spirit.

For to be carnally minded is death; but to be spiritually minded is life and peace. Because the carnal mind is enmity against God: for it is not subject to the law of God, neither indeed can be. So then they that are in the flesh cannot please God. But ye are not in the flesh, but in the Spirit, if so be that the Spirit of God dwell in you. Now if any man have not the Spirit of Christ, he is none of his. And if Christ be in you, the body is dead because of sin; but the Spirit is life because of righteousness. But if the Spirit of him that raised up Jesus from the dead dwell in you, he that raised up Christ from the dead shall also quicken your mortal bodies by his Spirit that dwelleth in you. Therefore, brethren, we are debtors, not to the flesh, to live after the flesh. For if ye live after the flesh, ye shall die: but if ye through the Spirit do mortify the deeds of the body, ye shall live. For as many as are led by the Spirit of God, they are the sons of God. The Spirit itself beareth witness with our spirit, that we are the children of God.[2]

LEADER:

"As some of us look back on our own lives the feeling is borne in upon us that there were times when God had a hand in our affairs. We may not be able to prove the fact to other people, and we may not care to try because of the intimate nature of the situations involved. But for ourselves we cannot escape the feeling that we were deliberately encouraged here and thwarted there, that we were prepared in advance for burdens and responsibilities later to fall upon us, that some of the best things which happened to us happened not merely without our own effort but actually in spite of it."[3]

We shall hear the story of a man who was willing to be led by the Spirit of God and whose influence has touched the lives of many people and helped to bring in the Kingdom of God.

STORY:

CHARLIE SOONG'S DESTINY

AT an early age a lad was left an orphan in the village of Kuisan on Hainan, an island off the coast of China. He was adopted by an uncle who was engaged in a silk and tea importing business and brought to Boston. Because of a dislike for his uncle's business, the boy determined to seek his fortune elsewhere. After talking with Chinese students, he decided that he wanted an education in American schools. His uncle, having no children of his own, wanted to pass on his silk and tea business to his nephew and was not interested in his going to school.

Being of a restless nature, the boy roamed along the Boston harbor, dreaming of the new learning which he intended to secure. His plans were indefinite; only one point was clear—he did not intend to become a merchant. Taking matters into his own hands, one day he boarded a second-class side-wheeler, the "Colfax," as a stowaway. Captain Charles Jones, the captain of the boat, was kind to the ambitious lad and immediately made him cabin boy.

During the autumn of 1880 Captain Jones came into port at Wilmington, North Carolina. He sought the pastor of the Fifth Street Methodist Church, T. P. Ricaud, and introduced the boy to him. It was the boy's first contact with Christians. He was converted to Christianity, and, when baptized, the Captain's name was added to his own family name, Soong. At last the orphan boy knew what he wanted to do—secure an education that he might return to China as a missionary to his own people.

When the "Colfax" left Wilmington, Charlie Soong remained behind. In a short while his friendly manner won for him a place in the hearts of the hospitable people. Temporary employment was secured for him in a printing shop, and at night he studied with Dr. Ricaud as tutor. At the meeting of the North Carolina Conference, Dr. Ricaud spoke to the ministers of the boy's desire for an education. General Carr, a layman of Durham, North Carolina, agreed to finance Charlie's education. Impressed by his fine qualities, General Carr took Charlie into his home and adopted him.

Charlie attended Trinity College, Durham (now Duke University), and later was graduated from Vanderbilt University, Nashville, Tennessee. At first the students at Vanderbilt paid little attention to him. He was small of stature, about five feet in height, quiet and reserved in manner, and was no more than a curiosity to them. Dr. John C. Orr, a fellow student, recounts that on a certain Sunday morning in the chapel of Wesley Hall, Charlie voiced his loneliness, saying, "I feel so little, so lonesome, so far from my people, so alone among strangers. I feel just like a little chip floating down the Mississippi River, but I know that Jesus is my Friend and my Comforter." He did not need to say more. The students crowded around him, expressing their interest and concern for him. After this he was included in their activities.

Charlie wrote to a relative in China, "I am in a great hurry to be educated so I can go back to China and tell you about the kindness of the friends in Durham. General and Mrs. Carr are good Christians and have been kind to me. Keep your ears open so you can hear what the Spirit says, and let your eyes look up so you can see the glory of God." He had a strong desire to study medicine as a further preparation to minister to his people. While General Carr was willing to finance his further study, there were others who advised him to return to China before he became too completely Americanized. Consequently, upon graduation from the School of Theology, he accepted work in the Methodist China Mission.

At last Charlie Soong was free to do the work for which he had been training, but there were obstacles to be overcome. Having been away from China for many years, he was almost like a foreigner to the Chinese. He was compelled to learn another dialect in order to work with the people in the province to which he was assigned. The authority exercised over him by the Superintendent of the Mission irked him. Writing to a friend in Durham, he said, "I am very much displeased with this sort of authority, but I must bear it patiently. If I were to take rash action, the people at home, especially my Durham friends, might think me an unloyal Methodist and a lawbreaker, so I have kept silent."

Later, however, Soong withdrew from the Mission, established a private printing business and for a number of years printed Bibles for the Chinese. His former experience as a printer helped him to render a great service to his countrymen. He was also manager of a large flour mill, the same business in which General Carr was engaged. His business prospered, and after a time he became a man of considerable wealth. Remaining loyal at all times, he used his means and influence to carry forward the work of Christian missions in China.

Soong was happily married to Miss Ni, a graduate of one of the Mission schools. Being a devout Christian, his wife was noted for her piety and good works. To this couple were born six children, three boys and three girls, all of whom were educated in America. The entire family, including sons-in-law and daughters-in-law became Christians. The daughters were given names which reflect Charlie Soong's happy temperament. Their names sound like the echo of distant temple bells: Chingling, Eling and Mayling. Translated into English, "ling" means "mood," hence the literal translation of their names are "Happy Mood," "Pleasing Mood," and "Beautiful Mood."

Each of the daughters married leaders who had prominent places in shaping the New China. Chingling is the widow of the late Dr. Sun-Yat-Sen, the Father of the Republic; Eling is the wife of Dr. J. H. Kung, a lineal descendant of Confucius; Mayling, the first lady of the land, is the wife of the Generalissimo, Chiang Kai-shek. The sons have also held important positions of national leadership. A large part of the leadership of the New Republic came through the Soong family, and because of their wide influence, the Christian religion is a potent force in the life of the nation today.

In 1916 General Carr visited China and was entertained in the home of Charlie Soong. The tables were turned; old friends were meeting under different circumstances. Soong was the host to his American benefactor in surroundings that rivaled the richness of the Carr home in Durham. The leaders who were shaping the destiny of China showed General Carr every courtesy. To them he was a symbol of America's goodwill toward China because of his kindness to Soong in the past. In appreciation for his former service, the Chinese government presented him with three exquisite porcelain vases.

When General Carr invested a few hundred dollars in the education of a youth, he set in motion a force that a generation later turned the leaders of China toward the Christian religion. In dedicating his resources to the Christian cause, he did not realize that the destinies of so many people were bound up in the lad, and one cannot estimate at the present time all that it may mean in promoting the Christian movement in Asia. General Carr was a great benefactor, but nothing he ever did was as far-reaching as the kindness shown to Charlie Soong. He invested in friendliness to a stranded boy a generation ago, and the returns today are friendly relations between two great republics.[4]

Poem:

> O gracious Father of mankind,
>   Our spirits' unseen Friend,
> High heaven's Lord, our hearts' dear Guest,
>   To thee our prayers ascend.
> Thou dost not wait till human speech
>   Thy gifts divine implore;
> Our dreams, our aims, our work, our lives
>   Are prayers thou lovest more.
>
> Thou hearest these, the good and ill,
>   Deep buried in each breast;
> The secret thought, the hidden plan,
>   Wrought out or unexpressed.
> O cleanse our prayers from human dross,
>   Attune our lives to thee,

— 153 —

Until we labor for those gifts
    We ask on bended knee.

Our best is but thyself in us,
    Our highest thought thy will;
To hear thy voice we need but love,
    To listen, and be still.
We would not bend thy will to ours,
    But blend our wills to thine;
Not beat with cries on heaven's doors,
    But live thy life divine.

Thou seekest us in love and truth
    More than our minds seek thee;
Through open gates thy power flows in
    Like flood tides from the sea.
No more we seek thee from afar,
    Nor ask thee for a sign,
Content to pray in life and love
    And toil, till all are thine.[5]

                —HENRY H. TWEEDY

PRAYER:

    Dear Father, Almighty God, Maker of all things, Judge of all men, hear us as we pray. Thou who didst set the stars in the sky and yet didst concern thyself with the life of an orphan lad, causing him to sit in high places and to do thy great works, be thou our guide. Thou whose wisdom is above all wisdom, whose sovereign hand is over all hands, direct our ways. Help us that we may, like thy servant Soong, keep our ears open to the leading of thy Spirit, that our wills may be directed by thee and our lives fashioned according to thy design. Overrule our mistakes; turn our errors into lessons, our failures into fortune, and our tragedies into triumphs. Grant that in our difficulties we may remember the example of thy Son, our Lord, who trusting in thee was obedient unto death, exchanging a cross for a crown. In the light of his devotion we blush with shame, for we have often been hesitant, vacillating, and fearful. Make us confident of thy guiding care and bold to do thy will. In the name of him whose will it was to do thy will, we pray. AMEN.[6]

THE HAND OF GOD IN THE AFFAIRS OF MEN

HYMN: "Spirit of God, Descend upon My Heart," or
"Breathe on Me, Breath of God," or
"Thou My Everlasting Portion."

BENEDICTION:

May we go from this service to follow the leadership of thy spirit in every decision that we make. AMEN.

SERVICE 21

PROPHET OF SOCIAL JUSTICE

PRELUDE: Hymn tune, "Nicaea."

CALL TO WORSHIP:

> God of the strong, God of the weak,
>   Lord of all lands and our own land,
> Light of all souls: from thee we seek
>   Light from thy light, strength from thy hand.
>
> In suffering thou hast made us one,
>   In mighty burdens one are we:
> Teach us that lowliest duty done
>   Is highest service unto thee.
>
> —RICHARD W. GILDER

HYMN: "We Thank Thee, Lord, Thy Paths of Service Lead," or "O Master, Let Me Walk with Thee."

SCRIPTURE:

But in the last days it shall come to pass, that the mountain of the house of the Lord shall be established in the top of the mountains, and it shall be exalted above the hills; and the people shall flow unto it.

And many nations shall come, and say, Come, let us go up to the mountain of the Lord, and to the house of the God of Jacob; and he will teach us of his ways, and we will walk in his paths: for the law shall go forth of Zion, and the word of the Lord from Jerusalem.

And he shall judge among many people, and rebuke strong nations afar off; and they shall beat their swords into plowshares, and their spears into pruninghooks: nation shall not lift up a sword against nation, neither shall they learn war any more.

He hath shewed thee, O man, what is good; and what doth the Lord require of thee, but to do justly, and to love mercy, and to walk humbly with thy God?

Blessed is the nation whose God is the Lord;
And the people whom he hath chosen for his own inheritance.
The Lord looketh from heaven;
He beholdeth all the sons of men.
From the place of his habitation he looketh upon all the
inhabitants of the earth.
He fashioneth their hearts alike;
He considereth all their works.
Behold, the eye of the Lord is upon them that fear him,
Upon them that hope in his mercy.
Our soul waiteth for the Lord:
He is our help and our shield.
For our heart shall rejoice in him,
Because we have trusted in his holy name.[1]

POEM:

> Friendless and faint, with martyred steps and slow,
> Faint for the flesh, but for the spirit free,
> Stung by the mob that came to see the show,
> The Master toiled along to Calvary:
> We gibed him, as he went, with houndish glee,
> Till his dimned eyes for us did overflow;
> We cursed his vengeless hands thrice wretchedly,—
> And this was nineteen hundred years ago.
>
> But after nineteen hundred years the shame
> Still clings, and we have not made good the loss
> That outraged faith has entered in his name.
> Ah, when shall come love's courage to be strong!
> Tell me, O Lord—tell me, O Lord, how long
> Are we to keep Christ writhing on the Cross!
> —EDWIN ARLINGTON ROBINSON

HYMN: "O Brother Man, Fold to Thy Heart," or
"Where Cross the Crowded Ways of Life," or
"Jesus Calls Us."

STORY:

PROPHET OF SOCIAL JUSTICE

IT is difficult to imagine that anyone could live such an inconspic-
uous life as that of Walter Rauschenbusch and yet make such a

splendid contribution as he did. His story proves the statement that if one really has something to offer, the whole world will beat a trail to one's doorstep. There was nothing ostentatious in his manner, pretentious in his behavior, nor showy in his dress or demeanor. He was reserved and modest to the extent that one might call him shy. His first great contribution to the religious thinking of the world was presented in such a manner that he might have been offering an apology. He gave to the publishers his manuscript, "Christianity and the Social Crisis" and left for Europe for further study. Yet when he returned to find himself famous, no one was more surprised than he.

The background of Rauschenbusch's life was such that unassuming modesty is to be expected. He was the son of a minister who was professor in the Rochester Theological Seminary. There was an unbroken line of ministers for seven generations in his family. Upon completion of his theological training he became pastor of the Second German Church, New York City. His parish, composed of immigrant laboring people, was in a crowded tenement district. For the eleven years that he served this church his salary was small—about six hundred dollars a year. He practiced rigid economy and self-denial in order to live as his people lived. Sharing their life, he was able to understand their problems. In this way he received his information about the conditions of underprivileged people and realized the need for a radical change in the thinking of Christian people.

Ministering to his people took the young minister into many strange places—into saloons on Saturday night, hospitals on Sunday, and police courts on Monday. He answered all calls and helped in every way that he could. With a willing spirit, sympathetic understanding, and great love he upheld them in their sorrow, comforted them in their distress, and helped to find a way out of their difficulties. He preached the simple gospel of love of God and personal salvation for those who believed on Christ.

His ministry was effective, yet he felt that something was wrong. It was impossible to make permanent progress. He could not sweep back the tide of unemployment, poverty, disease, and immorality. At best he could only pick up the driftwood, save a few human derelicts here and there, while the great mass of people in his parish remained victims of a system for which they were not responsible.

Being a sincere shepherd of his flock, he felt that he must find a solution for the problem. He read again Jesus' sermon in the synagogue at Nazareth: "The Spirit of the Lord is upon me, because he hath anointed me to preach the gospel to the poor; he hath sent me to heal the brokenhearted, to preach deliverance to the captives, and recovering of sight to the blind, to set at liberty them that are bruised, to preach the acceptable year of the Lord." He followed the example of Jesus as he denounced the rich for their greed and the religious leaders for their pretentions. He saw his own community organized for crime and graft, the fathers trying to feed their families on sweatshop wages and drowning their failures in drink. He saw children ill housed, with meager food and scanty clothing, begin a losing battle for existence, and he realized that conditions must be changed before any permanent good could be accomplished.

In this way Rauschenbusch discovered the far-reaching application of the teachings of Jesus to the life of his day. He realized that it was impossible to make any permanent improvement in the life of his people as long as the environment was against them. He believed that the simple gospel which he had been preaching to save individual sinners must also be applied to the society in which the people lived. He found support for his belief and discovered implications that had been hidden to the students of the Bible for many centuries. Thus the social gospel was born in the mind of Walter Rauschenbusch.

Two characteristics combined to make Rauschenbusch the great prophet of social righteousness—his keen, incisive mind and his devotion to his convictions. His keen mind was supported by a loyal and devoted spirit. It may have been that his intense desire to help his people fired his imagination and sent him to search the Scriptures for a solution. Being a devoted pastor, he answered the calls of his people regardless of circumstances. On one occasion when he had been ill, a call came from one of his parishioners who was in distress. Though he had not recovered from his illness and in spite of extreme cold weather, he answered the call. Exposing himself in his weakened condition cost him his hearing.

After the publication of his first book Dr. Rauschenbusch was recognized as an outstanding leader. He was offered a position as teacher in the Rochester Seminary, which he accepted. During the twenty-one years which he taught he bore with patience the handicap of deafness. Several books were written by him which elaborated his beliefs. *Christianizing the Social Order* and *Dare We Be Christians?* are titles which show the purpose of mind and heart of this great thinker and writer.

Walter Rauschenbusch never thought of himself as a great leader, for his modesty remained a dominant characteristic. Yet the flame that burned in his heart set on fire thousands of ministers who proclaimed the social injustice of society today. There was an insistent demand from leading ministers throughout the nation that the teachings of Jesus be applied to the problems of social life. There was given a new and broader interpretation of the words of Jesus, "Not every one that saith unto me, Lord, Lord, shall enter into the kingdom of heaven," and, "Why call ye me Lord, Lord, and do not the things which I say?" Much remains yet to be done in improving the social order, but there are ministers and consecrated young people who are laboring at the task more intelligently because of the contribution of Walter Rauschenbusch, the prophet of social justice.

POEM:

> I listen to the agony of God—
> I who am fed,
> Who never went hungry for a day.
> I see the dead—
> The children starved for lack of bread—
> I see, and try to pray.
>
> I listen to the agony of God—
> I who am warm,
> Who never yet have lacked a sheltering home.
> In dull alarm
> The dispossessed of hut and farm
> Aimless and "transient" roam.
>
> I listen to the agony of God—
> I who am strong,
> With health, and love, and laughter in my soul.
> I see a throng
> Of stunted children reared in wrong,
> And wish to make them whole.
>
> I listen to the agony of God—
> But know full well
> That not until I share their bitter cry—
> Earth's pain and hell—

Can God within my spirit dwell
To bring his kingdom nigh.[2]

—Georgia Harkness

LITANY OF SUPPLICATION:

Leader: Our Father, grant that we who have an abundance of material things

Group: May be willing to endure the personal inconvenience of privation in order to share with others;

Leader: That we who have more clothes than we need

Group: May be willing to share with those who suffer for lack of clothes;

Leader: That we who have more food than we can eat

Group: May divide with those who die for want of food,

Leader: That we who are warm and protected from cold

Group: May be mindful of those without shelter;

Leader: That we who enjoy thy bounty,

Group: May not be deaf to the cries of the poor.

Leader: Give us eyes to see, minds to understand, and hearts to feel the suffering of all people,

Group: We pray thee, O Lord.

Leader: Give us courage and strength sufficient to make the necessary changes in order to get rid of social injustice,

Group: We pray thee, O Lord.

Leader: Lead us by thy spirit into new insight and deeper understanding of thy rule of righteousness on earth,

Group: We pray thee, O Lord. AMEN.

HYMN: "That Cause Can Neither Be Lost nor Stayed," or
"God Send Us Men," or
"Rise Up, O Men of God."

BENEDICTION:

May the blessing of God our Father abide with you always. AMEN.

SERVICE 22

BREAKING THE SILENCE OF THE CENTURIES

PRELUDE: Hymn tune, "Wesley."

CALL TO WORSHIP:

> The Lord hath done great things for us;
> Whereof we are glad.
> Be thankful unto him, and bless his name;
> For the Lord is good.

HYMN: "Eternal God, Whose Power Upholds," or
"Guide Me, O Thou Great Jehovah."

SCRIPTURE:

God that made the world and all things therein, seeing that he is Lord of heaven and earth, dwelleth not in temples made with hands; neither is worshipped with men's hands, as though he needed any thing, seeing he giveth to all life, and breath, and all things; and hath made of one blood all nations of men for to dwell on all the face of the earth, and hath determined the times before appointed, and the bounds of their habitation; that they should seek the Lord, if haply they might feel after him, and find him, though he be not far from every one of us: for in him we live, and move, and have our being; as certain also of your own poets have said, For we are also his offspring.[1]

PRAYER:

O God, thou who art the Light of the world, have compassion upon those who sit in darkness, enlighten the ignorant and superstitious, and give freedom to the enslaved. Break down the walls that separate, and bind the people of all nations together in bonds of love and brotherhood. Widen our sympathies and interest that we may share the struggle of those who are oppressed and bear our part in making the advantages of education possible for them. Hasten the coming of that perfect day when none shall hurt nor destroy in all thy holy mountain, for the earth shall be full of the knowledge of the Lord as the waters cover the sea. In the name of Christ, our Lord. AMEN.

LEADER:

The Bible is printed in over a thousand languages and dialects, but it is still a closed book to three-fifths of the people of the world because they are unable to read. Nine-tenths of the non-Christians cannot read, and in order to understand the gospel they must first learn to read it.

Most people who cannot read know the world only through their immediate surroundings, and because of ignorance and prejudice their minds are closed to progress. Ninety per cent of them are in debt, and since they do not know how much they owe, they pass on the same debt to their children. Unscrupulous leaders rob, oppress, and enslave these victims, giving them no voice in the government.

We shall hear the story of the man who has done more than anyone of his generation to teach the masses to read and to share with them a more abundant life.

STORY:

LAUBACH, MIRACLE MAN

SINCE 1930 Frank C. Laubach has been the outstanding leader in the Campaign for World Literacy. He has carried through a colossal task by giving to the people speaking two hundred languages and dialects, living on four continents, a method by which in a short while they can learn to read their native tongues. While visiting India, Africa, South America, the Near East, co-operating with educators, he has developed charts to fit the myriad tongues of the masses. He is called the Miracle Man because he has demonstrated that any person of average intelligence can learn to read his native dialect in a few hours.

At the age of seventeen Laubach became interested in going to the Philippines as a missionary. This field was selected because of his contact with friends who were teaching there. When his study was completed at Columbia University, he went to the Island of Mindanao, for it seemed to be the neediest field. He found the Moros on this island a fierce, warlike tribe who looked upon all white people as enemies. They were living in a state of feudalism, at the point where our ancestors in Europe were a thousand years ago.

After the United States took over the Philippines in 1898, the Moros continued their resistance, waging war against the American forces based at the head of Lake Lanao. Their hatred was shown by their burning the school buildings erected for them. The feeling became so tense that all of them carried weapons. Laubach was the first white person to go among them unarmed.

He asked for the privilege of studying their four holy books with their Moslem leaders. As he became familiar with their background, he was able to point out the similarity between their religion and his. Through this exchange of knowledge they became co-operative, and their hatred changed to a warm friendship. His patient work among these hostile tribesmen produced a new method of teaching the masses to read.

Since the Moros did not have a written language, Dr. Laubach's first task was to learn their dialect and reduce it to writing. With the help of an intelligent native he learned the meaning of the various words and wrote them out according to their sounds. Since Arabic was too difficult for the masses, he adopted a Roman alphabet that was phonetic—one letter to a sound and only one sound to a letter. It was necessary to teach only a limited number of sounds rather than thousands of words. Their dialect contained only sixteen sounds—twelve consonants and four vowels.

Old methods of teaching were too slow, so Laubach experimented with new ideas. After several months he discovered a method which greatly simplified the process. He selected two or three key words which would use up all of the twelve consonants and in which only the vowel *a* was used. Around these keys he built up easy lessons which he illustrated. For example, the basis of his first lesson was the word "Malabanga," the name of a near-by coastal town. He separated the word into syllables which he taught the student to pronounce. Using these syllables, he worked out other combinations which formed the following words: *ma la* ("big"), *la ma* ("yard"), *ma ma* ("man"), *a ma* ("father"), *a la* ("God"). When these were learned, he substituted other vowels and formed additional words, such as *li ma* ("hand"), *a mi* ("to eat"), *bi bi* ("duck").

In his charts Dr. Laubach placed the syllables beside the whole word. In other columns he listed the various syllable combinations and used pictures to illustrate the meaning of the words. As the students pronounced the words, Dr. Laubach pointed to the pictures which indicated the meaning of the words. Thus, in a few hours the student learned to read such sentences as *Mala a lama* (the yard is big), or *Mala a ala* (God is great). The pupil tied up the picture with the sound of the word and the printed word as he recited the simple lessons from the chart.

As the interest in reading spread, requests for teachers came from many quarters. A Chieftain begging for a teacher said, "Not one person in our province can read. Won't you send us a teacher?" Laubach replied, "We have no money to send you a teacher, but if you can spare the time, we can teach you, and you in turn can teach your people." In a short while the new reader went away with charts and sufficient knowledge to begin his teaching.

Taking his pupils one at a time, humbly sitting beside them, Laubach helped them to get rid of any feeling of inferiority they might have. Instead of frowns, rebukes, and impatience, there were always kindness and gentleness. At every opportunity he praised and encouraged the slightest show of intelligence. By making the learning process pleasant he encouraged the pupils to do their best.

The Moros were amazed that educated people would take the time to teach them. They remarked, "No educated person except money lenders ever talked to us before. We can't understand why you care. Do you also want money?" The teacher replied: "We learned this from Christ, who was always ready to help. We find that when we help others as he did, our hearts sing. When you finish this lesson, we want you to teach someone, and your heart will sing also." This method was used to fix the lesson in the mind of the pupil and to give him a feeling of importance and self-respect. Thus the principle "Each one teach one" helped to spread the new learning.

The Moros were delighted at being able to read. The demand for reading material was such that a staff of volunteer workers was enlisted to help meet the need. A printing press was installed and a biweekly paper was published which gave in simple language the news, health rules, practical suggestions for planting rice, and the stories of ancient Moro heroes which had been handed down orally for many generations. These scraps of writing were treasured and read over and over again. Once a year this reading material was bound for each family, and thus their private libraries were started.

Because of the high rate of illiteracy in India a call for help came from that country, which Dr. Laubach answered immediately. He held conferences in more than two hundred strategic places, trained leaders to work out charts in native dialects, and demonstrated the

use of them in teaching the masses to read. The caste system compli-
cated the work; for when a low caste was invited to come to school, he
usually replied: "Who am I that I should learn to read? Am I better
than my fathers? Why should I try to be better than my caste?"

The premier of Bombay said, "Unless the people of India can get
the same spirit of service that missionaries have, we can never become
a literate nation. Teaching is more than can be put into mere words;
it is a thing of the spirit. It is the art of applying to education the
mysterious power of love that held together the early Christians."

On one occasion Dr. Laubach showed a chart, which he had completed in the Marathi language, to Mahatma Gandhi. His reply was,
"I doubt whether India ought to become literate."

"You are the first person I've heard say that. What do you mean?"
Laubach inquired.

"The literature you publish in the West is not fit for India to read.
Think of what you sell at railway stations. Many of the greatest ben-
efactors of the human race have been illiterate—Mohammed, for example."

"You are right," Laubach replied, "but, on the other hand, millions of us admire you and have read your books with great profit.
If we had not been able to read and if you had not written these
books, we should never have heard of you. The greatest single blessing that ever came to this world was the life and teaching of Jesus.
If his life had not been written and if we had not been able to read
the Gospels, we would know very little about him."

Gandhi replied: "I really do believe in literacy for India. I have
probably been instrumental in teaching thirty thousand indirectly,
but by far the largest question for India is how to feed her hungry
multitudes."

"This is exactly why India needs to become literate. The way to
lift the illiterate masses above hunger is to teach them to lift themselves. Literacy is the only road to their complete freedom," answered
Laubach.

The story of the success of the Laubach method has spread over the
entire world. He answered a call to go to Africa, where he worked
with specialists, making charts and training teachers in the use of the
simplified system. The Africans responded with the same eagerness
and learned as readily as people in other countries. One of the native
workers said: "I have watched you day by day teaching my countrymen, and I am convinced that this is the greatest hope that has come

to Africa since Livingstone's day. All we Africans ask of you is to give us your backing and financial help. We will do the rest."

Shortly after going to Africa, Laubach wrote to a friend, saying: "Eight men have reached the reading stage this week. One young fellow, upon learning the syllables and finding that he could pronounce new words without aid, shouted, 'Give me a book. I can read!' And he was as elated as was Columbus when he first sighted the coast of the New World. His shoulders became erect and his face radiant as a new world opened up suddenly before him."

As soon as the people learn to read, they are given practical lessons in arithmetic, hygiene, care of children, preparation of food, and other daily problems. There is great need for more workers to teach the masses and to prepare literature for the new readers.

When a man learns to read, he is in love with the printed word and believes everything he reads. The great task of the Church is to supply sufficient quantity of the right kind of reading material for the new readers. Whatever is sown in their minds the world will reap. Are they to be taught hatred and suspicion, or love and good will? The situation will be tragic if the right kind of ideas are not instilled in the minds of the thousands of new readers.

Dr. John R. Mott said: "The alphabet is the most dangerous weapon ever put in the hands of the people. It is like science—it may bless the world or destroy it. No one can stop science or literacy now—all we can do is to guide them."

Dr. Laubach's methods have been approved by Columbia University, from which he holds a Ph.D. degree. At the present time he is lent to the American church at large to work with the World Literacy Committee. As a result of his work, illiterate people in all parts of the world can learn to read and write their native languages in the incredibly short time of six or more lessons of a few hours each. He says: "If that terrible load of ignorance and superstition is lifted from the illiterate half of humanity, it will be one of the most glorious liberations in history. The greatest need of the world today is to break down the walls that separate the people—of race, religion, nationality, and class—so that the pure love of God can tie the world together." [2]

PRAYER:

O God, thou who dost guide the destinies of men to fulfill thy far-reaching purposes for mankind, be thou our guide. Keep our spirits sensitive to the still, small voice, and grant us courage to carry out the design for our lives that has been revealed to us. Although we have but one talent, may we never be willing to bury it.

We thank thee for all that has been accomplished by thy servants the missionaries, who have dedicated their lives to thy cause. Be near them in moments of discouragement, give them strength to continue in the face of difficulties, and grant them faith to attempt great things in thy name. Help us to support them by our prayers and offerings. Direct those who are carrying forward the World Literacy Campaign, and may we be generous in the support of this movement to liberate mankind from ignorance. In Jesus' name, we pray. AMEN.

HYMN: "O Gracious Father of Mankind," or
        "Heralds of Christ, Who Bear the King's Commands."

BENEDICTION:

Hasten the time when the gospel shall be carried to all people and righeousness shall cover the earth as the waters cover the sea. AMEN.

SERVICE 23

PRESSING TO REGIONS BEYOND

PRELUDE: Hymn tune, "Duke Street."

CALL TO WORSHIP:

Leader: Sing unto the Lord a new song:
       Sing unto the Lord, all the earth.
       Declare his glory among the heathen,
       His wonders among all people.

Group: Let the people praise thee, O God;
      Let all the people praise thee.
      O let the nations be glad and sing for joy:
      For thou shalt judge the people righteously,
      And govern the nations upon earth.[1]

HYMN: "Jesus Shall Reign," or
    "In Christ There Is No East or West."

RESPONSIVE READING:

Leader: Let us hear the words of Jesus as he entered
     upon his mission:
    The Spirit of the Lord is upon me,
    Because he hath anointed me to preach the
     gospel to the poor;
    He hath sent me . . . to proclaim deliverance
     to the captives,
    And recovering of sight to the blind,
    To set at liberty them that are bruised,
    To preach the acceptable year of the Lord.

Group: O Master of the waking world,
     Who hast the nations in thy heart—
    The heart that bled and broke to send

God's love to earth's remotest part:
Show us anew in Calvary
The wondrous power that makes men free.

Leader: Let us hear the words of Jesus as he gave the Great Commission to the disciples: Go ye therefore, and teach all nations, baptizing them in the name of the Father, and of the Son, and of the Holy Ghost: teaching them to observe all things whatsoever I have commanded you: and lo, I am with you alway, even unto the end of the world.

Group:
    On every side the walls are down,
      The gates swing wide to every land,
    The restless tribes and races feel
      The pressure of thy piercèd hand;
    Thy way is in the sea and air,
    Thy world is open everywhere.

Leader: To whom should the message be carried? Other sheep I have, which are not of this fold: them also I must bring, and they shall hear my voice; and there shall be one fold, and one shepherd.

Group:
    We hear the throb of surging life,
      The clank of chains, the curse of greed,
    The moan of pain, the futile cries
      Of superstition's cruel creed;
    The peoples hunger for thee, Lord,
    The isles are waiting for thy word.

Leader: When Jesus pointed out the need and the urgency he said: The harvest truly is plenteous, but the labourers are few; pray ye therefore the Lord of the harvest, that he will send forth labourers into his harvest.

Group:
    Thy witness in the souls of men,
      Thy Spirit's ceaseless, brooding power,
    In lands where shadows hide the light,
      Await a new creative hour:
    O mighty God, set us aflame
    To show the glory of thy name.[2]

PRAYER:

Our Father, bless those who have gone into difficult fields and unto distant lands to proclaim thy message to the people who are still in darkness. Grant unto them an abiding sense of thy presence that they may be able to persuade people to turn to thee; prosper them in their labors, and guide us as we strive to co-operate with them. Forbid that we should become complacent or satisfied with the attainments of the past; help us to think clearly and honestly and to act with sincere motives. Create within us a clean heart, and renew a right spirit before thee; touch our eyes that we may see the needs of the world; open our ears to the cries of the people in distress; and grant us wisdom and courage as we strive to help bring thy Kingdom on earth. In the name of the Master of us all, we pray. AMEN.

HYMN: "Rise Up, O Men of God," or
"March On, O Soul, with Strength."

STORY:

WALTER RUSSELL LAMBUTH, WORLD CHRISTIAN

WALTER RUSSELL LAMBUTH, the son of missionaries, was born in China in 1854. There was the urge and daring of the pioneer, the vision and passion of the missionary in his heritage. His first friends were the Chinese, and throughout his life he was able to make friends with all classes and races of people. He went to school in America; his undergraduate work was at Emory and Henry College, with postgraduate work in medicine and surgery at Vanderbilt University and later at Edinburgh, which fitted him to be a medical missionary.

His work began in Nanziang, China, where he traveled over a circuit of two hundred miles, treating patients suffering from many kinds of diseases. Since he could not send his patients to specialists, he served both as specialist and as surgeon. His work with persons addicted to the use of opium was successful to the extent that the government used his methods in an effort to stamp out the use of the drug. He established hospitals, but his work was not confined to the medical field alone. Some of the results of his labor in the field of education may be seen in Soochow University in China, Kwansei Gakuin and Hiroshima Girls' School in Japan, Anglo-Korean School in Korea, and Granberry College in Brazil. His combination of gifts enabled him to pioneer in opening missions in Japan, Cuba, Africa, Brazil, and Siberia.

Dr. Lambuth was never content with the conquests of today but pressed on into the regions beyond, entered new fields, and tried out new methods. Because of his unusual ability he was asked to return to America to serve as Secretary of the Board of Missions during a critical period. The people responded to his leadership; the giving to missions increased, young people volunteered as missionaries, and a new era of progress and development began under his influence. Honors were heaped upon him, and in recognition of his world-wide service he was made a Methodist bishop in 1910.

The first territory assigned to him as bishop covered the far western part of the United States, Brazil, and a new mission to be opened in Africa. On the journey to Africa he was accompanied by John Wesley Gilbert of Payne College, a gifted interpreter. Landing at the mouth of the Congo River, Lambuth realized a dream that he had held since boyhood when he read the life of Livingstone and planned to be a missionary to Africa. On their long trek of more than two thousand miles into the interior, they crossed rivers, waded swamps, camped in cannibal villages, endured fevers and other hardships. Gilbert always went ahead of the bishop that he might meet the danger first and thus protect his white friend. At that time money was of no value in the Congo territory, and sixty natives had to be employed to carry the cloth, salt, and other commodities which they exchanged for the things needed for the journey.

The Presbyterian Mission which had been in operation for twenty years in the Belgian Congo invited Lambuth to open his new mission adjoining theirs. In accepting this invitation he began with the Batetela tribe, an independent, self-respecting group that had never been conquered by the Belgians.

The chief, Wembo Niama, became interested and begged the bishop to bring new recruits as soon as possible to open up the mission. When Lambuth was detained in Brazil and could not keep his agreement with the chief, a message was sent asking for a six months' extension of time. The chief, in granting the request, sent his spear by the messengers as a guarantee of protection to the bishop upon his arrival in Africa. The spear had been used by the chief in killing a number of people whose flesh he had eaten. Lambuth felt that he had nothing to fear, for he had come on an errand of peace, but he appreciated the thoughtfulness of the chief in sending the spear.

At the appointed time Bishop Lambuth arrived with eight missionaries to open up the Belgian Congo Mission. He was welcomed by the chief, who showed every courtesy to the entire group. He was generous to the missionaries, steadfast in his friendship, and unshaken in his childlike confidence in his new friend, the bishop. When converted to Christianity, the chief was eager to learn more about the white man's religion. Lambuth worked patiently to share the good news of the gospel, for the miseries and tragedies of the simple, black people of the jungle touched him deeply. When he returned to America every effort was made to enlist other workers for the new mission.

Lambuth felt keenly the urgency in carrying the gospel to the remote regions. He pioneered in establishing missions on four continents and at sixty-seven years of age was planning to go into other countries. His physician had advised that he submit to a surgical operation, but Lambuth felt that he must visit the missions in the Orient and in Siberia before entering the hospital. The travel and the supervision of the work greatly taxed his waning strength.

Writing from Siberia to a friend, he said: "I realize that I am making my last trip in the Orient; I have had a part in the founding of our missions in Japan and Africa, and now I will feel satisfied if I can lay the foundation of this work in Siberia and Manchuria. The doctors told me not to come, but I want to found this mission first. Then I will be satisfied." He held a conference, attended to all details, then sought a warmer climate in Japan.

Writing from Yokohama, he told of welcoming to Japan five young missionaries and mentioned the need of a doctor and nurse for the mission. In closing he wrote, "I am feeling better. The wonderful work in Korea and in Siberia has been a tonic." Entering a U. S. naval hospital, he was relieved temporarily by the operation, but two weeks later, in September 1921, he passed away. His life began in China and ended in Japan, where he and his father had labored together to establish a mission.

Bishop Lambuth gave himself in service wherever his church called. As a missionary secretary he was unsurpassed; as editor of the *Review of Missions* he stirred the people with his sincere messages, urging them to give more generously and to send the gospel to all races of men; as a bishop he was wise in counsel and sympathetic in his dealings with the workers. In all of these positions he was broad-minded and liberal.

As physician, minister, editor, bishop, organizer of schools, hospitals, and missions, he was a world leader. He was not only a practical man of affairs but was also a man of vision, of culture, and of keen insight into the things of the spirit. He had a firm conviction that the truth as it is revealed in Christ is sufficient to save all the nations of the earth.

He was able wherever he went to win people to Christ and to enlist workers in the cause to which he devoted his life.[3]

This man of gentle speech, prophet of the far vision, and comrade of all races, has set a high standard. The unfinished tasks which he left behind challenge us to continue his work until the message of Christ is carried to all races everywhere.

PRAYER:

We are grateful, our Father, for the pioneer missionaries who faced many dangers and hazards to carry thy message to remote regions. We are thankful for the inspiration coming from these valiant souls; their tireless devotion and their spirit of daring encourages us to carry on the work. We pray that we may become worthy to be numbered with the company of the faithful who have carried the truth of the Christian gospel to other races. Equip us for the task; give us strength and courage that we may not become discouraged by opposition. We pray thee to have compassion on the nations that are still in darkness. Enable us to do all within our power to cause the light of the gospel to shine unto the uttermost parts of the earth and make thy truth known unto all people. Bless thy servants who are working in distant lands; give them a sense of thy presence, and prosper them in their labors. Give us grace to do our part in supporting the work with our prayers and our offerings. AMEN.

HYMN: "The Voice of God Is Calling," or
"O Zion, Haste."

BENEDICTION:

The grace of our Lord Jesus Christ, the love of God, and the fellowship of the Holy Spirit be with us evermore. AMEN.

SERVICE 24

FIGHTING FOR PEACE

PRELUDE: Hymn tune, *"Pax Tecum."*

CALL TO WORSHIP:

> This is the day which the Lord hath made;
> We will rejoice and be glad in it.
> The hour cometh, and now is, when the true
> worshippers shall worship the Father in
> spirit and in truth: for the Father seeketh
> such to worship him.[1]

HYMN: "Dear Lord and Father of Mankind," or
"Lead On, O King Eternal."

RESPONSIVE READING:

Leader: In the last days it shall come to pass, that the mountain of the house of the Lord shall be established in the top of the mountains,

Group: And it shall be exalted above the hills; and the people shall flow unto it.

Leader: And many nations shall come, and say, Come, and let us go up to the mountain of the Lord, and to the house of the God of Jacob;

Group: And he will teach us of his ways, and we will walk in his paths: for the law shall go forth of Zion, and the word of the Lord from Jerusalem.

Leader: And he shall judge among many people, and rebuke strong nations afar off;

Group: And they shall beat their swords into plowshares, and their spears into pruninghooks:

Leader: Nation shall not lift up a sword against nation, neither shall they learn war any more.

Group: But they shall sit every man under his vine and under his fig tree;

Leader: And none shall make them afraid: for the mouth of the Lord of hosts hath spoken it.

Group: For all people will walk every one in the name of his god, and we will walk in the name of the Lord our God for ever and ever.

Leader: And it shall come to pass, that before they call, I will answer; and while they are yet speaking, I will hear.

Group: The wolf and the Lamb shall feed together, and the lion shall eat straw like the bullock: and dust shall be the serpent's meat. They shall not hurt nor destroy in all my holy mountain, saith the Lord.[2]

Poem:

> God of the nations, near and far,
>   Ruler of all mankind,
> Bless thou thy people as they strive
>   The paths of peace to find.
>
> The clash of arms still shakes the sky,
>   King battles still with king;
> Wild through the frighted air of night
>   The bloody tocsins ring.
>
> But clearer far the friendly speech
>   Of scientists and seers,
> The wise debate of statesmen and
>   The shouts of pioneers.
>
> And stronger far the clasped hands
>   Of labor's teeming throngs,
> Who in a hundred tongues repeat
>   The common creeds and songs.
>
> From shore to shore the peoples call
>   In loud and sweet acclaim,

FIGHTING FOR PEACE

The gloom of land and sea is lit
With Pentecostal flame.

O Father, from the curse of war
We pray thee give release,
And speed, O speed the blessed day
Of justice, love, and peace.[3]

—JOHN HAYNES HOLMES

HYMN: "Heralds of Christ," or
"These Things Shall Be."

STORY:

GEORGE FOX, FIGHTER FOR PEACE

GEORGE FOX, an adventurous young man, came of the stock of martyrs. His parents were honest and respected people who brought him up in the state religion. From his childhood he was religious and observing beyond his years. Growing up in the country, he was assigned the task of shepherd. As a young man he was disturbed because of the condition of the world, the suffering and brutality which came as a result of the Thirty Years' War in Europe. Humanity was bleeding to death because of inhuman wars. The world was ill, but it seemed to him not beyond recovery.

Consequently, during the Reign of Charles I, Fox left the farm and wandered off into solitary places to find a solution for the ills of the world. He sought the priests for a remedy, but their replies did not satisfy him. Forsaking the church in which he had been brought up, he traveled from one village to another seeking the most religious people of each section. He talked to them of the meaning of the Christian life and the coming of the Kingdom of God, urging them to work and wait patiently.

After four years of meditation Fox came to the conclusion that the world situation would improve if leaders practiced humility, if Christians became more Christlike and learned the ways of peace. Being firm in his conviction, Fox dedicated himself to the task of teaching the ways of peace.

Before starting on his crusade for peace, Fox made for himself a suit of leather and a broad-brimmed hat to wear as a protection against the wind, rain, and sleet. The style which he adopted for these articles of clothing became at a later date the distinctive garb of the Quakers, the sect which he founded. His followers wore plain clothing, different from the fashion of the times. The Scripture—"Swear not at all"—forbade their taking an oath. They neither gave nor received any titles of honor, nor called any man master.

Fox selected from his followers a group of devout men and women whom he called the "Valiant Sixty" to forward the cause of peace. Within two years their number had increased to two thousand. They were called the Society of Friends but later were nicknamed "Quakers" because of the remark, "Fox made his enemies to quake and tremble at the word of the Lord." They were idealists who faced the world as it was but set out to improve it. Because of their beliefs they endured ridicule, fines, and imprisonment. Finally they were forbidden to hold meetings except in authorized places. When they persisted in their meetings, they were dragged off to prison, where many of them died. Under all of these persecutions they behaved patiently, for their beliefs did not permit them to take up arms in defense of themselves or of others. Nothing stopped them or caused them to turn aside.

When enemies struck him in the face for telling the truth, Fox wiped away the blood and continued with what he had to say. Instead of striking back he used a more powerful weapon—the weapon of reason pleading in the cause of justice. Because he wanted men to live peaceably, he was called an atheist, a traitor, and a dangerous character. Fox showed his contempt for pomp and vainglory by refusing to remove his hat in the presence of kings. He was thrown into prison for no greater crime than asking a group to stop disputing about Jesus and start obeying him. The jailor, thinking that he had beaten the crazy ideas out of his head, released him only to find that he still held to them. But his going to jail was always the means of bringing others out of their prisons.

In 1669 Fox married Margaret Fell, an attractive, wealthy widow who could have been a leader in society but chose rather to cast her lot with the Quakers. Her spacious home "Swarthmore Hall" was open for their meetings, and occasionally she went to jail in their behalf. At the time of their marriage the wedding gift from the King of England was a jail sentence for both of them. It was a strange union—a cultured lady wedded to a leader of a band of consecrated vagabonds—but there was a deep affection between them. During the twenty-five years they were married, only about five years were spent together, for Fox was busy traveling over the country preaching. When his wife urged him to come home and rest, he always replied, "There is no rest for me as long as there is injustice to be uprooted."

When Charles II came to the throne, the Quakers were accused of plotting against the crown, and as a result fifteen thousand were in prison at one time. They met this injustice with the same fortitude as that with which they had met other persecution. During the reign of James II they were treated with greater indulgence because William Penn interceded in their behalf. Their number had greatly increased, and at the time of the settlement of Pennsylvania many of them came to America.

Upon receiving word of the hardships of the Quakers in America, Fox immediately sailed for the new country. Landing in Boston, he learned that four of his followers had been executed for having set foot in Massachusetts against the wishes of the governor. He did everything within his power but could not induce the Pilgrims to relent in their treatment of his followers. He then advised the Quaker settlers to have a fearless attitude toward their persecutors at all times regardless of what happened, for Quakers compel others to yield instead of yielding themselves.

Returning to England when his presence was no longer needed, he went to Holland and Germany, where he continued to work for peace. Later in London on a cold winter day he preached a sermon on peace. Coming from the church he felt a chill which seemed to strike at his heart. Fearing that the end was near, he urged his followers to carry on the work, to teach that there is in the whole world but a single temple—the heart of man. He said: "It is here you will find the holy habitation of God, for God dwells in the human heart, in every human heart. In the divine scales of mercy, all men are equal. It is in silent worship alone that we can hear the still, small voice of truth." Thus ended the career of the leader of the Fighting Army of Peace, George Fox, the first of the Quakers.

Poem:

> Hatred and greed and pride shall die,
> Cannon and swords shall prostrate lie;
> Warring shall end, the world shall cry—
> For he shall speak peace.
>
> Rivers shall nevermore run red,
> Terror shall hide his bloody head,

Life shall no more for lust be shed—
　　For he shall speak peace.

They shall not strive in earth again,
Honor will come to dwell with men;
Children will bide in safety then—
　　For he shall speak peace.

Desolate plains, now bleak and cold,
Burst forth again in green and gold;
Birds of the trenches sing, as of old—
　　For he shall speak peace.[4]

—THOMAS CURTIS CLARK

HYMN: "Lead Us, O Father, in the Paths of Peace," or
　　"O God of Love, O King of Peace."

PRAYER:

O God, Father of all men, forgive us for our pride of race and clan, for greed, hatred, and selfishness, and for territorial aggression. Remove from our lives all enmity, self-seeking, and strife. Make us humble and teachable, and may we have only love and good will toward all people. Grant us wisdom as we strive to reconstruct our economic life; help us to rid ourselves of an exorbitant desire for profits, markets, or materials, or any other evil which will engulf us in war again. Guide us in our struggle to build a new world order in which war will be impossible. Lead all of the nations of the world into a co-operative manner of living, so that the needs of all people will be provided for and the weaker nations will be protected. Lead us into ways of peace, brotherhood, and good will. In the name of the Prince of Peace, we pray. AMEN.

BENEDICTION:

　　　Father, give thy benediction,
　　　　Give thy peace before we part;
　　　Still our minds with truth's conviction;
　　　　Calm with trust each anxious heart.
　　　Let thy voice with sweet commanding,
　　　　Bid our grief and struggles end;
　　　Peace which passeth understanding
　　　　On our waiting spirits send. AMEN.

—SAMUEL LONGFELLOW

SERVICE 25

CARRYING LIGHT INTO DARKNESS

PRELUDE: "He Shall Feed His Flock," by Handel.

CALL TO WORSHIP:

Leader: The earth is the Lord's, and the fulness thereof;
The world, and they that dwell therein.
Let the people praise thee, O God;
Let all the people praise thee.[1]

Group: All people that on earth do dwell,
Sing to the Lord with cheerful voice.
Him serve with mirth, his praise forth tell;
Come ye before him and rejoice.

HYMN: "O Worship the King," or
"Jesus Shall Reign," or
"O Zion, Haste."

SCRIPTURE:

From the rising of the sun even unto the going down of the same my name shall be great among the Gentiles; . . . for my name shall be great among the heathen, saith the Lord of hosts.

The Lord hath made known his salvation: his righteousness hath he openly shewed in the sight of the heathen.

The Gentiles shall come to thy light, and kings to the brightness of thy rising.

We have also a more sure word of prophecy; whereunto ye do well that ye take heed, as unto a light that shineth in a dark place, until the day dawn, and the day star arise in your hearts.

For God, who commanded the light to shine out of darkness, hath shined in our hearts, to give the light of the knowledge of the glory of God in the face of Jesus Christ.

Thy throne, O God, is for ever and ever: the sceptre of thy kingdom is a right sceptre.

O Zion, that bringest good tidings, get thee up into the high mountain; O Jerusalem, that bringest good tidings, lift up thy voice with strength;

Lift it up, be not afraid; say unto the cities of Judah, Behold your God!

How beautiful upon the mountains are the feet of him that bringeth good tidings, that publisheth peace; that bringeth good tidings of good, that publisheth salvation; that saith unto Zion, thy God reigneth! [2]

LITANY:

Leader: Light of the world, forbid that darkness should veil thee from any of us,

Group: We beseech thee, O Master of our lives.

Leader: Speak to us, and make thy presence known to us,

Group: We beseech thee, O Lord.

Leader: Give us an attentive mind, and attune our hearts to thy message,

Group: We beseech thee, O Lord.

Leader: Make us sensitive to human needs, and give us an overwhelming interest in a worthy cause,

Group: We beseech thee, O Lord.

Leader: Give us purity of life, a spirit of self-denial, and a consuming desire to be a fellow laborer with thee,

Group: We beseech thee, O Lord.

Leader: Help us to find that fulness of life which comes when we dedicate our lives to serving thee,

Group: In Jesus' name, we pray. AMEN.

HYMN: "We Thank Thee, Lord," or
"These Things Shall Be."

STORY:

MARY SLESSOR OF CALABAR

MARY SLESSOR became accustomed to hardships early in life, because her father was addicted to drink. On account of poverty in the home

— 182 —

she started working in a factory at eleven years of age and continued for fourteen years. By propping her book on the loom to read as she worked and by attending night school, she managed to keep up her studies.

The father's conduct cast a shadow over the home, but the mother and children hid their shame and misery and on Sunday were faithful worshipers at the church. From childhood Mary's life was shaped by deep religious feelings and motives. A portion of her free time was spent working with the poor in the slums. Her religion was not merely a refuge; it was an inspiration and stimulus to a richer, fuller life.

Mary wanted to go to Africa as a missionary, but after her father's death she was the main support of the family. Playing school as a child, she had little black children from Calabar as her imaginary pupils. Her brother had caught her missionary enthusiasm and was planning to go to Calabar. His early death caused her to begin making her own preparation to serve in Africa. It was not until she was twenty-eight that she was ready to sail for Nigeria on the west coast of Africa and from there to travel inland to Calabar.

At that time British influence had not penetrated beyond the coast, and conditions in the interior were appalling. Calabar with all its tropical splendor was a plague-ridden spot. Witchcraft and other fiendish customs terrorized the people, and the slave trade had reduced them to a most degraded position. It was a land of contrasts: in the midst of great natural resources there was abject poverty; in beautiful surroundings there were loathsome diseases and evil practices.

Mary was deeply touched by the utter disregard for human life. Men and women were bound and left by the waterside to perish, or they were fed to the alligators in an effort to appease the gods. When a crime was committed, the guilt of a person was determined by pouring boiling oil over his hands, and if blisters appeared, he was judged guilty. A mother giving birth to twins was banished, and the twins were put to death to placate evil spirits. At the death of a chief, his wives and scores of persons were put to death to keep him company in the spirit world. Mary waged a ceaseless war against these evil practices, seizing every opportunity to teach the people and to rid them of their fears and terrors.

She fought deeply intrenched evils, such as flogging women, offering human sacrifices, killing children, and other forms of violence. She visited the vilest hovels, nursed the sick, and tried to share with the people the fullness of life which she enjoyed. Realizing that preaching was not enough, she started schools in which chiefs were taught along with the children. In an effort to teach the people habits of industry and thrift, she opened up trade routes with the English and accompanied the first cargo of trade to the coast. When she would not allow the men to carry weapons, they complained, saying, "You make women of us. Did you ever see men go to a strange place without their weapons?"

Mary's tenderness, firmness, and shrewdness completely won the natives. For months at a time she was among warring tribes, but was never molested. Her health was affected because she ate native food in order to send her meager salary to her mother. She endured the discomforts of living in native huts, traveled through jungles infested with wild animals, and exposed herself to tropical diseases. But her interest in her work was such that she was indifferent to hardships.

The call of the country beyond was always urgent to Mary. On numerous trips into the interior she lodged in mud huts, slept on dirty rags, and shared the lot of the people. On all of these trips natives accompanied her to protect her from wild beasts and savage tribes. There was no privacy, for she shared quarters with the chief's wives, slaves, children, or even cows, goats, and other animals. She taught the women how to care for the children, to cook, and to keep house. When she preached, the entire population gathered to hear her message.

The British government appointed her a sort of consular agent to supervise the native courts. It required patience to listen to the tedious palaver, but she found that knitting helped to calm her nerves. Finally gathering all the evidence, she helped them to arrive at a just settlement as she gave her judgment in the case. The natives were kept in a constant state of wonder at her knowledge of conditions. She met tribes bent on war, compelled them to pile up their arms and discuss terms of a peaceful settlement. In all of the difficult situations there was not one instance of a native's refusing to abide by her decision.

As Mary went into the interior her fame went ahead of her, and people came from afar to see the woman who had transformed the lives of the people. They may have expected to see a powerful leader, surrounded with wealth and with many subjects to do her bidding. Instead they saw a frail little woman, moving among a motley crowd of people who stood in awe of her. It was incredible that angry mobs, drunken warriors, and cruel savages alike should come under her spell and vie with each other in an effort to serve her.

CARRYING LIGHT INTO DARKNESS

Recognition came from the King of England when the Order of the Hospital of St. John of Jerusalem was bestowed on her. It was with difficulty that her friends persuaded her to come to the coast to receive the badge of honor. With humility she declared that it was done in recognition of the work of the mission and not for herself personally.

After thirty-nine years of service, when forced to lay aside her work, she was far from any white person, but the natives flocked in to see the one whom they called "Everybody's Mother." Someone began to wail and immediately another protested, saying, "Do not cry. Praise God from whom all blessings flow, for she was a great blessing." When the doctor finally arrived, Mary was eager to slip away, and in January 1915 she died.

Mary Slessor's entire life was an act of self-denial, dedicated to the task of relieving human suffering. She did not go in her own strength alone, for underneath her were the everlasting arms bearing her up. She felt called of God to engage in the great adventure of helping to build a better world. At all times she believed that she was a co-worker with God and that her task was a part of the great enterprise which would eventually make fullness of life possible for all people.

PRAYER:

Almighty Father, we thank thee for the missionaries who have gone into distant countries to share the good news of the gospel with those who are still in darkness. We are grateful that through the past thy messengers have pressed on into the outposts of civilization and have been loyal to the truth as it was revealed to them. Bless those who are still serving thee at home and abroad. Give them courage, perseverance, patience, and humility. Hasten the time when thy light will reach into all the world and all men shall acknowledge thee as their Father. Grant unto all who work for freedom, justice, and equality a greater measure of faith, a courage and boldness of spirit; through Jesus Christ our Lord. AMEN.

HYMN: "The Voice of God Is Calling," or
"The Whole Wide World for Jesus."

BENEDICTION:

Thy Spirit guide us as we strive to share with those who have not heard the gospel message. AMEN.

SERVICE 26

OVERCOMING HANDICAPS

PRELUDE: "Jesu, Joy of Man's Desiring," by Bach.

CALL TO WORSHIP:

> God of the whole creation,
>   God of all life below,
> We seek thy nearer presence,
>   Thy grander life to know;
> When we, thy heightened splendor,
>   Thy greater glories see,
> Thou God of all creation,
>   We still shall worship thee. AMEN.
>   —THOMAS PAXTON

LITANY:

Leader: Our Father, from whom every good impulse comes, deliver us from coldness of heart and wandering of mind,

Group: We beseech thee.

Leader: Cleanse us of every unholy thought or desire and make us fit for thy holy presence,

Group: We beseech thee.

Leader: Prepare our hearts and minds to worship thee;

Group: Let thy praise be on our lips.

Leader: Set our affection on worth-while things, and show us the way wherein we should go,

Group: We beseech thee, O Lord.

Leader: Guide us in our effort to help bring thy Kingdom on earth,

Group: We beseech thee, O Lord.

Leader: Fill our hearts with kindness, compassion, and brotherly love,

Group: We beseech thee, O Lord.

Leader: Grant that we may put away all envious thoughts and rejoice in the success of others,

Group: We beseech thee, O Lord.

Leader: Grant us peace and calmness which comes only from communion with thee,

Group: In Jesus' name, we pray. Amen.

Hymn: "Awake, Awake to Love and Work, or
"When Morning Gilds the Skies."

Scripture:

Look not every man on his own things, but every man also on the things of others. Let this mind be in you, which was also in Christ Jesus: who, being in the form of God, thought it not robbery to be equal with God: but made himself of no reputation, and took upon him the form of a servant, and was made in the likeness of men: and being found in fashion as a man, he humbled himself, and became obedient unto death, even the death of the cross. . . . Do all things without murmurings and disputings: that ye may be blameless and harmless, the sons of God, without rebuke, in the midst of a crooked and perverse nation, among whom ye shine as lights in the world; holding forth the word of life.

But what things were gain to me, those I counted loss for Christ. Yea doubtless, and I count all things but loss for the excellency of the knowledge of Christ Jesus my Lord. That I might know him, and the power of his resurrection, and the fellowship of his sufferings. Brethren, I count not myself to have apprehended: but this one thing I do, forgetting those things which are behind, and reaching forth unto those things which are before, I press toward the mark for the prize of the high calling of God in Christ Jesus.[1]

Hymn: "Where Cross the Crowded Ways of Life," or
"Be Thou My Vision."

Story:

OVERCOMING HANDICAPS

Marian Anderson was educated in the public schools of Philadelphia. At six years of age she made her first public appearance, singing "The

Lord Is My Shepherd" with an older girl. Her father with much pride remarked at the close of the program, "The older girl's voice sounded like skimmed milk; Marian's was like corned beef and cabbage." The youthful singer was invited to join the junior choir of the Union Baptist Church, which the family attended, and she has been singing ever since.

Marian's father sold coal and ice to support the family. At his death when she was twelve, her mother did housework to keep the family together, but after a time became ill and had to give up her outside work. Friends in the church, realizing that the girl was gifted and should have an education, started a fund which they called "Marian Anderson's future." Voice teachers gave their services, local musicians donated the proceeds from concerts, and Marian added to the fund what she could from her own recitals.

At sixteen she began to study voice seriously. After her graduation from high school the principal of the school arranged for her to study with Giuseppi Boghetti of New York. Their first meeting was at the close of a full day's work when the instructor had little interest in any beginner. But when the girl sang "Deep River" he forgot his weariness, and from that time forward they were close friends. Since then she has studied with a number of instructors, but when in New York, he is still her teacher, for she attributes much of her success to him.

Boghetti entered his gifted pupil's name in a contest, the prize of which was the privilege of appearing as a soloist with the New York Philharmonic Orchestra. He feared that the competition would be too much for a novice. Marian sang at the close of a sultry August day when the judges were eager to finish. But after she began the judges gave evidence of their delight, and at the close there was a burst of applause. It was obvious to all present that none of the contestants could compare with her, and she was awarded the prize.

Her performance in the Lewisohn stadium with the New York Philharmonic Orchestra did not perturb her, for she had been singing before musically alert people for a number of years. The critics on this occasion were lavish in their praise of her voice. However, the next five years were very difficult because of the barriers erected by prejudice and racial discrimination. Promises were made to her, only to be broken. When one of New York's top managers failed to carry out his part of a contract, she wondered if she would ever overcome the handicap of race.

Had Marian been content to be satisfied with mediocrity, her problem would have been easier, but she demanded the best of herself and would not compromise her ideals in order to take a short cut. She lacked money to complete her education, but she determined to persevere, for she knew that she had the ability to produce great music. She continued to sing under Negro auspices, and her concerts brought from $100 to $150 each.

With the money she saved and with the help of the Julian Rosenwald scholarship she began her study in Berlin. When invited to sing, she always filled the concert halls. She sang in the chief cities of Europe before kings and queens and other celebrities. In 1931 her agreement was to give six concerts in Scandinavia, but before leaving she had given seventy-six. Three weeks in Russia lengthened to three months. In Paris she appeared before audiences equally as large as those of Kreisler.

When she sang in Salzburg, Toscanini remarked, "What I have heard today is not heard once in a hundred years." In Finland when she sang for the great Sibelius, he was so delighted that he dedicated his song "Solitude" to her, saying, "The roof of my house is too low for you." After singing in the chief musical centers of Europe she returned to her own country as humble and modest as ever.

It would seem that an artist who had sung before kings and queens would be able to sing in any concert hall in her own land. But in Washington she was refused the use of Constitution Hall, and no other hall of sufficient size could be secured because of her race. Protests came from many quarters. It was then that Secretary Ickes arranged for her to sing at the foot of the Lincoln Memorial. Her sponsors were cabinet members, senators, congressmen, and other national celebrities.

The newspapers, because she had been refused the use of a hall, gave the occasion much publicity, saying that Marian Anderson would give a free open air performance for all music lovers and believers in a true democracy. The occasion is still fresh in the memory of many who were fortunate enough to be among the seventy-five thousand who heard her sing. As the tall, grave girl stood near the towering statue of Lincoln, the crowd was not unmindful of the symbolism. Lincoln had done his utmost for her race, and she was fully aware of her responsibility as she looked at the sea of upturned faces, white and colored. But with her gift of soul and of music she was equal to the occasion.

There was a hush while the crowd waited for the first note. When it came it was deeper and more moving than ever before. Singing the spirituals as well as the great music of other countries, she held the vast audience throughout the entire performance. Following the concert the critics pronounced her one of the great singers of today.

When Marian Anderson travels in this country, she usually stays at the homes of members of her race. For a time she lived at the Harlem Y. W. C. A., but in recent years she has had a suite at the Algonquin Hotel. She practices self-discipline, travels without a maid or secretary, and her schedule of seventy-five concerts each year is heavier than that of most singers. She is usually booked two years ahead of time. Before the war her vacations were spent in Europe, where she prepared her programs for the next season. Naturally her social life is limited because of her art, but she is happily married to Orpheus Fisher, an architect.

Marian Anderson sings the great music of Italy, France, and Germany, but she prefers singing the spirituals. She herself worships and her audience is reverent as she sings "Were You There . . . ?" and "Jesus Walked This Lonesome Valley" and other spirituals. At the foundation of her art is a vital religious experience—a firm faith in God which sustains her in many trying situations which she faces because of prejudice against her race.

Miss Anderson's greatness is seen in the fact that she bears no ill will toward those who have caused her to suffer. In 1940 she was selected as the one who had made the greatest contribution to her city and was awarded the Bok prize of $10,000. Her spirit is shown by the fact that she donated the entire sum to provide scholarships for struggling young musicians, regardless of race, color, or creed.

POEM:

A Phantom out of deep midnight
Now flashes on our startled sight
   With a voice like glory flying!

A goddess carved of ebony
With poise and grace and symmetry
   And a voice like glory flying!

A woman, human as was Eve,
With a heart to love, rejoice and grieve,
   And a voice like glory flying!

A soul transcending every race,
God's radiance in a human face
And a voice like glory flying! [2]

—CHAUNCEY R. PIETY

SPIRITUALS: "Jesus Walked This Lonesome Valley," or
"Were You There When They Crucified My Lord?"

READING:

I am the person who was born to live in a skin with a different color from yours.

I could not choose my parents, nor you yours.

Thus, the color pigments embedded by the unchangeable hands of nature in your skin are perchance white, while mine are black, or brown, or yellow.

But, underneath I am just like you.

My muscles ripple in the same waves of power and thrill to the same throb of joyous action.

My mind is as good as yours.

I reach out, just as you do, in aspirations of the soul.

I love and hate, hope and despair, rejoice and suffer, along with you.

When my children lose their fair chance at life and become aware of the bitter road of prejudice they must tread, then I know what my color has cost.

I offer my hand in rebuilding an unjust world that you and I can make more Christian than we have found it.

I am the person in a different skin. [3]

—PERCY R. HAYWARD

POEM:

Take thou the burden, Lord;
I am exhausted with this heavy load.
My tired hands tremble,
And I stumble, stumble
Along the way.
Oh, lead with thine unfailing arm
Again today.

Unless thou lead me, Lord,
The road I journey on is all too hard.
Through trust in thee alone
Can I go on.

Yet not for self alone
Thus do I groan;
My people's sorrows are the load I bear.
Lord, hear my prayer—
May thy strong hand
Strike off all chains
That load my well-loved land.
God draw her close to thee! [4]

—TOYOHIKO KAGAWA

SOLO: "O Saviour, Hear Me," by Gluck (with violin obligato), or

HYMN: "Master, No Offering."

PRAYER:

Our Father, through the guidance of thy Holy Spirit direct each of us to the task thou hast for us; deliver us from the temptation of taking life too easily. We are prone to resent restrictions, deplore difficulties, and avoid hardships; yet we realize that it is through overcoming them that we develop. Grant that we may never be free from the things which spur us on to our best endeavor. Give us sufficient strength to rise above the temptations which so easily beset us and patience to persevere until we reach the attainment of our goals. Give us the diligence to prepare that we may make the most of our study. May we consecrate our talents to labor in thy Kingdom. During these days while we are striving to retain freedom and democracy in the world, help us to show our patriotism by being friendly to members of other races. Help us to avoid being a stumbling block to any person who seeks to develop his talents, and grant that we may grow in appreciation for the contribution which gifted members of other races have made to the world; through Christ our Lord. AMEN.

HYMN: "Awake, My Soul, Stretch Every Nerve," or
"Great Master, Touch Us."

BENEDICTION:

Grant us a determination to press on toward the mark of the prize of the high calling in Christ Jesus our Lord. AMEN.

SERIES FIVE

AROUND THE YEAR WITH GOD

Suggestions to the Counselor

IN this series a variety of worship services is offered for special days, some of which may be used on other occasions. During the Christmas season the resources of paintings, music, and poetry may be utilized to enrich worship. The following pictures are suitable to be used with the service "Love Came Down at Christmas": Hofmann, "The Worship of the Wise Men"; Lerolle, "The Arrival of the Shepherds"; Correggio, "Holy Night"; and Burne-Jones, "The Star of Bethlehem."

"Each Brought His Gifts" is presented in the form of a panel discussion which should be rehearsed until each speaker is familiar with his part. If a formal service is desired, there should be a processional led by two young men, one carrying the Christian flag and the other the flag of the country. When they reach the altar, they will place the flags in the standards and take their places with the audience. The speakers follow the choir in the processional and are seated on either side of the altar. During the discussion the speakers remain seated except to stand when the entire group stands. Before the offertory the leader will explain the meaning of Mission Sunday and mention the cause to which the offering is dedicated.

A worship center may be arranged by placing a globe of the world on the altar or table, and around it small flags of different countries may be set in standards. The room should be dimly lighted with a strong light thrown upon the worship center. At the close of the service the leader may help the group to discover practical ways to break down barriers between races and to show a spirit of friendliness.

"Along the Way" may be given at other times but is especially suitable for Easter. The pictures Rembrandt, "The Supper at Emmaus" or Uhde, "Christ at Emmaus" are effective with this service.

With the service "A Mother's Vow" a good picture of a mother and child, or Copping, "Samuel and Eli," or Whistler, "Whistler's Mother," may be used. The story should be mastered until it can be told without notes.

The service "Be Strong and of Good Courage" may be used on Columbus Day or on any patriotic occasion. The poem should be read slowly, distinctly, and with feeling.

With the service "Appreciating the Sanctuary" use Boughton, "Pilgrims Going to Church," or any good picture of a church or cathedral. In preparation for this service a study of Christian symbolism, types of architecture, a trip through the church with the pastor, or a visit to a neighboring church to discover symbols would be helpful. For background material use Stafford, *Christian Symbolism in the Evangelical Churches.*

SERVICE 27

LOVE CAME DOWN AT CHRISTMAS

PRELUDE: Hymn tune, "The First Noel."

CALL TO WORSHIP:

> O holy child of Bethlehem!
> Descend to us, we pray;
> Cast out our sin and enter in;
> Be born in us today!
> We hear the Christmas angels
> The great glad tidings tell;
> O come to us, abide with us,
> Our Lord Immanuel!
> —PHILLIPS BROOKS

HYMN: "Good Christian Men, Rejoice," or
"The First Noel."

DECLARATION OF FAITH:

I believe in Jesus Christ, and in the beauty of the gospel that began in Bethlehem.

I believe in him whose spirit glorified a little town; of whose coming only shepherds saw the sign, and for whom the crowded inn could find no room.

I believe in him whom the kings of the earth ignored and the proud could never understand; whose paths were among the common people, whose welcome came from men of hungry hearts.

I believe in him who proclaimed the love of God to be invincible; whose cradle was a mother's arms, whose home in Nazareth had love for its only wealth, who looked at men and made them see what his love saw in them; who by his love brought sinners back to purity, and lifted human weakness up to meet the strength of God.

I confess our everlasting need of God; the need of forgiveness for our greed and selfishness, the need of life for empty souls, the need of love for hearts grown cold.

I acknowledge the glory of all that is like Christ; the steadfastness of friends, the blessedness of homes, the beauty of compassion, the miracle of hearts made kind at Christmas, the courage of those who dare to resist all passion, hate and war.

I believe that only by love expressed shall the earth at length be purified.

And I acknowledge in Christ a faith that sees beyond the partial fact, a trust in life redeemed that looks beyond our present evil;

And I pray that this redemption may begin in us who kneel and pray the Lord's Prayer.[1]

THE LORD'S PRAYER.

HYMN: "As with Gladness Men of Old."

SCRIPTURE:

> The people that walked in darkness
> Have seen a great light:
> For unto us a son is given:
> And the government shall be upon his shoulder:
> And his name shall be called Wonderful, Counsellor,
> . . . The Prince of Peace.
> Of the increase of his government and peace
> There shall be no end,
> Upon the throne of David, and upon his kingdom,
> To order it, and to establish it with judgment and
> with justice from henceforth even for ever.[2]

POEM:

> The earth has grown old with its burden of care
> But at Christmas it always is young,
> The heart of the jewel burns lustrous and fair
> And its soul full of music breaks forth on the air,
> When the song of the angel is sung.
> The feet of the humblest may walk in the field
> Where the feet of the holiest have trod,
> This, this is the marvel to mortals revealed

LOVE CAME DOWN AT CHRISTMAS

When the silvery trumpets of Christmas have pealed,
That mankind are children of God.

—Phillips Brooks

Scripture:

And there were in the same country shepherds abiding in the field,
keeping watch over their flock by night. And lo, the angel of the Lord
came upon them . . . and they were sore afraid. And the angel said
unto them, Fear not: for, behold, I bring you good tidings of great
joy, which shall be to all people. For unto you is born this day in the
city of David a Saviour, which is Christ the Lord. And this shall be
a sign unto you; Ye shall find the babe wrapped in swaddling clothes,
lying in a manger. And suddenly there was with the angel a multitude
of the heavenly host praising God, and saying, Glory to God in the
highest, and on earth peace, good will toward men.[3]

Poem:

Now is the world all lovely,
   Waiting, hushed and still,
Ere angel voices herald
   Their tidings of good will.

Now are our hearts all ready,
   And we believe that still
A little Child shall show the world
   The meaning of good will.[4]

—Marjorie Elton Young

Directed Meditation:

Love came down at Christmas. But it was recognized only by the
very wise and the very simple, and its glory was celebrated by the
song of angels in a quiet countryside under the cold light of the stars.
It was crowded out of the main currents of life by the hurry and noise
of hot lust, meaningless ritual, and selfish strife. It found a haven in
the sacred loyalty of two young people to each other and to God. The
stable and manger were only incidental. We make so much of them
only because of our stupidity and love of romance.

Love came down at Christmas not because men deserved it but
because God was gracious. No man can merit the love of God. Yet
God loves all men, both ourselves and our enemies alike. Love is not
dependent upon the moral character of the person toward whom it is

exercised, and it does not imply any approval of what that person does. It creates character and makes people worthy of approval. Even though we be sinners and in no wise worthy, yet God's love toward us and toward all men cannot fail. It is his free gift for man's redemption.

Love abides in our love to others: in the conviction that there is an absolute difference between persons and things, and that persons ought never to be treated as things; in the attitude of respect toward every human being just because he is a person and not a thing; in the doing unto every other person as we would that he should do unto us. At our best we always will that another person understand us, respect us, and work with us for both his good and ours.

Respect for persons, however come by, is the final rampart which democracy, if it is to live, can never surrender. If we do not believe in the absolute difference between men and things, if we cannot respect as a person every human being regardless of color, creed, or economic condition, and if we cannot will to do unto every other person as we would that he should do unto us, then we have already lost democracy in the citadel of the human heart. If it is surrendered there, it can never be recovered or defended on a battlefield.

Love abides not by the power of lightning war but by the invincible strength of good will to those who least deserve or expect it. Because Love came down from God at Christmas, Love abides.[5]

HYMN: "Love Came Down at Christmas," or
"There's a Song in the Air."

POEM:

> The angels hover close in love tonight;
> All the wide world waits in a hush of snow,
> As though a thousand angels robed in light
> Were something not too wonderful to know;
> Almost as if the fringes of that star
> Might feel the brush of restless wings, or soon
> Three figures riding on the hill afar
> Should trace their patterns past the paling moon.
> These are not wonders to my singing soul—
> Music in darkness, and the beat of wings,
> Starry-eyed worship through whose pulses roll
> Faith and the vision of eternal things.
> Heaven bends near at Christmas-time to men

LOVE CAME DOWN AT CHRISTMAS

Weaving a hallowed poem of this place;
And now I hear the angels' song again,
And glimpse the Light upon a Baby's face.[6]

—ESTHER BALDWIN YORK

PRAYER:

Jesus, Master of our lives, thou who didst come into the world to
reveal the Father, help us to understand that love is stronger than
hate. Grant that we may rid our lives of everything which would
keep up from loving our fellow men. We thank thee that at the Christmas season our hearts are made kinder and that our sympathy goes out
to those who suffer.

Before we confess our love for thee, help us to find in all persons
something that is lovable. Before we ask for forgiveness for ourselves,
help us to forgive our enemies, or any who may despitefully use us.
Before we seek thy mercy, help us to show mercy to all with whom we
have dealings. As we strive to live by thy spirit, help us to find thy
spirit of love reflected in the lives of those with whom we associate.

Teach us thy ways of peace, and guide us as we strive to build anew
the City of God. Make us ambassadors of peace and good will, and
grant that we may be instruments of thine helping to bring peace to
a troubled world. Grant that Christ may come into our hearts and that
we may find new life because of his indwelling. AMEN.

POEM:

In the pure soul although it sing or pray,
The Christ is born anew from day to day;
The life that knoweth him shall bide apart
And keep eternal Christmas in the heart.

—ELIZABETH STUART PHELPS

HYMN: "It Came upon a Midnight Clear," or
"Silent Night, Holy Night."

BENEDICTION:

And now may love and peace abide in your hearts forever. AMEN.

SERVICE 28

EACH BROUGHT HIS GIFTS

PRELUDE: "Deep River," by Coleridge-Taylor.

PROCESSIONAL: Hymn, "America, the Beautiful."

CALL TO WORSHIP:

> At length there dawns the glorious day
>   By prophets long foretold;
> At length the chorus clearer grows
>   That shepherds heard of old.
> The day of dawning brotherhood
>   Breaks on our eager eyes,
> And human hatreds flee before
>   The radiant eastern skies.
>
> For what are sundering strains of blood,
>   Of ancient caste and creed?
> One claim unites all men in God
>   To serve each human need.
> Then here together, brother men,
>   We pledge the Lord anew
> Our loyal love, our stalwart faith,
>   Our service strong and true.
>   —OZORA S. DAVIS

SCRIPTURE:

Except the Lord build the house, they labour in vain that build it:
Except the Lord keep the city, the watchman waketh but in vain.
Blessed is the nation whose God is the Lord; and the people whom
  he hath chosen for his own inheritance.
Righteousness exalteth a nation: but sin is a reproach to any
  people.

One is your Master, even Christ; and all ye are brethren.

God . . . hath made of one blood all nations of men to dwell on all the face of the earth.

Therefore all things whatsoever ye would that men should do to you, do ye even so to them.

Bear ye one another's burdens, and so fulfil the law of Christ.

As we have therefore opportunity, let us do good unto all men.[1]

PRAYER:

Great God and Father of mankind, who didst make thy children of one blood, and dost desire them to dwell together in brotherhood, wilt thou strengthen the ties that bind and weaken the forces that divide? Forgive our mistakes; help us to be patient in our perplexities, calm in our fears, diligent in our duties, and honest in our dealings. Multiply our high moments of faith, and deliver us from our moods of doubt. Sustain us with the memory of thy past mercies and a sense of thy present nearness.

Grant, O God, that we may be worthy of the heroic sacrifices made for us. May the spirits of the noble dead and the fellowship of loved ones far away quicken our hearts to high endeavor and selfless sacrifice. Lead us so to commit our wills to thy purposes that thou canst guide our ways into thy Kingdom's program. Illumine the minds of our leaders; encourage the hopes of our people; and lift high the banners of thy church that we may form a fellowship of love for the sake of those who suffer, until peace and justice shall reign throughout the earth. This we ask through Jesus Christ our Lord. AMEN.[2]

HYMN: "These Things Shall Be."

INTERPRETATION OF AMERICAN CITIZENSHIP:

Leader: We the people of the United States love our country with its scenic beauty, its broad highways, its immense factories, its towering buildings, its beautiful churches, its spacious farms and ranches, its cities with parks and playgrounds, schools and colleges. We love America because it is a land of opportunity where people are free to worship God as they desire and to develop according to their own ideas. We are proud to be called Americans.

First Speaker: Who are we?

Leader: All of us except the American Indians have ancestors who have come from other countries. In the forty-eight states there are sixty different racial, religious, and national backgrounds. America is a nation of nations, related by blood to almost every other country of the world, yet we are one people.

Second Speaker: Why have these people come to America?

Leader: Some left their homeland to escape conditions which they did not like, and they came to a new country to have a part in building a better civilization. Some came for adventure or for love of money, but whatever the lure that brought our ancestors here, each brought his gift.

First Speaker: What gifts did they bring?

Leader: Irish lad and Scot, Englishman and Dutch, Italian, Greek, and French, Spaniard, Slav, Norse, Negro—all came bearing gifts which they laid on the altar of America. Dirge, dance, and wassail song, proud march and religious chant. All brought their music and their instruments for making music, those many children of the harp and lute—all brought their music.

Second Speaker: May we hear music from some of the countries?

Hymn tunes: "Vesper Hymn," by Bortniansky (Russian).
"Hymn to Joy," by Beethoven (German).
"Du Friedensfürst, Herr Jesu Christ," by Bach (German).
"Lucy," by Brahms (German).
"Finlandia," by Sibelius (Finnish).
"Creation," by Haydn (Austrian).
"Gloria" (French carol).
"W Zlobie Lezy" (Polish carol).[3]

Third Speaker: What other gifts were brought to America?

Leader: Winged tales of man's many passions, folk songs and psalms, ballads of heroes and tunes of the sea, lilting scraps caught from sky and field, or mighty dramas that tell of primal struggles of the profoundest meaning. All of these races brought their poetry.

First Speaker: May we hear some of their poetry?

EACH BROUGHT HIS GIFTS

Poem:

O thou, to whose all-searching sight
The darkness shineth as the light:
Search, prove my heart, it yearns for thee;
O burst these bonds, and set it free!

If in this darksome wild I stray,
Be thou my Light, be thou my Way:
No foes, no violence I fear,
No fraud, while thou, my God, art near.

When rising floods my soul o'erflow,
When sinks my heart in waves of woe:
Jesus, thy timely aid impart,
And raise my head, and cheer my heart.

Saviour, where'er thy steps I see,
Dauntless, untired, I follow thee;
O let thy hand support me still,
And lead me·to thy holy hill! [4]

—Nicolaus L. Zinzendorf

Second Speaker: What gifts were brought by others?

Leader: Fancies of the mind, woven in wood and wool, silk, stone, or metal—rugs and baskets, gates of fine design and modeled gardens, houses and walls, pillars, roofs, windows, statues, and painting—all brought their art and handcraft.

Third Speaker: Were any homely things brought?

Leader: Each brought some homely things, some touch of the familiar home, field or forest, kitchen or dress—a favorite tree or fruit, an accustomed flower, a style in cookery or in costume—each brought some homelike, familiar thing.

Second Speaker: Is this all they brought?

Leader: All brought hands with which to work; all brought minds that could conceive and hearts filled with home—stout hearts to drive the minds, and alert minds to direct the hands. These are the gifts that were brought to our shores.

First Speaker: What pledge did these people make when they came to America?

Leader: At the altar of America they gave allegiance to a single loyalty. They have bound themselves to sacrifice and struggle, to plan and to work for this one land. They have given that they may gain; they have surrendered that they may have a victory. They have taken an oath that the world shall have a chance to know how much of good may be gathered from all countries and how solid in its strength, how wise, how fertile in its yield, how lasting and sure is the life of a people who are one.[5]

Second Speaker: When they became American citizens, what pledge did they take?

Leader: They pledged allegiance to God, to our country, and to our flag.

Third Speaker: As Christians building a new world what pledge do we take?

Leader: We pledge allegiance to the truths that have been revealed concerning the worth and dignity of man: that all men are created equal and with certain inalienable rights. We pledge to defend this new world in the making, its ideal of democracy, of freedom, and of equality.

First Speaker: What are some of the beliefs on which our nation is founded?

Leader: We believe that God is our King, that our rights are derived from him, that every person is a child of God, that we are all members one of another, that we have the right to worship God according to the dictates of our own conscience, to know the truth and to form our own religious conclusions. We believe that no one is divinely appointed as the sole representative of God on earth; that no religious organization is the sole custodian of truth and therefore should not be permitted to hold spiritual authority over other groups.

Second Speaker: Who are the enemies of our nation?

Leader: Those who preach hatred against brothers, or incite creed against creed, race against race, or nation against nation.

Third Speaker: What must we do in order to preserve our American way of living?

Leader: We need to strive for a common belief in the ideals of liberty and accept the members of all races as equal partners, allow-ing them the freedom to be different and to build up an appreciation for the contribution of each racial group. We must get rid of racial discrimination and class distinction that there be no hatred between Gentile and Jew, Protestant and Catholic, white and colored races. Since America is the work of many hands and each racial group adds a new impetus to the discovery of a finer way of living, we need to build for unity even in the midst of diversity and to strive for a culture that will be the composite of all racial groups.

First Speaker: What can we as individuals do to realize our ideals?

Leader: That our American dream of freedom and equality be realized by all, we must do everything within our power to assure every person an education. We must give everyone a chance to prepare for a vocation, to secure himself against want, to enjoy the security of a happy home in healthful surroundings. We must make religious teachings available and extend justice and equal opportunities to all. We must get rid of hatred, intolerance, and prejudice against those who differ from us and strive to hasten the day when Americans can say to the countries across the sea:

"Give me your tired, your poor,
　Your huddled masses yearning to breathe free,
　The wretched refuse of your teeming shore,
　Send these, the homeless, tempest tossed to me,
　I lift my lamp beside the golden door!" [6]

POEM:

Not for our lands, our wide-flung prairie wealth,
　Our mighty rivers born of friendly spring.
Our inland seas, our mountains proud and high,
　Forests and orchards richly blossoming;
Not for these, Lord, our deepest thanks are said
　As, humbly glad, we hail this day serene;
Not for these most, dear Father of our lives,
　But for the love that in all things is seen.

We thank thee not for prestige born of war,
　For dauntless navies built for battle stress;
Nor would we boast of armies massed for strife;
　These all are vain, O Lord of kindliness.

What need have we of swords and bayonets,
  Of mighty cannon belching poisoned flame!
O, woo us from the pagan love of these
  Lest we again defile thy sacred name.

We thank thee, Lord, on this recurring day,
  For liberty to worship as we will;
We thank thee for the hero souls of old
  Who dared wild seas their mission to fulfil.
O, gird our hearts with stalwart faith in good,
  Give us new trust in thy providing hand,
And may a spirit born of brotherhood
  Inspire our hearts and bless our native land.[r]

—THOMAS CURTIS CLARK

OFFERTORY HYMN: "In Christ There Is No East or West."

RESPONSE: Hymn tune, "Pentecost."

> All things are thine; no gift have we,
>   Lord of all gifts, to offer thee;
>   And hence with grateful hearts today,
>   Thine own before thy feet we lay. AMEN.

CLOSING PRAYER:

Eternal God, in strange lands and in many tongues thy children cry to thee; they worship in diverse manners, but they worship the same God. There are the crushed, defeated souls, the sad and lonely hearts, the sick and the maimed, the homeless and the friendless—all come to thee seeking comfort and aid. Grant all of thy children wisdom that we may learn how to live together as brothers, free from tension and strife. Grant that we may be willing to bear one another's burdens, and when we have achieved a sustaining fellowship with thee, may we progress to a kinship with all mankind. AMEN.

RECESSIONAL: Hymn tune, "Hymn to Joy."

SERVICE 29

THIS DO IN REMEMBRANCE OF ME

The following service may be used as a consecration service, but when used with the Communion the minister will assume the leadership and administer the Lord's Supper. The service should be rehearsed until the speakers are familiar with their parts and can read with expression. They should stand in the background if the group is small. But if there is any difficulty in being heard, they should stand on either side of the altar. The material may be placed on reading stands at the proper height for reading. The entire service should be presented sincerely and in a spirit of worship.

PRELUDE: "The Holy Grail" from *Parsifal* by Wagner.

CALL TO WORSHIP:

> Behold, I stand at the door, and knock:
> If any man hear my voice, and open
> the door,
> I will come in to him, and will sup with
> him, and he with me.[1]

HYMN: "Dear Master, in Whose Life I see," or
"O Jesus, Thou Art Standing."

A DECLARATION OF BELIEF:

I believe in God, the creator of heaven and of earth, Lord of all power and might;

I believe in Jesus Christ, in whom the grace and glory of God became incarnate;

I believe in the Holy Spirit, by whom the heavenly flame is brought to human souls;

I believe in the Oneness of Him who is made manifest in all things great and good.

I acknowledge the law of God which is written in the majesty of suns and stars;

I acknowledge the truth of God within which alone we can be free;

I acknowledge the love of God by which alone we are redeemed;
I acknowledge the fellowship of all saints
Who learned of Christ and lived for him,
Who carried in their hearts the flame of consecration and of courage,
Who dared and endured and triumphed ever in defeat:
> The evangelists, the apostles, and the
>   martyrs,
> The singers of the triumph of the soul,
> The lovers and the servants of mankind,
> Who gave their lives, and in the giving
>   found all life fulfilled,
> Who in their gentleness were great.
> Through them and unto God I lift my soul
>   in thankfulness and in eternal praise.[2]

SCRIPTURE:

Hear what the Scripture saith to those of a humble and contrite heart:

If any man sin, we have an advocate with the Father, Jesus Christ the righteous: and he is the propitiation for our sins: and not for ours only, but also for the sins of the whole world.

This is a faithful saying, and worthy of all acceptation, that Christ Jesus came into the world to save sinners.

God so loved the world, that he gave his only begotten Son, that whosoever believeth in him should not perish, but have everlasting life.

Come unto me, all ye that labor and are heavy laden, and I will give you rest.

Hear the Beatitudes of our Lord Jesus Christ:
Blessed are the poor in spirit: for theirs is the kingdom of heaven.
Blessed are they that mourn: for they shall be comforted.
Blessed are the meek: for they shall inherit the earth.
Blessed are they which do hunger and thirst after righteousness: for they shall be filled.
Blessed are the merciful: for they shall obtain mercy.

Blessed are the pure in heart: for they shall see God.

Blessed are the peacemakers: for they shall be called the children of God.

Blessed are they which are persecuted for righteousness' sake: for theirs is the kingdom of heaven.

Blessed are ye, when men shall revile you, and persecute you, and shall say all manner of evil against you falsely, for my sake. Rejoice and be exceeding glad: for great is your reward in heaven: for so persecuted they the prophets which were before you.[3]

HYMN: "When I Survey the Wondrous Cross."

READING:

"GENTLEMEN—THE KING!"

First Reader:

> To all the neighbors and the common ken
> He came of plain and simple working folk,—
> The first-born of the village carpenter;
> A son of toil born to a son of toil.
>
> . . . .
>
> His face was winning in its glandsomeness;
>
> . . . .
>
> His strong calm eyes looked through the outer masks
> Of men and things, and saw what dwelt within,
> And whither it was tending, up or down.
> None upon whom that clear gaze dwelt but knew
> Its strange compelling power. It seemed as though
> Their very souls lay bare unto his sight,
> And none forgot that wondrous look of his.
>
> . . . .
>
> So, through long years he toiled unceasingly,
> Enriching all with loving thought and deed.
> And then there came to him a call, and he,
> Forewarned by his much thought that it must come,
> Left mother, home, and all, and followed it;
>
> . . . .
>
> His eyes were opened and he knew at last
> That God had meant him from the first to be
> His bearer of good tidings to mankind—

His chosen one to bring the world to him.
For man had fallen upon evil ways,
And God's great heart was very sore for him.
Yet, having made him freeman of his fate,
With power to choose his way, for good or ill,
He could not now revoke that mighty trust,
Annul the laws on which his world was based,
And make man good against his own desire;
He could but sorrow at his waywardness
And strive to win him to himself again.

Second Reader:

His race was bowed beneath the Roman yoke,
And longed, with soul-sick longing, to be free;

.   .   .   .

But, though they recked not, weightier bonds were theirs
Of their own making, but these galled them not.

.   .   .   .

Making vast show of outward righteousness
But careless of the rottenness within,

.   .   .   .

Their captive souls bore theirs full easily.
His work was plain,—to win them back to God.

.   .   .   .

For road-mates and companions he chose twelve,
All, like himself, of homeliest degree,
All toilers with their hands for daily bread,
Who, at his word, left all and followed him.
He told them of the Kingdom and its laws,
And fired their souls with zeal for it and him.
He taught a new sweet simple rule of Right
'Twixt man and God, and so 'twixt man and man,—
That men should first love God and serve him well,
Then love and serve their neighbors as themselves.

.   .   .   .

But, in the priestly places, fear of him
And his subversive teaching grew apace.
Envy and hatred, malice, all the powers
Of evil-vested interests were set
To stay the message and the messenger.

—210—

They strove to trap him with insidious talk,
But all their craft he turned so that they fell
Into the pits they digged for him;—and all
The common folk hung on his words the more,
And would acclaim him King.

First Reader:
For two full years he traveled all the land
With ever-growing anguish at its need;

. . . .

One thought alone filled all his days and nights,
One sole desire,—to win man back to God.

. . . .

So—slowly, surely, in his breaking heart
Was born the tragic sorrow of it all.
God had come down to man to give him life,
And man, earth-blinded, would have none of him.

. . . .

One other chance he still could give to man—
One crowning sacrifice could make—himself!
One final mighty effort he would make;
Perchance e'en now the people might be won,—
For men think much of those who die for them.

. . . .

But he went sadly when he saw that still,
In spite of all that he could do for them,
Their hearts were set on earthly things alone,—
And yet—"Perchance if One should die for them!"
They sat with him at table that last night,
And, as the shadows nearer, nearer drew,
He spoke with them more deeply than before,
And strove to hearten them for what should come,

. . . .

For greater love can no man show than this—
That for another he lay down his life.

SOLO: " 'Tis Midnight; and on Olive's Brow."

Second Reader:
Then, in the garden, whither he had gone
To seek God's help in that which should befall,

His loneliness fell on him like a wound.

.   .   .   .

And there—with swords and spears and rabble crew,
The rulers look him—
Took him with violence, as men would take
A malefactor to his rightful doom.

.   .   .   .

O grim black stain upon the book of life!—
The good was offered, and their own free will
Instead chose evil, as so oft since then
The world has chosen—and so chooses still!
Barabbas?—or the Love of God?
And they Barabbas chose
And endless infamy.
Barabbas?—or the Love of God?
Shall we join hands with them
In their apostasy?
In silence that spoke louder than all words,
In silence that has thundered down the years,
In silence that has never ceased to speak
To all men's souls through all the ages since,
He suffered all with patient dignity,
Knowing the end, and trustful for the rest.
With jeers and taunts they nailed him to a cross,
And then, with tearing flesh and riving bone,
Raised him on high that all might see their King,
And sat and watched him there.
And at last the gallant spirit sped
With one embracing prayer for all mankind,—
"Father—forgive!—they know not what they do." [4]

THE LORD'S SUPPER. (Here the minister will take charge and administer
the Holy Communion.)

PRAYER:

Our Father, through the fellowship of this hour, through the inspiration of thy Holy Word, and through our communion together
may we hear thee speaking to us. We acknowledge our sin which is
ever before us: we have walked in paths which are contrary to thy
will; we have done those things which are evil in thy sight. Forgive

us, we pray; absolve us from all evil; save us as individuals and as a nation. Save us from littleness of thought, from selfish pride and arrogance, from all hate or desire for revenge. Grant that we may seek to know thy will and to follow it all the days of our lives. In Jesus' name, we pray. AMEN.

HYMN: "In the Cross of Christ I Glory," or

"Christ of the Upward Way."

BENEDICTION:

Unto him that loved us and saved us from sins, to him be glory and dominion for ever and ever. AMEN.

SERVICE 30

ALONG THE WAY

PRELUDE: Hymn tune, "Easter Hymn."

CALL TO WORSHIP:

> My risen Lord, I feel thy strong protection;
> I see thee stand among the graves today;
> I am the Way, the Life, the Resurrection,
>   I hear thee say.
> And all the burdens I have carried sadly
> Grow light as blossoms on an April day;
> My cross becomes a staff, I journey gladly
>   This Easter day.
>
> —AUTHOR UNKNOWN

HYMN: "Come, Ye Faithful, Raise the Strain," or
"Sing with All the Sons of Glory."

PRAYER POEM:

> Lord, make my heart a garden,
>   As real a place of prayer
> As was night-hushed Gethsemane
>   When Jesus suffered there.
>
> Make it a place of flowers,
>   Whose fragrant cups distill
> The dews of living water
>   Ensweetened in thy will.
>
> Plant there the trees of kindness,
>   Where all who look above
> May find the shadows softened
>   By sunshine of thy love.

Fill it with Easter gladness
As fresh and new as spring.
Keep it the clean, pure dwelling
Of Christ, the risen, the King.[1]
—Esther Baldwin York

Scripture:

In the end of the sabbath, as it began to dawn toward the first day
of the week, came Mary Magdalene and the other Mary to see the
sepulchre. And, behold, there was a great earthquake: for the angel of
the Lord descended from heaven, and came and rolled back the stone
from the door, and sat upon it. His countenance was like lightning,
and his raiment white as snow: and for fear of him the keepers did
shake, and became as dead men.

And the angel answered and said unto the women, Fear not ye: for
I know that ye seek Jesus, which was crucified. He is not here: for he
is risen, as he said. Come, see the place were the Lord lay. And go
quickly, and tell his disciples that he is risen from the dead; and,
behold, he goeth before you into Galilee; there shall ye see him: lo,
I have told you.

And they departed quickly from the sepulchre with fear and great
joy; and did run to bring his disciples word. And as they went to tell
his disciples, behold, Jesus met them, saying, All Hail. And they
came and held him by the feet, and worshipped him. Then said Jesus
unto them, Be not afraid: go tell my brethren that they go into Galilee,
and there shall they see me.

Then the eleven disciples went away into Galilee, into a mountain
where Jesus had appointed them. And when they saw him, they worshipped him: but some doubted. And Jesus came and spake unto
them, saying, "All power is given unto me in heaven and in earth. Go
ye therefore, and teach all nations, baptizing them in the name of the
Father, and of the Son, and of the Holy Ghost: teaching them to
observe all things whatsoever I have commanded you: and, lo, I am
with you alway, even unto the end of the world.[2]

Poem:

Outside the city wall but near, there stands
A gnarled old olive tree, its twisted arms
Outspread to shelter from unholy hands
A fresh-hewn tomb. The Roman guards' alarms

Have made them double-seal it with a rock.
"He's there to stay!" They cursed and kicked it tight.
"You just can't trust these scheming Jews! They'll mock
At Rome and try to get him out tonight."

This was on Friday. None came near the spot—
The only sound the olive's whispering leaves.
The Sabbath passed, and some by now forgot
That yesterday a Jew had died with thieves.

Then early on the first day Mary came,
And holy love that nothing could confine
Burst through the walls of death to speak her name.
"Mary!" "Rabboni!" Mary's Lord and mine—
The living Christ was there, and all was light.

And still he speaks at dawn from out the night—
And still he breaks the bonds of death and sin
When Caesar tries to shut his body in.[3]

—GEORGIA HARKNESS

STORY:

ALONG THE WAY

IT was the Passover week. Jesus' disciples, after having followed him
for three years, had gathered in Jerusalem to observe the feast. Their
hearts were filled with the great hope that at last the time had come
when he would overthrow the power of Rome and set himself up as
King of the Jews. They believed that he was the promised Messiah,
that he would restore the former glory to their nation. They had
differed in their opinions about the kind of kingdom he would establish. With mingled feelings of hope and fear they came to the city
of David, their first great ruler.

Word had gone out that Jesus would be present at the Passover feast.
From many parts of the country the people flocked to hear him. They
came expectantly, but were totally unprepared for the events which
followed. The crucial time had come. If Jesus intended to set up a
new kingdom, the first step was to put down the power of Rome.
But, to the surprise of the disciples, instead of conquering the enemy,
Jesus gave himself up without any struggle whatsoever.

Jerusalem, which was usually a joyous city at the time of the feast, held nothing but gloom for the disciples. Their leader had been put to death shamefully, and with his death their hopes had also died. It had been such a glorious dream, but it had all vanished. This was their first waking moment to what seemed stark reality.

Peter slowly picked up his fishing net to return to his former occupation. There was nothing else left to do, for with the burial of Jesus his hopes were buried also. Of course, he thought that Jesus would arise at the final Judgment, but that was too far distant to bring much encouragement to him in his present disappointment. This feeling was tersely expressed in the words, "We had hoped that it was he who would redeem Israel."

On the third day following the crucifixion Cleopas and another follower of Jesus were returning from Jerusalem. They talked of the mighty works of the young leader and of the strange ending of his ministry. Along the way a Stranger joined them. They discussed at length the recent events which puzzled them. The Stranger entered into their conversation and opened up to them the meaning of the Scriptures. Though they did not recognize him, they felt a strange power burning in their hearts.

While he was still speaking to them, they came to the home of Cleopas. The day being far spent, Cleopas invited the Stranger to join them at their evening meal. He shared their simple fare, and in his giving thanks and breaking the bread they recognized Jesus, their leader, who had been crucified. They were filled with wonder, for as they gazed at him, he disappeared from their midst.

In amazement Cleopas remarked, "Did not our hearts burn within us while he talked with us along the way? How clear he made the mysterious sayings of the prophets! Isn't it strange that we did not recognize him until he gave thanks and broke the bread?"

For some time Cleopas and his friend talked about the strange events. They realized that they had been slow to grasp the meaning of the new kingdom. Now it was clear that Jesus' kingdom was not an earthly one, but a rule of righteousness in the hearts of his followers. Though their hopes had been buried when he was placed in the tomb, his resurrection had brought them to life again. His enemies had put him to death, but they could not keep him in the tomb. He was alive! He was still their leader!

A new light came into Cleopas' eyes as he said: "I understand now —Jesus did not come to live in a palace and be served as a king. He came to give himself in service to others. He walks the dusty road, shares our poverty, and breaks bread with us in our humble homes. He knows our needs and sympathizes with us in our sorrows. He came not to rule over us but to reign in our hearts. Not only is he alive, but his spirit is in our lives. Let us return even now to Jerusalem to tell the others."

LITANY:

Leader: O Master of our lives, be as evident in the world today as in the days of thy ministry.

Group: Give us discerning hearts, we pray.

Leader: Be as much alive in our midst as in the days of thy flesh.

Group: Grant us a clear vision of thee, O Lord.

Leader: As thou didst walk the dusty road to Emmaus,

Group: Come, travel the road with us.

Leader: As the pilgrims along the Emmaus way felt their hearts strangely warmed,

Group: Make us aware of thy presence along the way.

Leader: As thou didst share the simple fare with the travelers,

Group: Come, share our common joys and sorrows.

Leader: As thou didst revive their faltering hopes,

Group: Kindle within us the fires of faith.

Leader: As thou didst reveal thyself in the breaking of bread,

Group: May we find thee in the simple tasks of everyday life.

Leader: As thou didst come into the lives of the disciples,

Group: Come and abide with us, for the day is far spent. AMEN.

HYMN: "Again, as Evening's Shadow Falls," or
   "Christ the Lord Is Risen Today."

BENEDICTION:

And now may the blessing of the Father, Son, and Holy Spirit be with you now and evermore. AMEN.

SERVICE 31

A MOTHER'S VOW

PRELUDE: "Ave Maria," by Bach-Gounod.

CALL TO WORSHIP:

> Happy the home when God is there,
>   And love fills every breast;
> When one their wish, and one their prayer,
>   And one their heavenly rest.
>
> Happy the home where prayer is heard,
>   And praise is wont to rise;
> Where parents love the sacred Word
>   And all its wisdom prize.
>
>   —HENRY WARE

SCRIPTURE:

> Who can find a virtuous woman?
> For her price is far above rubies.
> The heart of her husband doth safely trust in her,
> So that he shall have no need of spoil.
> She will do him good and not evil all the days of her life.
> She seeketh wool, and flax,
> And worketh willingly with her hands.
> She is like the merchants' ships;
> She bringeth her food from afar.
> She riseth also while it is yet night,
> And giveth meat to her household,
> And a portion to her maidens.
> She considereth a field, and buyeth it:
> With the fruit of her hands she planteth a vineyard.
> She girdeth her loins with strength,
> And strengtheneth her arms.

She perceiveth that her merchandise is good:
Her candle goeth not out by night.
She layeth her hands to the spindle,
And her hands hold the distaff.
She stretcheth out her hand to the poor;
Yea, she reacheth forth her hands to the needy.
She is not afraid of the snow for her household:
For all her household are clothed with scarlet.
She maketh herself coverings of tapestry;
Her clothing is silk and purple.
Her husband is known in the gates,
When he sitteth among the elders of the land.
She maketh fine linen, and selleth it;
And delivereth girdles unto the merchant.
Strength and honour are her clothing;
And she shall rejoice in time to come.
She openeth her mouth with wisdom;
And in her tongue is the law of kindness.
She looketh well to the ways of her household,
And eateth not the bread of idleness.
Her children arise up, and call her blessed;
Her husband also, and he praiseth her.
Many daughters have done virtuously,
But thou excellest them all.
Favour is deceitful, and beauty is vain:
But a woman that feareth the Lord, she shall be praised.
Give her of the fruit of her hands;
And let her own works praise her in the gates.[1]

HYMN: "O Happy Home," or
"O Thou Whose Gracious Presence Blessed."

PRAYER:

O God, Giver of all good things, we thank thee for our mothers, for their devotion and sacrifice, their patient struggle in our behalf, their hope and faith in our achievement, their loyalty to Christian ideals, and their worthy example. We are grateful for the love and fellowship which we enjoy in our homes. Help us to become more worthy of the blessings we enjoy. Grant us purity of thought, word, and deed, and give us strength to live according to our highest ideals. Protect us in times of danger, encourage us in adversity, strengthen us in times of weakness, and lead us in the paths of righteousness; through Jesus Christ our Lord. AMEN.

LEADER:

All great mothers have been created by their sons or their daughters. Many great women have achieved fame as women, have won their positions as rulers, artists, musicians, scientists, educators, but no great mother has done this.

We know the ruler as ruler, the artist as artist. It's Mme Curie, the scientist; Mary Lyon, the educator; Jane Addams, the social worker. But whenever we say "mother," we search for the son, the daughter. The great mother is created by a great son. She is dependent. Through him she becomes triumphant. The son and the daughter create her. No matter how intrinsically great as a mother she may have been, history accords her no such recognition if the son or the daughter fails her.

Who would have heard of Mary, the Madonna, had Jesus of Nazareth failed her? The Magnificat, the song upon Mary's lips before his birth, would have been lost among the million songs of a million mothers if he had not exalted them of low degree. Raphael's "Sistine Madonna" would not hang in the Dresden Gallery today had Christ in cowardice refused the cross. The inestimable influence of Mary "the mother of God" would never have reached the hearts of countless girls had he been less Godlike. We know Mary, the peasant-girl of Galilee, because of Jesus, the carpenter-son of Nazareth.

Who was the mother of Judas? No one knows. Did she not love him? Were there no dreams in her mother heart? Had she fondly hoped her child might be the Messiah? We do not know. We do know that Judas failed her. And thus she, like all mothers, was dependent —dependent upon a son who might have led her into triumphant immortality but who broke her heart instead.[2]

We shall hear the story of a mother who is remembered because of the greatness of her son.

STORY:

THE VOW OF HANNAH

WITH a heavy heart Hannah had gone to Shiloh with her husband, Elkanah, to observe the feast day. Suddenly he looked up to see her weeping.

With deep concern he said, "Hannah, why do you weep? Am I not better to you than ten sons?"

She did not reply but joined mechanically in the festivities with her eyes turned to the temple. Her own prayer for a son would be offered there once more. Surely the Lord could not withstand the cry of her need forever.

She looked at the great doors of the temple. Old Eli sat there, bowed with age. His sons, Hophni and Phinehas, were evil. When Eli was gone, who would administer justice and bring the word of Jehovah?

Suddenly a thought burned through her brain as though it had been a live coal from the altar. She walked swiftly toward the temple, moved toward the altar of the outer court, and fell upon her knees. She raised her hands before her.

"O Lord of hosts," prayed Hannah, "if thou wilt indeed look on the afflication of thine handmaid and remember me! If thou wilt give unto me a man-child, then I will give him unto the Lord all the days of his life! O Lord of hosts, if thou wilt remember me, I will give him unto thee. I will give him . . ."

Suddenly a voice spoke behind her. "How long will you remain drunken? Put away your wine!" Hannah rose bewildered. Eli had mistaken her frenzied posture, her moving lips, her very presence in that unaccustomed place.

"No, my lord," she answered, "I have drunk neither wine nor strong drink. But I am a woman of a sorrowing spirit, and I have poured out my soul before the Lord. Out of the abundance of my grief have I been praying."

They faced each other in the stillness of the holy place: the young woman who had no son and the old man whose sons were vile. The pain in the eyes of the one challenged the pain in the eyes of the other, but the woman's conquered.

"Go in peace," Eli said slowly, "and the God of Israel grant you the petition that you have asked of him."

Hannah bowed low before him and slipped between the curtains out into the street. A miracle had touched her, and her heavy heart was gone. She felt light and eager, for a consuming confidence possessed her. She had added to her petition a vow which Jehovah could not disregard, and upon it the man of God had pronounced a blessing.

After the birth of the son, Elkanah heard Hannah say, "His name must be Samuel, because I asked him of the Lord."

As the weeks and months passed, the neighbors said that they had never seen such a perfect child as little Samuel. To Hannah, a new world had been freshly created. She feasted her starved heart upon the baby's beauty. Her days became breathless with happy activity, and her nights were alive with loving care.

Time passed, and once more it was time for the feast at Shiloh. In all their rejoicing over the coming of the child there had been one subject that was not mentioned between them. That was the vow. Elkanah had waited for his wife to speak, and she had been silent. Now on the eve of the departure for Shiloh he asked, "Will you not go up to Shiloh on the morrow with the child? You have not forgotten the vow?"

"The vow!" she echoed through white lips as they faced each other. "I will not go up until the child is weaned, and then I will bring him, that he may appear before the Lord—and—there—abide—forever," she said. The last words were a whisper.

"Do what seems best to you," he replied gravely. "Tarry, if you will, until you have weaned him. Only, the Lord establish his word!"

When he had gone, Hannah sat down dazedly, clutching Samuel to her. It had come at last. The vague dark cloud of fear that had hovered far in the background of her joy had drawn close, had taken form, had fastened itself irrevocably upon her. The vow that her lips had given long ago in the temple was cut now upon her heart.

Until he was weaned! As little Samuel grew in beauty and in stature, not once had Hannah's high courage seemed to waver. She spoke constantly of the time, now so near, when she would take the child up to Shiloh and dedicate him forever to the service of the temple. Her eyes grew bright as she spoke of it.

Through the days Hannah thrilled as she thought of Samuel grown, his baby beauty graven in strength. She saw him instead of old Eli in the ephod of blue with its hem of golden bells and pomegranates. She saw him in the courts of the temple, burning the sweet incense of oblation, offering with holy hands the evening sacrifice. She saw him, a man of God, judging the people righteously, and swaying Israel by the word of his counsel—her son!

When the last day came, the leave-taking was very quiet. Elkanah, his face set, his eyes suffering, saw to the loading of the sacrifices upon the pack donkey. Hannah came, carrying the child's neat bundle of clothing, her face very calm, very white, her eyes shining with a fierce, unreal exaltation.

On the way she pointed out the flowers, the birds, the strange villages, and answered the child's endless questions. As they neared Shiloh she caught the boy closer to her. The light on her face grew brighter. She spoke of nothing but the glory of the temple to which they were going. Little Samuel peered eagerly with round, childish eyes.

When they stood at last in the presence of Eli, Hannah advanced and knelt before him. "O my lord," she began in her low vibrant voice, "I am the woman who stood here once, praying in the temple. For this child I prayed, and the Lord has given me the petition which I asked of him. I made a vow to the Lord that I would give him my child. And as long as he lives he shall be lent to the Lord!"

The old man raised his trembling hands: "Blessed be the child and they that have brought him to the house of the Lord! Jehovah has not left his dwelling desolate, but has raised up youth and beauty within it." He reached his hand toward Samuel, and the little child went to him.

Hannah raised her head, clasped her hands, and the words poured swiftly from her lips:

> "My heart rejoiceth in the Lord,
> For there is none beside thee:
> Neither is there any rock like our God!
> He will keep the feet of his saints,
> And the wicked shall be silent in darkness!"

Elkanah stepped back as Hannah began to speak; Eli's lips moved with the echo of her words. Then suddenly, all was as it had been before. As Hannah rose from her knees, Samuel ran to her. They walked through the courts of the sanctuary to see the place that from that day forth was to be the home of the child.

When they started on their journey back to Ramah, Hannah, with white lips set, fixed her eyes on the road before them. "It is a pleasant enough little room he will have," the man said awkwardly at last. "There is a pallet and chair, and a table for the candle. It is near the room of the priest. He would hear if the child . . ." There was no answer, and they rode on. When they reached home Hannah's lips were set as when they left Shiloh.

Hannah moved through the rooms, touching the table where he had eaten his last meal, the little pallet, still unrolled, where he had slept, a plaything left behind, the little tunic too worn to send with him! She touched them one by one, as if she were a stranger to them.

Surely the Lord must measure the greatness of her gift by her suffering now, instead of by her song in the temple! Perhaps some time after endless tomorrow had passed, she would again know her holy dreams of aspiration for her boy—her pride, her hope. But tonight there were no visions—only a stark desolation. Elkanah stood desperate, helpless. The dusk became darkness. Out of it Hannah slowly raised her head. A voice came, half whisper, half sob: "I shall make him a little coat, woven with my own fingers and embroidered. Day by day I shall work on it. Year after year I shall make him a little coat and take it up to the feast, so that he may not forget me."

Elkanah sank down beside her and drew her close to him as she continued, "A little coat. Year after year . . . a little coat."[3]

READING (in unison):

My soul doth magnify the Lord, and my spirit hath rejoiced in God my Saviour.
For he hath regarded the low estate of his handmaiden:
For, behold, from henceforth all generations shall call me blessed.
For he that is mighty hath done to me great things; and holy is his name.
And his mercy is on them that fear him from generation to generation.
He hath shewed strength with his arm;
He hath scattered the proud in the imagination of their hearts.
He hath put down the mighty from their seats, and exalted them of low degree.
He hath filled the hungry with good things; and the rich he hath sent empty away.
He hath holpen his servant Israel, in remembrance of his mercy; as he spake to our fathers, to Abraham, and to his seed, for ever.

Glory be to the Father, and to the Son, and to the Holy Ghost;
As it was in the beginning, is now, and ever shall be, world without end. AMEN.[4]

SOLO: "Ave Maria," by Bach-Gounod (with violin obligato), or "Songs My Mother Taught Me," by Dvořák.

POEM:

God bends his loving heart down close
To altars everywhere:

To polished rails of wood and plush
    In dim-lit halls of prayer;

To rustic boards beneath a tent,
    Where, humbly in the straw,
Men kneel as shepherds did of old
    Before the Christ they saw.

To bedsides where tired mothers lay
    A full day's cares and joys;
To mothers' laps where clasp the hands
    Of little girls and boys;

To forest solitudes and hills
    And clean, wide, windswept spaces,
Where something deep within the soul
    Looks up. Around all places

Where men seek God with yielded hearts
    And simple, earnest prayer,
He draws his great encircling arms,
    And they will find him there! [5]
               —ESTHER BALDWIN YORK

PRAYER:

O God, Giver of all life, we thank thee for thy protecting care and for the ties which bind our families together. We are grateful for the security, joy, and comfort we possess in our homes. Forgive us that we have been content to accept these gifts without giving thought to those who are denied these pleasures. Touch our hearts that we may see our mothers in every woman who toils in the factory, shop, or office. Hasten the day when the lot of the mothers of the poor shall be made easier, and their needs shall be met and suffering prevented.

We feel unworthy of the sacrifice which our mothers have made for us. In times of weakness keep us firm; strengthen us in temptation; preserve us in danger; and assist us in every good work that we may become worthy sons and daughters. Grant us wisdom that we may understand the depth and constancy of our mothers' love, the incentive which pushes us on to our best endeavor. Fill us with all spiritual benediction and grace that we may live together as thy children in peace and in love. AMEN.

HYMN: "A Charge to Keep I Have," or
      "I Would Be True."

BENEDICTION:

And now as we wait before thee, grant to all thy children the benediction of that inner peace which passeth understanding. AMEN.

SERVICE 32

BE STRONG AND OF GOOD COURAGE

PRELUDE: Hymn tune, *"Veni Immanuel."*

CALL TO WORSHIP:

Leader: Our help is in the name of the Lord, who made heaven and earth.

Group: Give unto the Lord, ye kindreds of the people, give unto the Lord glory and strength.

Leader: Honour and majesty are before him: strength and beauty are in his sanctuary.

Group: Blessed be the name of the Lord from this time forth and for evermore.[1] AMEN.

HYMN: "He Who Would Valiant Be," or
"Stand Up, Stand Up for Jesus."

SCRIPTURE:

Be strong and of a good courage: for unto this people shalt thou divide for an inheritance the land, which I sware unto their fathers to give them. Only be thou strong and very courageous, that thou mayest observe to do according to all the law, which Moses my servant commanded thee: turn not from it to the right hand or to the left, that thou mayest prosper whithersoever thou goest. This book of the law shall not depart out of thy mouth; but thou shalt meditate therein day and night, that thou mayest observe to do according to all that is written therein: for then thou shalt make thy way prosperous, and then thou shalt have good success. Have I not commanded thee? Be strong and of a good courage; be not afraid, neither be thou dismayed: for the Lord thy God is with thee whithersoever thou goest.

Be of good courage, and he shall strengthen your heart, all ye that hope in the Lord.

Wait on the Lord: . . . wait, I say, on the Lord.[2]

BE STRONG AND OF GOOD COURAGE

LITANY OF PRAISE:

> We praise thee, God, for harvests earned,
>   The fruits of labor garnered in,
> But praise thee more for soil unturned
>   From which the yield is yet to win.
>
> We praise thee for the harbor's lee,
>   And moorings safe in waters still;
> But more for leagues of open sea,
>   Where favoring gales our canvas fill.
>
> We praise thee for the conflicts won,
>   For captured strongholds of the foe;
> But more for fields whereon the sun
>   Lights us when we to battle go.
>
> We praise thee for life's gathered gains
>   And blessings in our cup that brim;
> But more for pledge of what remains
>   Past the horizon's utmost rim.
>   —JOHN C. ADAMS

SOLO: "Lord, Make Me Strong," by Eville.

HYMN: "Go, Labor On," or
      "My Soul, Be on Thy Guard."

STORY:

MARKHAM, POET OF THE PEOPLE

IN the late sixties of the last century, when the thunder of buffalo stampedes could still be heard on the prairie and belated "Forty-Niners" in ghostly covered wagons were still groping through Death Valley on their way to Eldorado, a boy on a calico pony rode into the embers of a California sunset. Undismayed by the dusk, he urged his pinto on with bare feet, which for all their sturdiness caressed rather than prodded:

"Get up, Aristotle! It's a long way to Oregon."

But Aristotle did not get up. He stopped suddenly as a burley figure with a black beard emerged from the mesquite at the edge of the bridle trail.

"Don't be afraid," the newcomer said in a voice that was almost musical. "I've worked with you all summer on the threshing crew and have been watching you. You're a good man. I can use you in my business. I've been wanting someone to hold the gun while I take the tickers. Tickers are watches. That's what we call them in the trade. You may as well learn the lingo now as later. Come with me and I'll show you some of them."

By a tortuous bypath he led the boy on a balking Aristotle to a cache in a hollow tree. Out of it he pulled a burlap sack bulging with watches, heavy gold chains, jeweled charms, gold coins, and currency. The boy's eyes were bulging too.

"I got those last spring," the highwayman explained. "This fall ought to be better. The stages are crowded. What d'ye say? Do you want to shake the chaff out of your pants and put something there that matters?"

The boy shifted uneasily. Aristotle, with something of the discretion and ethics of his ancient namesake, pawed the ground restlessly as if to suggest a running flight. The boy shared the pony's innate honesty.

"No," he said, "I can't be a bandit. I have to go to Oregon and be a poet."

The brigand thought he knew all the answers. But this one was different. With a bristling contempt for anyone who chose to write poems when he might have robbed stagecoaches, he whirled away, beard and Babylonian baggage, and was soon only a muffled "klop-klop-klop" in the next valley; while the boy, riding Aristotle, as Quixote must have ridden Rosinante, went on to Oregon "to be a poet"—for the bandit was "Black Bart," whose shaggy beard under a bandana handkerchief and over a horse pistol had terrorized the Southwest; and the boy was Edwin Markham.[3]

Edwin Markham lived in a manner that will astonish the world when it discovers the facts. On one occasion when he was taken to a hotel for a luxurious meal, a friend noticing his uneasiness asked what bothered him. He said as simply as a child, "I cannot bear to be sitting down to this wasteful meal when I think of the thousands of people who do not have enough to eat. Why do we not eat in some moderate place and save the money for others? I do not believe, if we are followers of the lowly Nazarene, and take him seriously, that we have any right to eat more than necessity requires."

It was difficult to get him to ride in Pullman cars except on long trips. He says that he used the coach for two reasons, to save the extra expense and to ride with the common people. He dressed simply, even poorly, with an old battered hat, an old overcoat that some friend had given him. It is doubtful whether he ever willingly indulged in luxury on his own account. He lived as simply as a peasant, and yet he was gloriously happy.

When he was about eighty years of age, he walked and talked as a man of thirty. When most men were burned out at his age, he still had glowing within him the fires of youth. He often started on a three months' trip through ten states, filling two and three speaking engagements a day; laughing, shouting, exuberant, boyish; making friends on every train, in depots, hotel lobbies; giving himself to every person he met.

As the Nile River yearly renews and enriches the soil along its banks, so Markham restored hope and spirit in those who came in touch with him. To shake his hand was to know the touch of a prophet; to hear him speak was to listen to the trumpet call of truth.

Markham was the great pioneer of the social gospel in America. When more recent social prophets have been forgotten, the name and fame of "The Man with the Hoe" will go echoing down the centuries. Before the champions of the social gospel were heard of, he was beating down oppression, injustice, and slavery.

Dr. William L. Stidger tells the following story about Markham:

While visiting in my home in Boston several years ago, he was working on a secret poem which he carried about with him and promised to read to me when he completed it. It was the story of a man who fought against great odds, and it has a timely challenge for these days when courage is greatly needed.

Markham's eyes were flashing fire and pride when he came downstairs the morning of October 12, waving his poem above his long white hair.

"William, here's the poem on that brave explorer who had courage and faith," and he proceeded to read the poem at the breakfast table. "It is the story of a man who went to the Court of Spain with his dream that the world was round and with the statement that he could find a short path to the Indies. When ridiculed in the Court, Columbus was not baffled, for he knew that he was a servant of God."

I asked, "Did Columbus actually think that he was called of God to do this important thing?"

"Yes," replied the poet seriously, "I have read every book available, including the Diary of Columbus, and it is clear to me that he looked upon himself as a servant of God on that eventful voyage."

At last Columbus got his financial support from the Queen of Spain and started. There is the story of the long days and nights, the baffled and bewildered sailors, the mutinies; the day the needle seemed to feel some secret jar and also seemed to shake the polar star. His men wanted to turn back, but the sheer courage of Columbus kept them going on into the West. Then came that historic climax—the discovery of the American continent.

When the poet finished, I asked what he meant by the concluding lines. He said: "I mean that God in his heavens, the stars and planets in their courses, the sun and moon and stars, the seasons in their cycles, all history, time and eternity and the very angels in heaven are always on the side of the daring, the audacious, the courageous—the man who catches his vision, feels that he is God's servant, and goes ahead regardless of obstacles!" *

Let us listen to the poem honoring the great adventurer.

POEM:

Out of deep mystery he came:
A vapor hangs around his name.
What was his origin? Who knows
The cloud from which his birth-star rose?
Seven towns of Homer's ancient earth
Claimed they had cradled him at birth.
Seven also claimed this later one
After his daring deed was done.

This vagabond adventurer,
Touched by a vision's magic spur,
Rose into glory, rose to be
Spain's bold knight-errant of the sea.

Yet once he wandered ghast and grim,
While wolves of hunger followed him.
He journeyed on from year to year,
And cried to every listening ear.
He cried even at the courts of Kings
His story of incredible things.
"You know," he said, "that Plato told

BE STRONG AND OF GOOD COURAGE

Of old Atlantis, realm of gold.
We see its buried peaks and shores
Where rise the distant dim Azores.
Antilla and Zumpango wait
My coming at the ocean gate.
Dreams of these islands in the west
Disturb me, will not let me rest.
And far beyond the western seas
Slumber the vast Antipodes.
So sliding down the ocean wind
I'll touch the golden shores of Ind."

"What fantasy!" the courtiers shout:
"Delusion wraps him all about.
Here is a clown, a poor buffoon,
Toucht by some madness of the moon!"

They blew his dream away like chaff:
They blew it with a fleering laugh.
They speared him with a cruel jest:
They left the arrow in his breast.
Yet nothing could stop his march, nor **mar**
His vision lighted by a star.
He knew he was (his constant boast)
A servant of the Holy Ghost.
Some whisper from the vast Unseen
Held him erect, austere, serene;
Until the heat of his fiery brain
Melted the iron will of Spain.
The great hour came with triple ships
Then sudden fervor stirred his lips:
"On, on, into the west," he cried:
"I know and will not be denied.
The world is round: by the western gate
The riches of the Indies wait.
Lift sail, my men, the hour has come
For shipwreck or millennium.
Lift sail, my men, the hour is here
To probe the secret of the sphere."

The long day and the longer night,
And seas rushed by in eager flight.
Then frightened sailors raised a cry:
"We feel the terror of the sky.
Turn back, great Admiral," they moan:
"We cannot dare the dark unknown.
Soon we shall totter on the brink,
Soon into utter darkness sink!"
"No, no," the daring chief replied:
"The earth is round, the sea is wide:
Keep all the sails aloft, and steer
Into the west: the shores are near!"

They plowed and plunged for days and days,
Then horror struck and wild amaze.
The Needle felt some secret jar
And seemed to shake the Polar star.
The pilots paled with sudden awe:
Nature seemed crashing out of law.
Had they then swung to another realm?
Would the void open and overwhelm?
But no fear shook the Captain, none,
From sunset to the rise of sun.
He stood there sleepless on the prow,
With whipping cloak and troubled brow,
With wild hopes singing in his breast,
With grey eyes glued upon the west.
He stood there, beating against bars—
Stood all the night till drunk with stars.
At last near twelve, he suddenly saw
A thing of mystery and awe:
It was a light afar—a light:
It moved, and there was no more night!
Now let this startling thing be said:
If land had not been on ahead,
So mighty had been his gallant dare,
God's glad hand would have put it there! [5]

—EDWIN MARKHAM

BE STRONG AND OF GOOD COURAGE

PRAYER:

Our Father, we thank thee for the courageous souls who would not accept defeat, but who turned their failures into triumphs. Help us to accept the things which cannot be changed, and strengthen our courage as we struggle to change those things which should be changed. Reveal thy truth that the way ahead may be plain as we try to follow thy guidance. Forgive our mistakes, and may we use them as stepping stones by which we rise to higher things. Enable us to endure hardship as good soldiers. May we realize that we do not have to go in our strength alone, but that we can avail ourselves of divine resources which will turn our weakness into strength. Increase our faith and courage as we lose ourselves in serving thee. AMEN.

CLOSING HYMN: "Be Strong! We Are Not Here to Play," or
"A Charge to Keep I Have."

SERVICE 33

APPRECIATING THE SANCTUARY

PRELUDE: "In the Cathedral," by Pierne.

CALL TO WORSHIP:

> I was glad when they said unto me,
> Let us go into the house of the Lord.
> Surely the Lord is in this place; . . .
> This is none other but the house of God,
> And this is the gate of heaven.
> Enter into his gates with thanksgiving,
> and into his courts with praise.[1]

HYMN: "Let All the World in Every Corner Sing," or
"All People That on Earth Do Dwell."

SCRIPTURE:

One thing have I desired of the Lord, that will I seek after;
That I may dwell in the house of the Lord all the days of my life,
To behold the beauty of the Lord, and to enquire in his temple.
How amiable are thy tabernacles, O Lord of hosts!
My soul longeth, yea, even fainteth for the courts of the Lord: my heart and my flesh crieth out for the living God.
Yea, the sparrow hath found an house, and the swallow a nest for herself, where she may lay her young, even thine altars, O Lord of hosts, my King, and my God.
Blessed are they that dwell in thy house: they will be still praising thee.
Blessed is the man whose strength is in thee; in whose heart are the ways of them.
For a day in thy courts is better than a thousand. I had rather be a doorkeeper in the house of my God, than to dwell in the tents of wickedness.

For the Lord God is a sun and shield: the Lord will give grace
and glory: no good thing will he withhold from them that walk
uprightly.
O Lord of hosts, blessed is the man that trusteth in thee.[2]

PRAYER:

Almighty God, who hast given us grace, at this time, with one accord
to make our common supplications unto thee, and dost promise that,
when two or three are gathered together in thy name, thou wilt grant
their requests; fulfill now, O Lord, the desires and petitions of thy
servants, as may be most expedient for them, granting us in this world
knowledge of thy truth, and in the world to come life everlasting.
AMEN.

—ST. CHRYSOSTOM

POEM:

> The groves were God's first temples. Ere man learned
> To hew the shaft, and lay the architrave,
> And spread the roof above them—ere he framed
> The lofty vault, to gather and roll back
> The sound of anthems; in the darkling wood,
> Amid the cool and silence, he knelt down,
> And offered to the Mightiest solemn thanks
> And supplication. For his simple heart
> Might not resist the sacred influences
> Which, from the stilly twilight of the place,
> And from the gray old trunks that high in heaven
> Mingled their mossy boughs, and from the sound
> Of the invisible breath that swayed at once
> All their green tops, stole over him, and bowed
> His spirit with the thought of boundless power
> And inaccessible majesty. Ah, why
> Should we, in the world's riper years, neglect
> God's ancient sanctuaries, and adore
> Only among the crowd, and under roofs
> That our frail hands have raised? Let me, at least,
> Here, in the shadow of this aged wood,
> Offer one hymn—thrice happy, if it find
> Acceptance in his ear.

—WILLIAM CULLEN BRYANT

STORY:

BUILDING THE HOUSE OF GOD

FROM the time Solomon built the temple at Jerusalem about 1000 B.C. to the present time people have consecrated their finest treasures and their labor to building the house of God. Skilled craftsmen and artisans have devoted their lives to building and adorning their place of worship. One of the greatest accomplishments of man has been the translation of the genius of religion into the Gothic cathedral. The story of this accomplishment, told even in brief form, shows how the religious needs of the people were met in the various stages of development by the use of the available materials, meager though they were.

During the time of the persecution of the early Christians there was no development of church buildings. Services were held secretly in private homes or in the catacombs underground, but in A.D. 311 Constantine issued the Edict of Toleration, which made Christianity the legal religion and placed it on an equal footing with other religions of that time.

Coming out of the catacombs, the Christians adopted the building of the Roman court of justice as the type best suited for their worship. This basilica, as it was called, was a large rectangular hall, supported by rows of columns which divided it into aisles. The center aisle was wider than the others and led to the magistrate's seat. This was a semicircular space, separated from the rest of the hall by a screen of marble or bronze, and became the chancel when used for Christian services.

When Constantine moved his capital to Byzantium, a new style was introduced in the churches which he erected. In these structures the dome was the controlling feature. Fitting a circular dome upon a square or many-sided base created problems, but it resulted in one of the most original types of building. In addition to the large dome there were smaller half domes jutting up around the circumference. The Roman arch and vault were blended in perfect unity. This style is called Byzantine, taking its name from the capital. It developed almost entirely in church buildings and covered the period from the fifth to the fifteenth century. Artistry and inventiveness came into play in the decorations, the colored marbles and mosaics, the altars, thrones, and shrines. Many of them were made of solid gold and silver, set with precious stones and jewels. St. Sophia, at Istanbul, Turkey, erected by Justinian, is one of the churches of this period and still remains one of the great buildings of the world.

The Romanesque style developed from the ninth to the twelfth century. Its main features are the round arch, the vault, thick walls, small windows, and horizontal lines. In Italy it was known as the Lombard style, while in England it was called the Norman style. During the ninth century hordes of invaders swept over Europe, destroying the church buildings by the hundreds. The tenth and eleventh centuries brought confusion and depression, but with the twelfth century came a revival in church building. Out of this came the Gothic style, which is the most inspiring of all styles of architecture.

Roman architecture with its vaults and arches was static, whereas the Gothic leaped with life at every point. A live load or thrust was met by a live and active resistance. Columns carried some of the weight of the vault, but the greater portion was carried by the buttresses. The Gothic builders, having chosen this principle of design, followed it with a boldness never seen before. By putting weight upon slender columns they produced a grandeur and grace which could be obtained in no other way.

Church building came to its fullest development during this period. The Gothic building, which may never be entirely finished, typifies the everlasting Church. Artisans and craftsmen of many generations worked on a building and attempted to show in visible form the glory of the heavenly city, the power of the Church triumphant, and the majesty and dominion of the Kingdom of God. The Gothic church became the crowning work of man dedicated to the glory of God.

Inside the building many Christian symbols are found. The nave is intersected by the transepts and thus forms a cross—the best known of the Christian symbols. The cross, also seen on the altar, mounted on a pyramidal base, signifies the sacrificial death of Christ. The candles on either side of the cross represent the humanity and divinity of Christ, and when lighted remind the worshiper that he is the light of the world. The empty cross of the Protestant churches signifies the risen Christ as the source of strength in this world and hope in the world to come. Flowers on the altar are usually placed between the cross and the candles and are thus dedicated to the glory of God.

In Protestant churches the central pulpit denotes the prominence given to the spoken word in worship. In churches where the pulpit is at one side the emphasis is shifted from the speaker to the altar as a constant reminder that the worship of God is of greatest importance. The pulpit is often balanced by a lectern, or reading stand, on the other side of the altar. The open Bible on the lectern signifies the accessibility of the written Word to all men. Laymen, taking part in a service, usually stand on this side. The center aisle leads to the altar, which becomes the focal point and suggests that nothing should separate the worshiper from God. Thus in the construction of the building, in the arrangement of the properties, in the color and design of the windows, there are messages to the worshiper as he seeks fellowship with God.

The principles which the ancient builders used in erecting their magnificent structures are ours today. Even a limited knowledge of these truths will heighten our appreciation of well designed churches, though they be smaller and less adorned. It is not the size but the quality of the building which determines the emotional response and the reverence which it inspires. The small church, utilizing the principles that have been discovered in the past, may make the worship experience as meaningful as the larger church. Architects and craftsmen should be artists as well as builders, and by using the heritage of the past they should endeavor to meet today the needs of Christians worshiping and studying together in their churches.

During the Middle Ages, when books were rare and those who read rarer still, the magnificent churches with their sculpture, stained-glass windows, and other treasures of art were the textbooks of the Christian Church. Chartres Cathedral has over fifteen hundred hand-carved figures and 130 stained-glass windows. Each tells its own story and brings an eloquent message. For over seven hundred years this building has spoken to succeeding generations about the Christian ideals which it portrays. Man has attempted to set forth in such buildings the sentiments which he could not express in words. The Gothic church has become his sublime expression, the acme of his gratitude and devotion to a Supreme Being. It speaks of the importance of the worship of God and by its presence makes more vivid such values as faith, courage, and steadfastness.

The Gothic church may soar above other buildings in massive form and still be delicate, or it may be small and unassuming and yet tell its story. Upon entering such a structure, one receives the impression of infinity, and at the same time a feeling of enclosure and protection. The vaulted ceiling suggests the upreach toward higher spiritual values, and, looking toward the altar, one becomes aware of the presence of God. The Gothic church is a constant reminder of man's search for companionship with God.[3]

APPRECIATING THE SANCTUARY

POEM:

Wherever souls of men have worshipped, there
Is God: where old cathedrals climb the sky,
Or shining hillsides lift their heads on high,
Or silent woodland spaces challenge prayer,
Or inner chambers shut the heart from care;
Where broken temples of old faiths now lie
Forgotten in the sun, or swallows cry
At dusk about some crossroads chapel bare,
Alike of bells and beauty; where saints walked
Of old with speaking presences unseen,
Or dreaming boys with quiet voices talked
In pairs last night on some still college green;
Where Moses' Sinai flamed, or Jesus trod
The upward way apart: there, *here,* is God! [4]

—HERBERT D. GALLAUDET

SOLO: "How Lovely Are Thy Dwellings," by Liddle, or

HYMN: "Glorious Things of Thee Are Spoken," or
"I Love Thy Kingdom, Lord."

POEM:

The church is dim and vibrant with a peace
That hovers in the air on quiet wings.
My spirit, pausing, finds a sweet release,
And deeply drinks from soul-refreshing springs.
How hallowed are these moments, how sublime
The rolling organ tones that ebb and swell,
As though there were no death, no space, no time,—
But only this great place, where God can dwell!
From archèd heights the windows crystallize
His face in radiant hues of jewelled glory,
And I can feel on me those kindly eyes,
And know once more the wondrous old, old story:
I shall go out in sunlit streets again
To live these moments with my fellow men. [5]

—ESTHER BALDWIN YORK

PRAYER:

Our Father, we are grateful for the great builders of the past who
left us a rich heritage in church buildings. As we think of the sacrifice,

labor, and devotion required, we feel unworthy, for we have not been as generous with our time or our possessions. Grant us a new insight into the ideals for which the church stands. Forgive us for our lack of devotion and for our contentment with ugliness in our church buildings. May we labor zealously to make them beautiful that they may be an inspiration to all who worship within them. Grant that they may express strength and stability and point the people to thee. Help us to be more worthy of the fellowship and inspiration which come from worshiping in thy house. May thy spirit guide us as we strive to serve the cause for which the church stands. In Jesus' name. AMEN.

HYMN: "We Would Be Building," or
    "The Church's One Foundation," or
    "Lead On, O King Eternal."

SERVICE 34

CHRISTMAS IS A MIRACLE [1]
by Joyce Vernon Drake

The following play should be a part of a complete worship service and should be attempted only in a reverent mood. It may be given in a one-room church or in a more elaborate setting. Because of its simplicity it may be given equally as well in the small church as in the large sanctuary. If necessary, it may be simplified still further by omitting all of the angels except the Golden Angel, and by including only three tableaux. There should be no attempt to change the appearance of the chancel or the platform of the church where the play is to be given. The usual arrangement of a chancel with altar and pulpit is satisfactory.

Special lighting effects may be worked out for the tableaux and the scenes on the chancel steps. At the beginning the sanctuary should be in semidarkness with only enough light to seat the audience. During the processional the candlelighters come down the aisle, light the candles in the windows and the tall candelabra by the chancel, and retire to the rear of the room. The vested choir enters singing and takes its place in the choir loft. The music may be simple hymns or elaborate selections from oratorios or cantatas.

Those who take part should set aside other things in order to give sufficient time for preparation; they should live and act in harmony with the character they portray; and a waiting list may be kept year after year of those who desire to take part. The first time the play is given, a group of girls may be candlelighters. The second year the angels for the tableaux are selected from this group. The third year one of them may take the part of Mary, while another portrays the Golden Angel. In like manner a group of boys may be shepherds the first year, and the second year one is promoted to take the part of Uncle Jed.

A director with skill and imagination will greatly increase the effectiveness of the play.

ORGAN PRELUDE: "Pastoral Symphony," from Handel's *Messiah*.

CALL TO WORSHIP:

For unto us a child is born, unto us a son is given: and the government shall be upon his shoulder.

INVOCATION.

RESPONSE: "Threefold Amen."

HYMN: "Joy to the World."

READING:

In the back country in this state, or any state, are many small church buildings which, though once centers of community activity, are now deserted. With the coming of swift transportation, people have passed by these little churches and have gone into towns and cities for their church activities.

The scene of the play is laid in the chancel of one of these deserted churches. Although people have long since ceased to worship here, Uncle Jed, the old caretaker, is still faithful. He lovingly cares for the building and keeps it in repair, always hoping and believing that sometime the people will return. Every Christmas eve he rings the old bell, and there has been built up a legend of those things which happen when the bell rings. Some say a miracle takes place, that the organ plays and angels sing. Some even say that Mary and the Holy Child appear.

On this Christmas eve Nickie, a crippled boy, has come with Uncle Jed to the old church. Nickie is so awed by the place that when Uncle Jed rings the bell he imagines he sees the story of the first Christmas relived. The old church becomes an ancient sanctuary in which the shepherds have taken refuge from the winds on the plains of Bethlehem. The faded statue, in its niche on the wall, becomes Mary. Nickie himself and Uncle Jed are shepherds of long ago and the sacred mystery of the first Christmas is unfolded in lovely fantasy.

THE PLAY:

CHRISTMAS IS A MIRACLE

Setting:

The more simple the setting and arrangements, the more effective will be the result. Much can be left to the imagination or skilfully sug-

—244—

gested. There must be steps leading from the auditorium level to the platform or chancel. There is an entrance to the chancel from the left. This chancel or platform looks much as it always does. It has a table or altar with candle holders or candelabra and the usual fittings. At the back is an alcove for the tableaux and angel scenes. If possible this should be elevated and curtained, with entrances behind curtains. If the alcove cannot be elevated, the altar or table must be put to one side. If it cannot be curtained, screens may be used, these being folded open and shut by girls in white robes or by boys in choir robes. There is no front curtain.

Characters:
  Part I
    Uncle Jed, the old caretaker
    Nickie, a crippled boy
    Mary, the Golden Angel
    Three Little Angels
  Part II
    Jediah, an old shepherd (Uncle Jed of Part I)
    Nickie, the crippled shepherd lad
    Nathan, a shepherd
    Jehrod, a young shepherd
    Three Shepherd Lads
    Three Wise Men
    Mary
    Four Angels
    Three Little Angels
    Six Girl Candle Lighters

PART I

Time: This Christmas Eve.

Place: An old church.

The scene is the chancel of a deserted church. The usual arrangement of a pulpit-platform, altar or chancel is carried out. Unlighted candles in polished holders are on the communion table or altar. Flowers or greenery are placed stiffly about. In spite of Uncle Jed's efforts to beautify it, the place has a cold feeling of emptiness and loneliness. The alcove at the back is curtained in material harmonizing with the furnishings of the chancel.

While the audience is gathering only dim lights are in the audi-
torium. The chancel is unlighted. The alcove curtains are closed until
actors reach chancel.

The organ plays "O Come, All Ye Faithful." A hidden choir hums
and a soloist raises the melody above the organ and singers. The audi-
torium is now in darkness. As the singing ceases Uncle Jed and Nickie
enter down center aisle. They are carrying a spray of ivy. Nickie has
one crutch. Only their flashlights are at first discernible. They flash
the lights about as they come slowly down. The organ is silenced.
Uncle Jed, who is walking ahead of Nickie, stops at the chancel steps,
throws his light on Nickie.

Uncle Jed: Are you coming, Nickie boy?

Nickie: O yes, I'm coming. It is dark, isn't it? Are you sure you have
some candles?

Uncle Jed: (*Goes up steps into chancel*) There are always candles in a
church, Nickie.

Nickie: Even a deserted church?

Uncle Jed: (*Groping for match and lighting it*) Yes—if there is such a
thing as a deserted church. (*He lights several candles. Lights come*
up. Curtains in alcove are partly open, dimly revealing young woman
posed as a standing statue of Virgin Mary. Uncle Jed and Nickie
stand with backs to audience looking into chancel. They remove
caps.) There, that's much better with some light.

Nickie: (*Turns, looking about; Uncle Jed watches him.*) Why, it is
beautiful in here! Hardly rusty and cobwebby at all. Do you come
here every day?

Uncle Jed: Not every day, but often enough. I arrange the flowers,
polish the candlesticks, and keep the church clean. You see, we
can't have God's house stand neglected.

Nickie: Is it still God's house, even though no one worships here?
Here are the candles and the altar and even the lovely statue. Is it
just like it was years ago?

Uncle Jed: Only older—very much older.

Nickie: Uncle Jed, what did you mean when you said, "if there is
such a thing as a deserted church"?

Uncle Jed: I mean that if His spirit once dwelt here, it's here now; and
where He is it is never lonely and never deserted. Here, Nickie, hand
me that ivy. (*Nickie removes coat then assists with ivy.*) That's it,
we'll lay it along here. That looks fine, doesn't it? We'll dust a little

—246—

and then it will be time to ring the bell. (*Gets dust cloth from behind pulpit or organ.*)

Nickie: My grandmother says you ring the bell every Christmas Eve. That seems strange when no one ever comes.

Uncle Jed: Some one might come, though. (*Dusts at intervals*) Some one who needs it might come in to worship some time, and they'll find the candles burning and the bell ringing.

Nickie: Then I'm glad I came here with you, tonight. You see, I can't walk fast so I didn't go with the carolers, and I think you need me. You must feel very alone.

Uncle Jed: No, Nickie, not alone. After I ring that bell I don't feel alone. When I come back into this room it all seems different. I'm not old and tired any more; I feel young. This place is not dusty and dingy, but shining and clean, and even the old faded statue is so bright it almost glows. Sometimes it seems the organ begins to play and the place is full of music and angels.

Nickie: Angels? Uncle Jed, that would be a miracle! Do you mean you see a miracle when you ring the bell?

Uncle Jed: Christmas is always a miracle, Nickie. It is always a miracle because it is just what each one makes it in his own heart. If you have loved Him and kept yourself pure and good—when you think of *him* here as a little Baby you can almost see him and all his angels in your heart. I guess that's a miracle, Nickie. I don't know, but it would seem to me it is. (*Looks at watch.*) Well, I guess it's time to ring the bell. (*Starts left.*)

Nickie: (*Softly and wonderingly*) Go on and ring the bell, Uncle Jed; maybe I'll see a miracle, too. Ring it loudly, won't you? I'll stay here and watch and listen, like you said—in my heart.

(*Uncle Jed slowly exits left. Soon bell is heard ringing. Nickie is transfixed. When bell has rung a second or two, the organ begins playing in softest tones. A dim rosy light glows on statue. The organ continues and bell ceases.*)

(*Slowly the curtains open. Light from right increases on statue. Very slowly, so slowly as to be almost imperceptible, the statue moves. The head and eyes of the statue are raised from attitude of prayer and hands unclasp from breast. Softly and unbelievably, as the music swells, the statue becomes the living maiden, Mary. The light from R. has become a glowing amber and Mary gazes in rapture toward the light. Slowly, with uplifted face, she sinks to her knees, folds hands*) *upon breast as Golden Angel enters alcove R. The Angel extends hand in benediction. Organ continues softly.*)

Golden Angel: Hail! Thou art highly favored, the Lord is with thee. Be not afraid, Mary, for I have come to tell you of a great gift which God, our Heavenly Father is giving you. There shall be born unto you a son and you shall call his name Jesus. When he is a man he shall be very great and shall teach all the people and the influence of his life shall never cease.

Mary: My soul shall be glad in God my Saviour.

(*Music increases. Golden Angel extends hand. Mary, putting her hand in the hand of the Angel, rises, then sits on bench C. back of the alcove. Golden Angel tenderly beckons off L. Little Angel enters with halo which she places upon Mary's head. Little Angel steps back L., clasps hands in attitude of adoration. Golden Angel beckons off R. Second Little Angel enters R. with flowers which she gives to Mary, then takes place opposite first Little Angel in same pose. Golden Angel silently glides out R. as Tinest Angel enters R. with flowers and kneels at Mary's knee.*)

(*Tableau as curtain slowly closes.*)

Nickie: (*Stands a moment after curtain closes and music dies away, then makes his way to L. entrance shouting joyously*) Uncle Jed! Uncle Jed! I have seen a miracle!

Nickie exits L. as music swells.

PART II

Time: The First Christmas Eve.

Place: An old sanctuary on plains of Bethlehem.

The scene is the same as in Part I. The chancel is dimly lighted as before. Alcove curtains closed.

Jediah (*the Uncle Jed of Part I*) *is now an old shepherd, who comes down the center aisle, enters the chancel and looks about, then beckons to others who have stopped about half-way down the aisle. The Three Small Shepherds are grouped about Nathan, the older man. The little shepherds are cold and Nathan has his arm protectingly about one of them.*

Jediah: (*Beckoning*) Come. This is the place, the shelter which we seek. Come in and be warmed.

Nathan: (*Advancing*) It is well, for the lads are cold from the winds of the field.

(*Small Shepherds go into chancel awesomely, investigating.*)

First Lad: Jediah, this place, this shelter to which you have brought us—is it not a holy place?

Second Lad: See, a candle burns on the altar. We should not rest in here. We should worship and bow down. (*Goes C. and kneels on steps.*)

Jediah: It is a holy place but to rest will not profane the altar.

Nathan: (*Kneels, then rises*) I will return to keep watch over the flock, Jediah. You remain here with the lads.

Jediah: We will relieve you and the others at the next watch. (*Exit Nathan.*) (*Jediah turns to lads, lays his hand on heads in blessing.*) Take your rest in peace. (*Other two lads kneel on steps, then lay themselves down to rest on steps. Jediah waits until all are resting, then kneels. Enter Jehrob, a young shepherd, followed by Nathan.*)

Jehrob: (*Breathlessly*) Jediah, ah, Jediah!

Jediah: (*Rising*) Who calls? What sends you here?

Jehrob: It is about Nickie, the crippled shepherd lad. He has seen a vision. Come and talk to him.

Jediah: Nickie? Is this like the vision he saw before, months ago?

Jehrob: This one was different. He was watching alone at the far field and suddenly the angel of the Lord came upon him and the glory of the Lord shown round about him and—and—

(*Curtains open revealing Angel with outstretched hand. The Angel is standing upon low white covered bench to give elevation. Jediah and Jehrob gaze spellbound. Little Shepherds rise. One runs to Jediah and Jehrob who cling together L.; one kneels where he is. Another stands R. Choir sings exultantly "Glory to God in the Highest," to any good musical setting or anthem, in jubilant mood. At an interlude in the anthem the Angel, seeing the shepherds are afraid, speaks sweetly to them. Organ continues.*)

Angel: Fear not, for behold I bring you good tidings of great joy which shall be unto all people. For unto you is born this day in the city of David a Saviour which is Christ the Lord. And this shall be a sign unto you—you shall find the babe wrapped in swaddling clothes lying in a manger.

(*As Angel finishes speaking she lifts arms in praise and turns slightly to R. Soft light beams on her face. Four Angels glide into alcove, two L., two R., moving slowly and softly with upraised faces and folded hands. Two take positions at each side of first Angel; others kneel, one slightly in front of other. They, too, lift arms in exaltation. If the anthem is long the Angels may change positions to down-cast eyes and folded hands, then, after interval, back to original position. Every movement must be coordinated, slow, graceful, flowing and part of the rhythm of the whole scene. Expression of faces must be in mood of praise, then of prayer.)*

(Curtains at close of anthem.)

Jehrob: (*Wonderingly*) This is that which Nickie saw.

Jediah: This is a holy night in a holy place.

First Lad: Jediah, let us go—even unto Bethlehem, just as the Angel said.

Second Lad: Let us stop in the fields, for I shall take a lamb as a gift to the Babe.

First Lad: We must tell Nickie so he can go and see this thing which has come to pass.

Jediah: Alas. Poor Nickie must travel slowly because of his twisted foot.

Third Lad: (*Pulls at Nathan*) Come, Nathan, let us hasten.

(All Shepherds exit C. aisle or L.)

Jediah: (*Returns and kneels in prayer on steps*) He shall feed his flock like a Shepherd. He shall carry them in his bosom and shall gently lead those that are with young. They that wait upon the Lord shall renew their strength. They shall mount up with wings as eagles, they shall run and not be weary, they shall walk and not faint.

(Jediah continues to kneel in prayer. Three Wise Men are coming slowly down aisle. Just before reaching chancel they stop. As Third Wise Man raises arms and repeats Scripture from Old Testament, Jediah rises and goes up steps onto platform.)

Third Wise Man: Comfort ye, comfort ye, saith your God.

> Speak ye comfortably to Jerusalem and
> cry unto her.
> That her warfare is accomplished
> For her iniquity is pardoned.
> O Zion that bringeth good tidings
> Get thee up unto the high mountain.

(All Wise Men kneel on step, then slowly rise. Third and First stand R. on steps, Second L. Jediah is on platform. He faces them.)

Jediah: Peace be unto you upon this holy night.

First Wise Man: We are seeking shelter where we may rest for the night.

Second Wise Man: Some shepherds who were preparing to journey to Bethlehem directed us here.

First Wise Man: We have come far and are weary.

Jediah: I am a humble shepherd. With my companions I have rested here, using this place as a haven from the winds of the field.

Third Wise Man: Have you heard of a vision of which the shepherds spoke?

Jediah: Did they reveal it unto you? (*Eagerly*) Did they tell you of the angel of the Lord, of the heavenly host and the glad message?

Second Wise Man: All this and more.

Jediah: I pray this vision may come unto you as you find rest in the peace of this sanctuary. I go to join my companions, that I too may worship this new-born king.

First Wise Man: We should inquire concerning—(*Jediah is hurrying off.*)

Jediah: Peace, Masters. (*Bows, exit L.*)

Third Wise Man: It is the vision that has caused him thus to depart.

Second Wise Man: The shepherds spoke of the angels' message concerning a Babe. Could that be the one whom *we* seek?

First Wise Man: Far across the desert we have come, my comrades, always following the star. It would be unseemly that a group of lowly shepherds should first receive these tidings.

Second Wise Man: The news of the birth of a King would first be revealed to a King! Remember our royal degree.

Third Wise Man: It is written that those in high places shall be made low and that the meek shall be exalted. The glory of his birth has been made known to the shepherds of the fields. I believe it is he whom we have been seeking.

First Wise Man: If this be true, let us hasten with gladness to his feet.

Second Wise Man: Let us bear our costliest treasures and kneel before him.

(*Turn as though to depart side aisle R. Nickie enters vestibule L., dressed as shepherd boy.*)

Nickie: O please Sirs—do not go. Let me talk to you. It is urgent, Sirs. (*Wise Men return front.*)

First Wise Man: Why do you detain us? We are seeking a new-born King.

Nickie: I can tell you about him. It was I, Sirs, who saw the vision.

Second Wise Man: Tell us.

Nickie: I was alone at the end of the field. Suddenly there was a bright star in the sky . . .

Third Wise Man: A star?

Nickie: O Sirs, a radiant star and a beaming light. Then the angels, hosts of angels—all singing of the new-born King.

First Wise Man: It is he. Let us again follow the star.

Nickie: That is what the shepherds said, Sir. They ran and hastened that they might see him. They each took a new-born lamb or a fleece as a gift to the King. I tried so hard to follow but I could not and fell behind. See, Sirs, I too, have a gift. (*Shows fleece.*) It is a fleece, so white and soft. It would keep a baby warm. Could you take me, too, Sirs, that I might bring my fleece?

First Wise Man: We could not take you, little shepherd—you could not travel so far.

Nickie: O Sirs—I beg you, Sirs.

Second Wise Man: Let us bear your gift, the fleece.

Nickie: Have you brought gifts? (*Wise Man opens box.*) Oh, jewels, gold, perfume! Then take mine too, Sirs; and offer it with yours.

Third Wise Man: We will bear your gift faithfully, little shepherd.

Nickie: (*Handing fleece to Third Wise Man*) Tell the Little King the fleece is from my littlest lamb. Tell him it's from Nickie and—O Sirs, tell him I wanted to see him.

Third Wise Man: You shall see him, little shepherd, some day. And you shall run and not be weary, you shall walk and not faint.

Nickie: Thank you, Sirs. That is what Jediah says. I will say those words at the altar while you bear my gift to him.

(*Wise Men exit slowly down center aisle. Nickie kneels on steps facing altar in attitude of prayer.*)

Nickie: They that wait upon the Lord shall renew their strength. They shall mount up on wings like eagles, they shall run and not be weary, they shall walk and not faint.

(*Nickie remains a moment in prayer, then wearily places his crutch by his side, lies on steps and falls asleep. Music of "Silent Night" from organ. Two Little Angels steal in, look lovingly at Nickie, then bring his coat, worn in Part I, and cover him. They sit on top step, hands folded on breasts, and tenderly guard him, one Angel right, one Angel left.*

(*As they sit, six white-robed Girls carrying candles, move down aisle, two by two in rhythm with music. They go into chancel and light candles which are still unlighted. When the candles are lighted, Choir begins softly singing "Silent Night." The six Girls kneel as curtain in alcove opens revealing scene of Mary at the manger.*

(At second stanza two of the Shepherd Lads enter and kneel wonderingly and reverently before manger, then slowly exit.

(At third verse Third Wise Man enters; he kneels, presents box of jewels, which Mary accepts and lays to one side. He then presents Nickie's fleece. Mary holds it a moment, then tenderly wraps it about the Baby in the manger. She takes first position. Mary and Wise Man motionless for tableau.

(The curtains close.

(The music now modulates into the "Away in a Manger," "Jesu Bambino," "Lo, How a Rose E'er Blooming," or any cradle song or carol. Plays through, then Choir or soloist sings first stanza.

(Curtains open with singing. In the alcove two beautiful Angels bend in worship over the manger. Tableau. Curtain closes.

(Re-open on manger with the Tiniest Angel standing with clasped hands gazing at the Baby. Tableau. Choir finishes song. Curtain closes.

(The organ now returns to the music of "Silent Night." The six kneeling Girls rise, extinguish all candles in chancel. Then they go out by way of center aisle as they entered. While Girls are leaving the chancel, the two Little Angels guarding Nickie step in front of him, facing audience. This forms a screen behind which Nickie quickly puts on his overcoat and picks up modern crutch. As last girl marches out, the two Little Angels walk out behind them as part of the group. The music ceases. Nickie rises and stands, with crutch, on platform, looking into chancel as in close of Part I. The scene is exactly the same. The bell rings, the curtain slowly parts a trifle, revealing statue as in Part I. When bell ceases, Uncle Jed, as in Part I, enters L.)

Nickie: O Uncle Jed, I saw it! It all happened—just as you said—

Uncle Jed: *(Arm about Nickie at top of steps)* Yes, and just as I always shall say—Christmas is a miracle!

(The two walk down steps, down C. aisle, and exit as organ peals and Choir sings "O Come, All Ye Faithful.")

The End

The Tableaux:

The most important elements of the play are the tableaux and angel scenes. If these are done painstakingly the compensation in beauty will be great. Every movement must be carefully planned, every pose and position worked out to the minutest detail. Even inexperienced players can produce a lovely and worshipful effect if all movements are deliberate and flowing and if face and eyes express mood. When movement is static let entire body be absolutely motionless. Study pictures for grouping, poses, and effects.

If a more simple production is being attempted, all the angels except Golden Angel and the Angel of the Shepherds could be omitted and no tableaux used except annunciation to Mary, annunciation to shepherds, and manger scene.

Lighting:

Small floodlights may be placed in front pews to light the chancel. Dull amber globes or amber gelatin is effective. When the candles are lighted this makes enough light. If the alcove is elevated, the candles on altar will not interfere with lighting of the alcove. If the alcove is on platform level the altar or tables must be to one side. The alcove must be lighted independently. Strips on each side of alcove interior may easily be arranged. Red, blue, and amber globes are a minimum variety. Care must be used in using red, using old enough to cast a glow, for red changes ordinary colors in a startling manner. A small baby spot over R. entrance to alcove is used for first tableau as Golden Angel appears. Use blue lights in scene where Mary is alone at manger. Use a shade of red in foot or low strip with Angel scenes. Also amber with touch of blue for Golden Angel. Touch of red with blue and amber on the statue.

If strips are impossible with screens, use the regular overhead light, veiled with amber gelatin or cellophane; then with extension cords and double sockets use different colored globes held at a height suitable for the different scenes.

All lighting must be tried with the costumes to note carefully any change of color.

Costumes:

Uncle Jed in Part I wears a shabby suit, a worn overcoat, and an old cap. In Part II he dresses like the other Shepherds.

Nickie in Part I wears old corduroy trousers, a colored shirt, cap and overcoat. He has an ordinary crutch. In Part II he wears a blue tunic reaching just above knees, and a white skin over his shoulders. His crutch is a crude stick with crosspiece nailed on the top.

Mary's costume for Part I is a sleeveless foundation of pale rose, soft cotton material gathered at the neck. Over this is draped a lighter rose or peach-colored length of cloth which covers her arms. A very pale pink drapery is over her head. Take care that the drapery is securely fastened and that it does not cast a shadow on her face. In Part II she wears the same rose robe. Over it is a full robe of royal blue, open down the front, and a royal blue drapery over her head.

The Golden Angel wears a robe of gold sateen made after the pattern of Mary's and with a gold girdle. An over-drape of double width ecru net gives an ethereal appearance.

All Angel robes are white, made alike. Lengths of thin, soft gauze or cheesecloth are tacked to the shoulders and fastened to the wrist. Drapes are softer and more graceful than wings for angels. Robes for Little Angels are straight lengths gathered on to elastic and held under the arms, leaving shoulders bare. No drapes. All halos are made with wire wound with silver or gold tinsel. All Angels and Candle Lighters wear white ribbon around the neck, crossed in front and tied in back above waist, in Grecian effect.

Girl Candle-Lighters wear the same type of white robes as Angels. Use blue cheesecloth or gauze drapery over shoulders but not fastened at wrist.

Men Shepherds wear ankle-length robes of coarse cloth, with rough drapery and flowing scarves. Dull colors: brown, gray, or tan. Sandals. Use twisted, rough sticks, not traditional crooks, for Shepherds. Little Shepherds' costumes are short, knee-length tunics of burlap or monks' cloth with a narrow cord at waist. Skins around shoulders. Smallest Shepherd wears shorts with fur to simulate skins, over hips and shoulders. All Small Shepherds are barefooted.

Wise Men dress in rich robes and draperies of silk and velvet. Lengths of brocade or any rich material for turbans. If necessary, cheap cotton material of rich color may be used, but made in traditional Oriental fashion.

Properties:

Candles: those in chancel; those carried by six girls. Candle holders or candelabra. Candle snuffers.

Appointments for altar.

Flashlights for Uncle Jed and Nickie. Matches. Ivy for altar.

Crutches for Nickie. Have extra crutch on steps so that in Part II Nickie may change from crude stick to regular crutch.

Fleece. May be made of white wool tacked on muslin in shape of animal skin.

Gifts of Wise Men.

Manger. Covers and white draperies for manger.

Low bench draped in white, in alcove. Angels stand upon this if higher level is needed. Mary sits upon it.

Flowers for Little Angels.

Halo carried by Little Angel to place upon Mary's head.

Music:

There is such a wealth of material for Christmas that any director or organist has a free selection. With a large, well-trained choir, anthems, glorias, chants, jubilates, may all be dramatically included at many points. With a small volunteer choir, simple hymns and carols will be found to create a reverent mood in a beautiful manner.

The music, pageantry, and action must be completely co-ordinated.

NOTES

SERVICE 1, IMPRISONED SPLENDOR

1. John 18:38; 14:6; 8:31-32, 36; II Tim. 2:15; Ps. 91:4.
2. Adapted from *Madame Curie,* by Eve Curie, copyright 1937 by Doubleday, Doran & Co., Inc.
3. From *The Glory of God,* by Georgia Harkness. Used by permission of the publishers, Abingdon-Cokesbury Press.

SERVICE 2, SINGER IN LIGHT AND COLOR

1. From *The Prophet,* by Kahlil Gibran. Used by permission of the publisher, Alfred A. Knopf, Inc.
2. Ps. 96:1-4; Eccles. 3:11; Ps. 96:6-9, 11-13.
3. From *A Book of Prayers for Youth,* by J. S. Hoyland. Used by permission of the Society for Promoting Christian Knowledge.
4. From *The Human Side of Greatness,* by William L. Stidger. Used by permission of the publishers, Harper & Bros.
5. A short biographical sketch as well as a complete list of his windows may be found in *Who's Who in America.* Dr. Connick died Dec. 28, 1945.
6. From *Prayers of the Social Awakening,* by Walter Rauschenbusch. Used by permission of the publisher, The Pilgrim Press.

SERVICE 3, SEEING THE INVISIBLE

1. Used by permission of the author.
2. Ps. 27:1, 7-14.
3. Adapted from *The Story of My Life,* by Helen Keller, copyright 1902, 1903. Reprinted by permission of Doubleday, Doran & Co.
4. From *The American Magazine* (June 1929), by permission of The Crowell-Collier Publishing Co.

SERVICE 4, THE CHOICE GOES BY FOREVER

1. Ps. 119:1-2, 9-11, 33-34.
2. Adapted from an article in the *New York Times Magazine* by Sidney Shalett. Used by permission of the *New York Times* and the author.
3. Mark 8:35.

SERVICE 5, SHARING THE CHAINS OF OUR BROTHERS

1. Ps. 130.
2. From *A Book of Prayers for Youth,* by J. S. Hoyland. Used by permission of the Society for Promoting Christian Knowledge.
3. Luke 6:27-38.

SERVICE 6, THE SCAFFOLD SWAYS THE FUTURE

1. Isa. 40:31; Ps. 27:14.
2. Matt. 5:10-12; and "Be Strong," by Maltbie D. Babcock.
3. Used by permission of the author.
4. Phil. 1:12-14, 18, 21, 27-30. From *The Bible—An American Translation,* by Smith and Goodspeed. Used by permission of the University of Chicago Press.
5. Used by permission of the authorized publishers, Houghton Mifflin Co.

SERVICE 7, WAITING JUSTICE SLEEPS

1. Heb. 11:13, 32-40; 10:32-33, 35-36. From *The Bible—An American Translation,* by Smith and Goodspeed. Used by permission of the University of Chicago Press.
2. Used by permission of the publishers, Houghton Mifflin Co.

SERVICE 8, A LAMP UNTO OUR FEET

1. II Pet. 1:21; II Tim. 3:16; Acts 17:11; Matt. 4:4; and a hymn by William Cowper.
2. Adapted from *William Tindale,* by Robert Demaus. Used by permission of the publishers, Abingdon-Cokesbury Press.
3. From *Selected Poems,* by John Oxenham. Used by permission of Erica Oxenham.

SERVICE 9, FRIEND OF THE SOIL

1. Ps. 95.
2. Deut. 8:6-11; Isa. 28:24-26; 1:19.
3. From an article in the *Pilgrim Highroad* by Percy R. Hayward. Used by permission of the author.
4. Adapted from *The Story of John Frederick Oberlin,* by A. F. Beard. Used by permission of the publisher, The Pilgrim Press.
5. Copyright 1932. Used by permission of the Co-operative Recreation Service, Delaware, Ohio. Set to music in *Hymns and Songs of Christian Comradeship,* No. 92.

SERVICE 10, PRACTICING THE PRESENCE OF GOD

1. Used by permission of the author.
2. "The Little Gate to God." Reprinted by permission of Mrs. Walter Rauschenbusch.
3. Pss. 139:1, 4, 6-12, 17-18, 23-24; 46:7.

NOTES

4. From *A Book of Prayers for Youth,* J. S. Hoyland. Used by permission of the Society for Promoting Christian Knowledge.
5. From *The Glory of God,* by Georgia Harkness. Used by permission of the publisher, Abingdon-Cokesbury Press.

SERVICE 11, BE STILL AND KNOW

1. From the *Christian Advocate.* Used by permission.
2. "A Silent Te Deum," from *Selected Poems,* by John Oxenham. Used by permission of Erica Oxenham.
3. Used by permission of the author.
4. By Archibald Rutledge. From the *American Magazine* (Feb. 1929). Used by permission of the Crowell-Collier Publishing Co.
5. Used by permission of the author.
6. Hab. 2:20; Pss. 42:1-2; 51:1-3, 7, 9-10, 12.

SERVICE 12, BESIDE STILL WATERS

1. Ps. 100:1-3.
2. John 10:7-11, 14-16, 27-30.
3. From *The Book of Common Prayer.*
4. From "Picture Interpretations" in the *Upper Room,* by A. E. Bailey. Used by permission of Roy H. Short, editor. A copy of the picture may be obtained from Curtis Publishing Co., Philadelphia, Pa.
5. Ps. 23.

SERVICE 13, HE SHALL BE LIKE A TREE

1. Ps. 1.
2. "Te Deum of the Commonplace," from *Selected Poems,* by John Oxenham. Used by permission of Erica Oxenham.
3. Ps. 104:24-25, 30-33.
4. "Victory in Defeat." Used by permission of Virgil Markham.
5. Jer. 17:7-8.
6. From *Altars Under the Sky,* by Dorothy Wells Pease. Used by permission of the publishers, Abingdon-Cokesbury Press.
7. Words by Joyce Kilmer, music by Oscar Rasbach. Published by G. Schirmir Music Co., New York.

SERVICE 14, LET THIS MIND BE IN YOU

1. Phil. 4:8; John 18:37; 8:32; Titus 1:15-16; Rom. 12:17; Phil. 2:3-5. From *The Bible—An American Translation,* by Smith and Goodspeed. Used by permission of the University of Chicago Press. Isa. 26:3 (A. V.).
2. From *The Methodist Hymnal.*
3. From *The Gospel in Art,* by A. E. Bailey, pp. 435, 436.
4. From the Latin, 12th century. Trans. Henry S. Coffin.

5. From *Jesus and Human Personality,* by A. E. Day. Used by permission of the author.
6. Used by permission of the author, Earl Marlatt. Music in *The Methodist Hymnal,* No. 178.
7. Used by permission of the author.

SERVICE 15, I BELIEVE IN MAN

1. Used by permission of Virgil Markham.
2. Ps. 8:3-9.
3. From *The Ritual of the Methodist Church.* Used by permission of the Methodist Publishing House.
4. From *Developing Christian Personality,* by Sterling W. Brown. Used by permission of the publishers, the Christian Board of Publication.
5. From an article in the *International Journal of Religious Education* by John Keith Benton. Used by permission of the author.
6. From articles in the *International Journal of Religious Education* and *Church School* by John Keith Benton. Used by permission of the author.

SERVICE 16, I BELIEVE IN THE CHURCH

1. Matt. 16:13-19; Acts 2:38, 41-47.
2. By William Henry Boddy. Reprinted from the *International Journal of Religious Education.* Used by permission of the Board of National Missions of the Presbyterian Church, U. S. A.
3. From *Prayers of the Social Awakening,* by Walter Rauschenbusch. Used by permission of the publisher, The Pilgrim Press.

SERVICE 17, I BELIEVE IN THE KINGDOM OF GOD

1. Gen. 28:16-17; Pss. 100:4; 84:10, 1-4.
2. From *The Ritual of the Methodist Church.* Used by permission of the Methodist Publishing House.
3. By John L. Davis. Reprinted from the *International Journal of Religious Education* (Oct. 1943). Used by permission of the author.
4. From the Findings of the Madras Conference.
5. "Building God's Kingdom." Used by permission of the author.
6. Heb. 1:1-2, 8-9; Luke 13:18-21; Matt. 13:44-48; Luke 12:29-31; Rom. 14:17.

SERVICE 18, I BELIEVE IN JESUS

1. Luke 4:16-22.
2. From *The Ritual of the Methodist Church.* Used by permission of the Methodist Publishing House.
3. "The Shadow of a Great Rock." Used by permission of the author.
4. From an article by W. A. Smart in the *Church School.* Used by permission of the author and the Methodist Publishing House.
5. *Ibid.*

NOTES

SERVICE 19, I BELIEVE IN GOD

1. A creed in the words of St. John, from *The Book of Worship*. Used by permission of the Methodist Publishing House.
2. "Consecration." Used by permission of the author.
3. From an article by James Gordon Gilkey in the *International Journal of Religious Education*. Used by permission.
4. From "The Marshes of Glynn." Used by permission of the publishers, Charles Scribner's Sons.
5. Summarized from "I Believe in the Holy Spirit," by W. A. Smart, in the *International Journal of Religious Education*. Used by permission.
6. "Each in His Own Tongue," by William Herbert Carruth. Used by permission of Mrs. Carruth.
7. Pss. 63:1-4, 7-8; 107:1.

SERVICE 20, THE HAND OF GOD IN THE AFFAIRS OF MEN

1 Isa. 55:6-7.
2 I Cor. 3:16; Rom. 8:1-4, 16.
3. By Henry Sloane Coffin. Quoted in the *International Journal of Religious Education*. Used by permission of Dr. Coffin.
4. Adapted from *The Chiangs of China*, by Elmer T. Clark. Used by permission of the publishers, Abingdon-Cokesbury Press.
5. Used by permission of Funk & Wagnalls Co.
6. By Albert R. Ashley. Used by permission.

SERVICE 21, PROPHET OF SOCIAL JUSTICE

1. Mic. 4:1-3; 6:8; Ps. 33:12-15, 18, 20-21.
2. "The Agony of God," from *The Glory of God*, by Georgia Harkness. Used by permission of the publishers, Abingdon-Cokesbury Press.

SERVICE 22, BREAKING THE SILENCE OF THE CENTURIES

1. Acts 17:24-28.
2. Adapted from *The Silent Billion Speak*, by Frank C. Laubach. Used by permission of the Friendship Press.

SERVICE 23, PRESSING TO REGIONS BEYOND

1. Pss. 96:1, 3; 67:3-4.
2. Luke 4:18-19; Matt. 28:19-20; John 10:16; Matt. 9:37-38; and a hymn by Frank Mason North.
3. Adapted from *Walter Russell Lambuth*, by W. W. Pinson.

SERVICE 24, FIGHTING FOR PEACE

1. Ps. 118:24; John 4:23.
2. Mic. 4:1-5; Isa. 65:24-25.

3. "God of the Nations." Used by permission of the author.
4. "He Shall Speak Peace." Used by permission of the author.

SERVICE 25, CARRYING LIGHT INTO DARKNESS
1. Pss. 24:1; 67:3.
2. Mal. 1:11; Ps. 98:2; Isa. 60:2; II Pet. 1:19; II Cor. 4:6; Ps. 45:6; Isa. 40:9; 52:7.

SERVICE 26, OVERCOMING HANDICAPS
1. Phil. 2:4-8, 14-16; 3:7-8, 10, 13-14.
2. Used by permission of the author.
3. "The Person in a Different Skin." Used by permission of the author.
4. "The Burden," from *Songs from the Slums,* by Toyohiko Kagawa, copyright 1935. Used by permission of the publishers, Abingdon-Cokesbury Press.

SERVICE 27, LOVE CAME DOWN AT CHRISTMAS
1. From *Lift Up Your Hearts,* by Walter Russell Bowie. By permission of The Macmillan Co., publishers.
2. Isa. 9:2, 6-7.
3. Luke 2:8-14.
4. Used by permission of the author.
5. From "And Now Abideth . . . Love," by John Keith Benton, in the *Elementary Teacher* (Dec. 1940). Used by permission of the author and the Methodist Publishing House.
6. "Christmas Eve." Used by permission of the author.

SERVICE 28, EACH BROUGHT HIS GIFTS
1. Pss. 127:1; 33:12; Prov. 14:34; Matt. 23:8; Acts 17:26; Matt. 7:12; Gal. 6:2, 10.
2. By Ralph W. Sockman. Used by permission.
3. With the aid of the Index of Composers and Sources of Tunes these hymn tunes may be found in almost any denominational hymnal. In *The Methodist Hymnal* they are Nos. 45, 12, 52, 600, 73, 66, 108, 105.
4. This poem, set to music, is No. 360 in *The Methodist Hymnal.* Other poems may be selected from various countries.
5. Adapted from "Our World," by Franklin K. Lane.
6. From "The New Colossus," by Emma Lazarus. Used by permission of the publishers, Houghton Mifflin Co.
7. "We Thank Thee." Used by permission of the author.

SERVICE 29, THIS DO IN REMEMBRANCE OF ME
1. Rev. 3:20.
2. From *Lift Up Your Hearts,* by Walter Russell Bowie. By permission of The Macmillan Co., publishers.

NOTES

3. From *The Ritual of the Methodist Church*. Used by permission of the Methodist Publishing House. Also I John 2:1-2; I Tim. 1:15; John 3:16; Matt. 11:28; 5:3-12.
4. From *Gentlemen—The King!* by John Oxenham. Copyright, the Pilgrim Press. Used by permission.

SERVICE 30, ALONG THE WAY

1. "Easter Prayer." Used by permission of the author.
2. Matt. 28:1-10, 16-20.
3. From *The Glory of God*, by Georgia Harkness. Used by permission of the publishers, Abingdon-Cokesbury Press.

SERVICE 31, A MOTHER'S VOW

1. Prov. 31:10-31.
2. From *Behold Thy Mother*, by G. Bromley Oxnam. By permission of The Macmillan Co., publishers.
3. Adapted from *Far Above Rubies*, by Agnes S. Turnbull. Used by permission of the publishers, Fleming H. Revell Co.
4. From *The Book of Worship*. Used by permission of the Methodist Publishing House. Also Luke 1:46-55.
5. "Altars." Used by permission of the author.

SERVICE 32, BE STRONG AND OF GOOD COURAGE

1. Ps. 125:8; I Chron. 15:28; Pss. 96:6; 113:2.
2. Josh. 1:6-9; Pss. 31:24; 27:14.
3. From *Lands Away*, by Earl Marlatt. Used by permission of the publishers, Abingdon-Cokesbury Press.
4. Summarized from *More Sermons in Stories*, by William L. Stidger. Used by permission of the publishers, Abingdon-Cokesbury Press.
5. "Ode to Columbus." Reprinted by permission of Mr. Virgil Markham.

SERVICE 33, APPRECIATING THE SANCTUARY

1. Ps. 122:1; Gen. 28:16-17; Ps. 100:4.
2. Pss. 27:4; 84:1-5, 10-12.
3. Adapted from *The Dictionary of Architecture*, by Russell Sturgis.
4. "Holy Places." Used by permission of the Christian Century Press.
5. "The Sanctuary." Used by permission of the author.

SERVICE 34, CHRISTMAS IS A MIRACLE

1. By Joyce Vernon Drake. Copyright 1944, by Walter H. Baker Co. A pamphlet edition of this play may be supplied by Walter H. Baker Co., Boston, Mass., at $.35 per copy.

SELECTED BIBLIOGRAPHY

WORSHIP FOR YOUNG PEOPLE

Bailey, Albert Edward. *The Gospel in Art*. Boston: The Pilgrim Press, 1916.
———. *The Arts and Religion*. New York: The Macmillan Co., 1944.
Bowie, W. Russell. *The Story of the Bible*. Abingdon-Cokesbury Press, 1934.
Chase, M. E. *The Bible and the Common Reader*. New York: The Macmillan Co., 1944
Clark, Elmer T. *The Chiangs of China*. Abingdon-Cokesbury Press, 1943.
Herman, Nicolas (Brother Lawrence). *The Practice of the Presence of God*.
Jones, E. Stanley. *Abundant Living*. Abingdon-Cokesbury Press, 1942.
———. *The Christ of the American Road*. Abingdon-Cokesbury Press, 1944.
Jones, Rufus M. *New Eyes for Invisibles*. New York: The Macmillan Co., 1943.
Lockhart, J. C. *Drama for Church Services*.
Marlatt, Earl. *Lands Away*. Abingdon-Cokesbury Press, 1944.
Oxnam, G. Bromley. *Behold Thy Mother*. New York: The Macmillan Co., 1944.
Page, Kirby. *Living Creatively*. New York: Farrar & Rinehart, 1932.
———. *Living Triumphantly*. New York: Farrar & Rinehart, 1934.
Palmer, A. W. *Aids to Worship*. New York: The Macmillan Co., 1944.
Pease, Dorothy Wells. *Altars Under the Sky*. Abingdon-Cokesbury Press, 1942.
Quimby, C. W. *Jesus as They Remembered Him*. Abingdon-Cokesbury Press, 1941.
Reid, A. C. *Invitation to Worship*. Abingdon-Cokesbury Press, 1942.
Rice, Merton S. *My Father's World*. Abingdon-Cokesbury Press, 1943.
Sadler, Alfred J. *Out of Doors with God*. Abingdon-Cokesbury Press, 1940.
Smart, W. Aiken. *The Contemporary Christ*. Abingdon-Cokesbury Press, 1942.
Smith, H. Augustine. *Lyric Religion*. New York: D. Appleton-Century Co., 1931.
Toner, Helen L. *When Lights Burn Low*. Abingdon-Cokesbury Press, 1942.

POEMS

Armstrong, O. V. & Helen. *Prayer Poems*. Abingdon-Cokesbury Press, 1942.
Clark, T. Curtis. *Poems of Justice*. Chicago: Willett, Clark & Co., 1929.
Clark, T. C. & Gillespie, E. A. *1000 Quotable Poems*. Chicago: Willett, Clark & Co., 1937
Gibran, Kahlil. *The Prophet*. New York: Alfred A. Knopf, 1923.
Harkness, Georgia. *The Glory of God*. Abingdon-Cokesbury Press, 1943.
Hill, Caroline. *The World's Great Religious Poetry*. New York: The Macmillan Co., 1923.
Kagawa, Toyohiko. *Songs from the Slums*. Abingdon-Cokesbury Press, 1935.
Markham, Edwin. *Selected Poems*.
Marlatt, Earl. *Cathedral*. New York: Harper & Bros., 1937.
Morgan, Angela. *Selected Poems*. New York: Dodd, Mead & Co., 1926.
Mudge, James. *Poems with Power to Strengthen the Soul*. New York: The Abingdon Press, 1907, 1909.
Oxenham, John. *Gentlemen—the King!* Boston: The Pilgrim Press, 1928.

SELECTED BIBLIOGRAPHY

——. *Selected Poems*. London: Methuen & Co., Ltd.

——. *All Clear*. London: Methuen & Co., Ltd.

——. *Bees in Amber*. London: Methuen & Co., Ltd.

——. *All's Well*. London: Methuen & Co., Ltd.

——. *The Fiery Cross*. London: Methuen & Co., Ltd.

——. *Hearts Courageous*. London: Methuen & Co., Ltd.

Piety, Chauncey R. *General Sam Houston*. Emory University: Banner Press, 1943.

Van Dyke, Henry. *Collected Poems*. New York: Charles Scribner's Sons, 1920-25.

PRAYER

Bowie, Walter Russell. *Lift Up Your Hearts*. New York: The Macmillan Co., 1939.

Cavert, Walter Dudley. *Remember Now . . .* Abingdon-Cokesbury Press, 1944.

Fox, S. F. *A Chain of Prayers Across the Ages*. New York: E. P. Dutton, 1943.

Hoyland, J. S. *A Book of Prayers for Youth*. New York: Association Press, 1939.

Morton, R. K. *A Book of Prayers for Young People*. Abingdon-Cokesbury Press, 1935.

Rauschenbusch, Walter. *Prayers of the Social Awakening*. Boston: The Pilgrim Press, 1925.

STORIES

Bartlett, Robert M. *They Dared to Live*. New York: Association Press, 1937.

——. *They Did Something about it*. New York: Association Press, 1939.

——. *They Work for Tomorrow*. New York: Assocation Press, 1943.

Bolton, Sarah. *Famous Men of Science*. New York: The Thomas Y. Crowell Co., 1941.

By an Unknown Disciple. New York: Harper & Bros., 1927.

Cather, K. Dunlap. *Boyhood Stories of Famous Men*. D. Appleton-Century Co., 1916.

——. *Girlhood Stories of Famous Women*. New York: D. Appleton-Century Co., 1924.

de Kruif, Paul. *Microbe Hunters*. New York: Harcourt Brace & Co., 1926.

——. *The Fight for Life*. New York: Harcourt Brace & Co., 1938.

Eastman, Fred. *Men of Power*. 5 vols. Abingdon-Cokesbury Press, 1938-40.

Erdman, Walter C. *Sources of Power in Famous Lives*. Nashville: Cokesbury Press, 1936.

——. *More Sources of Power in Famous Lives*. Abingdon-Cokesbury Press, 1937.

Griggs, Edward Howard. *Moral Leaders*. Abingdon-Cokesbury Press, 1940.

Holt, Rackham. *George Washington Carver*. New York: Doubleday, Doran & Co., 1943.

Lotz, Philip Henry. *Creative Personalities*. 3 vols. New York: Association Press, 1940-41.

Mathews, Basil. *Book of Missionary Heroes*. New York: Geo. H. Doran Co., 1922.

Parkham, Mary R. *Heroines of Service*. New York: D. Appleton-Century Co.,

Sawyers, Mott R. *Famous Friends of God*. New York: Fleming H. Revell Co., 1933.

Stewart, Mary A. *A King Among Men*. New York: Fleming H. Revell Co., 1915.

Stidger, William L. *The Human Side of Greatness*. New York: Harper & Bros., 1940.

——. *There are Sermons in Stories*. Abingdon-Cokesbury Press, 1942.

——. *More Sermons in Stories*. Abingdon-Cokesbury Press, 1944.

Thomas, Henry and Dana Lee. *Living Biographies of Religious Leaders*. New York: Garden City Publishing Co., 1942.

Turnbull, Agnes S. *Far Above Rubies*. New York: Fleming H. Revell Co., 1926.

Wallace, Archer. *In Spite of All*. Abingdon-Cokesbury Press, 1944.

——. *Overcoming Handicaps*. New York: Harper & Bros., 1927.

——. *Stories of Grit*. New York: Harper & Bros., 1930.

INDEX OF STORIES

SOURCES FOR HYMNS

CODE: The letter refers to the hymnal, and the number to the page on which the hymn is found in the hymnal.

A ....New Hymnal for American Youth
B ....Broadman Hymnal (Baptist)
C ....Common Service Book (Lutheran)
D ....Church School Hymnal for Youth (Presbyterian U. S. A.)
E ....American Student Hymnal
F ....Hymnal for Youth (Presbyterian U. S. A.)
H ....The Hymnal (Presbyterian U. S. A.)
I ....Inter-Church Hymnal
J ....Christian Worship (Baptist and Disciples)
M ....Methodist Hymnal
P ....Pilgrim Hymnal (Congregational)
S ....Abingdon Song Book (Methodist)
T ....Presbyterian Hymnal (U. S.)
W ....Cokesbury Worship Hymnal (Methodist)

Abide with Me
A—20; B—179; C—476; D—14; E—368; F—293; H—33; M—520; S—248; T—470; W—205.

A Charge to Keep I Have
B—203; C—376; E—379; I—74; J—373; M—287; P—500; S—186; T—289; W—74.

Again as Evening's Shadow Falls
M—42.

A Glory Gilds the Sacred Page
C—170; M—388.

All Creatures of Our God and King
A—45; E—307; M—65; W—236.

All Hail the Power of Jesus' Name
A—135; B—1; C—131; D—135; E—362; F—122; T—116; M—164.

All People of the Earth
M—508.

A Mighty Fortress Is Our God
A—210; B—38; C—195; D—51; E—351; H—266; I—85; M—67; P—259; S—6; T—308; W—82.

Are Ye Able
A—205; B—396; E—174; M—268.

As with Gladness Men of Old
A—95; C—38; D—96; F—77; H—135; M—90; S—259.

Awake, Awake to Love and Work
M—455; W—171.

Awake, My Soul, Stretch Every Nerve
A—195; B—201; C—380; E—165; H—278; I—76; M—359; P—252; T—291.

Be Still, My Soul
B—479; C—181; M—73.

Be Strong! We Are Not Here to Play
A—182; D—186; E—105; F—229; H—488; I—272; M—300; P—253; S—182.

Be Thou My Vision
A—236; F—115.

Book of Books
A—69; E—337; M—390.

Break Thou the Bread of Life
A—71; B—81; D—157; E—101; F—
133; H—216; I—27; J—461; M—387;
P—412; S—235; T—381; W—88.

Breathe on Me, Breath of God
A—61; B—146; D—152; E—98; F—
130; H—213; I—438; M—180; P—201.

By Roads That Wound Uphill and Down
D—110; F—88.

Christ of the Upward Way
A—235; D—215; F—230; H—277.

Christ the Lord Is Risen Again
A—129; B—33; C—111; D—126; E—
331; F—104; T—118; M—154.

Come, Thou Almighty King
A—38; B—32; C—164; D—24; E—
354; F—33; H—52; I—1; J—122; M—
2; P—10; S—10; T—1; W—9.

Come unto Me
D—165; M—350; T—165.

Come, Ye Faithful, Raise the Strain
C—108; F—108; H—168; M—151.

Dear Lord and Father of Mankind
A—152; B—63; D—236; E—80; F—
150; H—302; I—29; J—411; M—342;
P—224; S—137; T—242; W—79.

Dear Master, in Whose Life I See
H—507; M—376; P—265.

Draw Thou My Soul, O Christ
A—149; D—234; H—297; P—232;
T—250.

Eternal God, Whose Power Upholds
M—476; S—225.

Fairest Lord Jesus
A—137; B—102; D—136; E—58; F—
119; H—195; I—80; J—261; M—111;
P—465; S—55; T—72; W—170.

Faith of Our Fathers
A—256; B—249; D—203; E—109; F—
224; H—267; I—13; J—348; M—256;
P—220; S—104; T—210; W—86.

For All the Saints
A—330; C—249; D—332; E—345; F—
290; H—429; M—527; S—250; T—
309.

For the Beauty of the Earth
A—46; B—309; C—292; D—55; E—
357; F—42; H—71; I—100; J—167;
M—18; P—168; S—16; T—16; W—
105.

Glorious Things of Thee Are Spoken
C—197; D—247; F—139; H—339; I—
35; M—382; P—376; T—352.

God of Grace and God of Glory
F—236; M—279.

God of the Strong, God of the Weak
A—212; E—217; M—457.

God Send Us Men
A—255; F—276; I—224; P—323.

God, Who Touchest Earth with Beauty
A—223; F—178.

Go, Labor On
B—206; F—249; H—376; I—89; M—
292; P—330; T—285.

Good Christian Men, Rejoice
F—80; H—130; M—110.

Great Master, Touch Us
A—222.

Guide Me, O Thou Great Jehovah
B—181; C—261; E—366; H—104; M—
301; T—29; W—44.

Hark, Hark, My Soul
A—329; B—62; D—331; E—343; H—431; F—289; M—532; S—252; T—434.

Have Thine Own Way
B—254; F—162.

He Leadeth Me
B—422; D—71; F—54; T—46; M—242.

Heralds of Christ
A—258; F—235; T—407; M—482.

He Who Would Valiant Be
A—204; E—169; F—233; H—276; J—364; M—265; P—250.

Holy Spirit, Faithful Guide
B—152; I—204; J—276; M—243; P—132; S—92; T—132; W—23.

Holy Spirit, Truth Divine
A—60; E—100; F—128; H—208; I—319; M—173; P—496; W—20.

How Beauteous Were the Marks Divine
M—116.

I Bind My Heart This Tide
A—121; E—143; F—205; H—243; J—302; S—202.

I Know Not What the Future Hath
A—332; M—517.

I Love Thy Kingdom, Lord
A—311; B—247; D—248; E—381; F—140; H—337; I—43; J—429; M—379; P—404; T—353; W—8.

In Christ There Is No East or West
A—299; D—314; F—243; H—341; I—235; J—480; M—507; P—389; S—221; W—166.

I Need Thee Every Hour
A—150; B—193; D—237; F—155; T—303; M—232.

In the Cross of Christ I Glory
A—124; B—180; C—62; D—117; E—377; F—95; H—154; M—149; S—43; T—94; W—28.

It Came upon a Midnight Clear
A—78; B—141; C—29; D—76; E—245; F—64; T—58; M—92.

I Would Be True
A—177; D—225; I—158; J—361; P—469; S—119; W—184.

Jesus Calls Us
A—144; B—443; D—168; E—106; F—198; T—284; M—233.

Jesus Shall Reign
A—305; B—260; C—219; D—310; E—380; F—248; H—377; I—21; M—479; P—373; S—220; T—392; W—13.

Jesus, with Thy Church Abide
C—207; D—251; M—380; T—350.

Joyful, Joyful, We Adore Thee
A—43; B—52; D—48; E—49; F—6; H—5; I—306; M—12; P—25; S—3; T—25.

Joy to the World
A—76, B—98; C—34; D—77; E—360; F—65; H—122; I—10; J—190; M—89; P—78; T—57; S—29; W—217.

Lead On, O King Eternal
A—199; B—210; D—208; E—177; F—226; H—371; I—51; J—363; M—278; P—251; S—210; T—301; W—21.

Lead Us, O Father, in the Paths of Peace
I—302; H—262; M—271; P—281; T—41.

Let All the World in Every Corner Sing
C—287; F—16; H—9; M—8; W—240.

Light of the World, We Hail Thee
A—9; D—5; E—19; F—281; H—422; M—114; T—398.

Lord, for Tomorrow and Its Needs
A—317; B—259; T—360; M—314.

Lord of All Being
A—33; E—1; F—56; M—62; H—87;
S—18.

Lord, Speak to Me That I May Speak
A—251; C—212; D—293; E—216; F—
196; T—279; M—460.

Love Came Down at Christmas
H—133; M—94.

March On, O Soul, with Strength
A—184; D—220; E—110; F—234; H—
273; J—359; M—264; P—247; S—192;
T—300.

Master, No Offering
A—252; D—277; E—229; H—407;
M—464; T—277.

Mid All the Traffic of the Ways
A—159; F—165; H—322; M—341;
S—165; T—237.

My God, I Thank Thee
A—51; B—49; D—361; E—204; F—
11; H—73; I—122; M—9; P—11.

My Sout, Be on Thy Guard
B—177; C—272; I—79; J—370; M—
277; T—295; P—256.

No Distant Lord Have I
D—145; F—113.

Now on Sea and Land Descending
M—45; P—57; T—462; S—23.

O Brother Man, Fold to Thy Heart
A—24; B—275; D—283; E—258; F—
260; H—403; J—515; M—466; P—310;
W—172.

O Come, All Ye Faithful
A—83; B—90; D—89; E—298; F—74;
H—116; I—20; M—96; P—105; S—
30; T—253.

O Come, O Come, Immanuel
A—75; C—1; F—63; H—108; M—83

O for a Closer Walk with God
T—256; M—228.

O God, Our Help in Ages Past
B—435; H—77; M—533; P—177; S—
145; T—19; W—196.

O Gracious Father of Mankind
A—66; D—72; E—34; H—85; M—305;
S—163.

O Happy Home
A—313; D—263; E—382; F—262; J—
601; M—427; T—320.

O Jesus, I Have Promised
A—196; B—193; D—187; E—369; F—
174; H—268; I—52; M—226; P—196;
T—253; W—52.

O Jesus, Prince of Life and Truth
D—224; F—182; P—257.

O Jesus, Thou Art Standing
A—148; B—242; C—322; D—174; E—
375; H—228; I—77; M—197; P—246;
T—170; W—132.

O Love That Wilt Not Let Me Go
A—154; B—231; C—343; D—196; E—
37; I—38; M—318; P—289; S—130;
T—26; W—211.

O Master, Let Me Walk with Thee
A—197; B—274; D—182; E—214; F—
166; H—264; I—12; J—306; M—259;
P—291; S—116; T—271; W—50.

O Master Workman of the Race
A—98; D—106; E—74; H—140; M—
118; P—328; S—59; T—82; W—58;
F—85; J—210.

Once to Every Man and Nation
D—184; E—240; H—373; M—263; P—
326.

SOURCES FOR HYMNS

Open My Eyes That I May See
B—351; W—89.

O Son of Man, Our Hero
A—109; E—79; F—114; H—177.

O Son of Man, Thou Madest Known
A—188; D—207; E—175; M—121; S—61; P—329.

O Spirit of the Living God
H—207; M—182; S—78.

O Thou in Whose Presence
M—346; S—173.

O Thou Whose Gracious Presence Blessed
A—314; F—266.

O Worship the King
A—36; B—2; C—294; D—29; E—59; H—2; I—15; M—4; P—5; T—7; W—7.

O Young and Fearless Prophet
M—266; S—213; W—179.

O Zion, Haste
A—306; B—151; C—224; D—308; E—270; H—382; I—145; M—475; P—372; S—222; T—395; W—16.

Praise the Lord
A—30; B—38; C—300; D—26; E—384; F—8; H—10; I—254; M—11; P—7; T—10.

Rise, My Soul
H—264; M—524.

Rise Up, O Men of God
A—254; B—186; D—288; E—224; H—401; I—292; M—267; P—313; S—203; T—274; W—147.

Saviour, Breathe an Evening Blessing
B—221; C—467; H—47; M—50; T—469; W—118.

Saviour, Like a Shepherd Lead Us
B—13; C—565; H—458; I—137; M—337; P—492; T—323; W—69.

Send Down Thy Truth, O God
A—268; E—242; M—181.

Silent Night, Holy Night
A—81; B—146; C—530; D—83; E—302; F—73; T—60; M—106.

Sing with All the Sons of Glory
M—150.

Soldiers of Christ, Arise
C—384; D—205; E—171; F—220; H—269; M—282; S—317; T—296.

Spirit of God, Descend upon My Heart
A—62; B—150; D—148; E—99; H—204; I—110; M—179; P—233; S—75; T—125.

Spirit of Life, in This New Dawn
A—63; E—22; M—178; S—74.

Stand Up, Stand Up for Jesus
A—201; B—31; D—204; E—170; F—225; T—288; M—283.

Stay, Master, Stay
M—122.

Still, Still with Thee
A—6; B—4; E—20; F—53; H—107; I—138; J—136; M—40; P—50; T—454; W—114.

Strong Son of God, Immortal Love
A—215; D—188; E—70; H—175; I—188; M—206; P—153.

Sun of My Soul
A—215; B—177; C—463; D—113; E—93; H—37; I—64; M—56; P—61; S—25; T—457; W—204.

Take My Life, and Let It Be
A—198; B—174; C—382; D—221; E—142; F—175; T—272; M—225.

Take Thou Our Minds
F—168.

That Cause Can Neither Be Lost nor Stayed
F—237; S—125; W—169.

The Church's One Foundation
A—308; B—406; C—198; D—246; E—
347; F—138; H—333; M—381; S—
234; T—345; W—81.

The First Noel
A—79; B—140; D—82; E—328; F—
70; H—129; M—97; S—35.

There's a Song in the Air
A—84; F—79; M—98.

There's a Wideness in God's Mercy
A—55; B—64; C—256; H—93; I—192;
M—76; P—180; T—18.

These Things Shall Be
A—293; D—289; E—189; F—283; H—
423; I—276; J—507; M—512; P—378.

The Spacious Firmament on High
D—53; H—69; I—144; M—66; P—
160; T—8.

The Voice of God Is Calling
E—235; M—454; P—337; W—168.

The Whole Wide World for Jesus
D—313; F—242.

This Is My Father's World
A—39; D—52; E—51; H—70; I—226;
M—72; P—464; T—332; W—106; S—
11.

Thou Didst Leave Thy Throne
A—101; B—138; C—541; D—112; F—
167; M—95; S—158; T—79; H—231.

Thou My Everlasting Portion
B—223; M—235.

'Tis Midnight; and on Olive's Brow
I—143; M—133; P—119; T—96.

Truehearted, Wholehearted, Faithful and
Loyal
F—177; M—255.

Walk in the Light
M—378; W—98.

We May Not Climb the Heavenly Steeps
M—120; W—70.

We Plow the Fields and Scatter
A—323; C—486; E—356; F—55; M—
544.

We Thank Thee, Lord, Thy Paths
A—249; D—287; E—223; F—203; H—
367; J—495; M—458; P—340; S—206.

We Would Be Building
F—204; S—113.

We Would See Jesus
A—100; B—219; D—105; H—263; I—
246; J—400.

When I Survey the Wondrous Cross
A—123; B—191; C—97; D—118; E—
376; F—96; T—88; M—148.

When Morning Gilds the Sky
A—2; B—2; C—410; E—201; F—10;
H—3; I—33; J—135; M—31; P—41;
T—453.

Where Cross the Crowded Ways of Life
A—265; B—276; E—60; F—253; H—
410; I—61; J—61; J—519; M—465; P—
140; T—330; W—195.

Work, for the Night Is Coming
B—243; M—293.

YOUTH leaders in all churches will welcome this collection of thirty-four worship services, grouped in five unified series, which not only aid in making religion a living reality to young people, but also emphasize numerous ways of applying Christian principles to everyday life.

Each of these usable services is built around a central theme which is strengthened and given deeper meaning by carefully chosen prayers, hymns, poems, and stories. Although all are completely planned, they allow for ample creativity on the part of the individual youth groups.

Suggestions to the counselor preface each of the five series and contain valuable ideas on lighting, worship-center arrangement, and other means for effective presentation.

Prepared with a secure knowledge and understanding of today's youth, these services are certain to arouse a lively interest and response in all who use them.

ALICE A. BAYS, a native Tennessean, was educated at Hiwassee College and the University of Tennessee. She is constantly in demand at youth assemblies and conferences because she understands young people and their needs as well. Her wide experience in leadership among Christian youth has been recognized. Well known are her articles on worship and worship leadership which appear in numerous church periodicals. Other volumes from her pen are: *Worship Services for Purposeful Living, Worship Programs and Stories for Young People, Worship Programs in the Fine Arts,* and *Worship Programs for Intermediates.*